About the Rules of Evidence for the New International Criminal Court

About the Rules of Evidence for the New International Criminal Court

Fernando del Cacho, Phd, London, 2002

libros en red

www.librosenred.com

C.E.O.: Marcelo Perazolo
Contents Director: Ivana Basset
Cover Design: Patricio Olivera
Interior Design: Viviana Bellante

Design, typesetting, and other prepress work by LibrosEnRed
www.librosenred.com

ISBN: 987-561-071-2

First english edition - Print on Demand

LibrosEnRed
A trade mark of Amertown International S.A.
editorial@librosenred.com

A mi padre, in memoriam

Abbreviations

Ar	Aranzadi
BGH	Bundesgerichtshof
BJC	Boletín de jurisprudencia constitucional
BOCG	Boletín Oficial de las Cortes Generales
BVerfGE	Bundesverfassungsgericht
ECHR	European Convention on Human Rights
CGPJ	Consejo General del Poder Judicial
EMRK	Europäische Menschenrechtskonvention
EOMF	Estatuto Orgánico del Ministerio Fiscal
EuGRZ	Europäische Grundrechte Zeitschrift
EuRHÜ	Europäischen Rechtshilfeübereinkommes
FJ	Fundamento jurídico
KMR	KomentarMenschensrecht
LOTJ	Ley Orgánica del Tribunal del Jurado
NJW	Neue Juristische Wochenschrift
NStZ	Neue Zeitschrift für Strafrecht
RDP	Revista de Derecho Procesal
RDPI	Revista de Derecho Procesal Iberoamericano
RGD	Revista General de Derecho
StPO	Strafprozessordnung
STC	Sentencia del Tribunal Constitucional
STS	Sentencia del Tribunal Supremo
StV	Strafverteidiger
ZStW	ZeitschriftStrafrechtWochenende

CHAPTER I

Expository Analysis

A. Right to Present Evidence in the Criminal Trial: Principles and Guarantees

A1. Rome Statute of the International Criminal Court (ICC)

The inseparability of the right to present evidence from the right to a defense is underscored in the Rome Statute, primarily in article 67 entitled "Rights of the accused." The first paragraph of this article deals with the "right to be heard" ("auf rechtliches gehör"): the right to a trial or the right to confront opposing witnesses and evidence, which we will analyze in depth in the sections that follow dealing with the Spanish and German constitutions.

This right to a trial is complemented by article 67.2, which states that the Prosecutor is required to disclose to the accused evidence under his or her possession or control that might

[*] Translation by Jessica Miller (Michigan, USA), revised by the author.

prove the innocence or "mitigate the guilt" of the accused or "affect the credibility of prosecution evidence." Furthermore, specific reference to the right to a defense is made several times throughout this provision (article 67.1 (b), (d), (e), (h), and (i)).

The language of article 67.1 (e) is similar to that of article 6 of the European Convention on Human Rights (ECHR). However, it is important to take special notice of the reference made in article 67.1 (e) to the accused's right to present "other evidence admissible under this Statute." In light of that statement, as we will later see, the criteria for admitting evidence and ruling evidence inadmissible set out in the Statute are subject to a fair share of criticism. The Statute repeatedly likens admissibility to relevance and uses the term "relevant" to describe situations that are not related to evidence; for example, article 61 makes reference to the "relevant" functions of the Pre-Trial Chamber.

The clause forbidding any reversal of the burden of proof or onus of rebuttal (article 67.1 (i)) is unnecessary if the principle of presumption of innocence as defined in the doctrine and jurisprudence of the States Parties is taken into account. The Statute specifically addresses this principle in article 66 entitled "Presumption of innocence," which summarizes the right in three concise sections that warrant comment. The first section provides that the accused shall be presumed innocent and that guilt must be proved. It provides the following two conditions:

1) The accused must be proved guilty before the Court, which means that the following procedural due process guarantees must be observed:

The right to confront and cross-examine opposing witnesses or evidence

The guarantee that both parties are on an equal footing (principle of equality)

The right to oral argument

A public trial[1]

The decision maker must be present at the trial[2]

2) The accused must be proved guilty in accordance with applicable law. This statement is unnecessary when we consider that criminal law is governed by the "principle of legality," which dictates that the letter of the law must be followed without deviation. Procedural law is also governed by this principle, without prejudice to "urgent cases" that might require the adoption of "provisional rules" mentioned in the Statute (article 51, see infra C).

Regarding the first point mentioned above and to corroborate

---

[1] Exceptions to the general rule requiring a public trial are listed in article 64.7 of the Rome Statute. See also article 68.2 for restrictions placed on public trials for the purpose of protecting victims, witnesses "or an accused."

[2] The Rome Statute itself makes reference to a fair trial in which the rights of the accused are respected. Article 64.2 states: "The Trial Chamber shall ensure that a trial is fair and expeditious and is conducted with full respect for the rights of the accused... ."

that technically we can only refer to evidence when all of the procedural due process guarantees are observed; that is, during the trial (with the exception of those cases in which evidence is examined beforehand respecting all due process guarantees), article 74.2 of the Statute provides that "The Court may base its decision only on evidence submitted and discussed before it at the trial."

Article 66, section 2 provides that it is the Prosecutor's duty to "prove the guilt of the accused." Without prejudice to any doubts and criticism arising from the use of the term "guilt," the language in this section corroborates the established principle requiring that the burden of proof rest with the accuser, a concept to which the Statute itself explicitly refers in its next article (article 67.1 (i)).

And lastly with regard to the presumption of innocence, article 66.3 states that "the Court must be convinced of the guilt of the accused beyond reasonable doubt" in order to convict. This means that if there is any doubt as to the guilt of the accused, the Court must find in favor of the defendant and in doing so, it recognizes the time-honored principle in dubio pro reo.

The controversial (at least in recent times) principle of material truth is reflected in article 65 of the Statute. When the accused confesses, the article requires the Trial Chamber to determine whether the "admission of guilt is supported by the facts of the case" and consider the admission "together with any additional evidence presented." However, this principle is contradicted by rule 69 of the Rules of Procedure and Evidence, which allows "agreements as to evidence."

This activity is contradictory even though such agreements may be based on the strict criteria of the Court.[3]

A2. Spanish Constitution

The right to present evidence, which is inseparable from the right to a defense,[4] is understood as the right to carry out an activity during the trial that involves the "use" of means of proof to shape the opinion of the decision maker. However, certain restrictions may be placed on this activity. We will later have the opportunity to examine these restrictions through an analysis of the discovery, admission, and sifting of evidence and its "relevance" as seen by the Court.[5]

Furthermore, if finding the legal nature of a principle entails

---

[3] Rule 69: "The Prosecutor and the defense may agree that an alleged fact, which is contained in the charges, the contents of a document, the expected testimony of a witness or other evidence is not contested and, accordingly, a Chamber may consider such alleged fact as being proved, unless the Chamber is of the opinion that a more complete presentation of the alleged facts is required in the interests of justice, in particular the interests of the victims." Agreements are also allowed relating to the "order and manner in which the evidence shall be submitted to the Trial Chamber" (rule 140.1).

[4] STC97/20 June 1995 FJ 4.

[5] See STC89/6 June 1995 FJ 5 which states: "En lo que concierne al derecho a los medios de prueba pertinentes para la defensa, hemos

identifying the general legal category under which it might be classified,[6] the nature of the right to present evidence is clearly procedural, as it can only be exercised during the proceedings. We can say that the right to a defense encompasses the right to present evidence, as it is not just limited to the parties' right to have a defender (technical defense) or to defend themselves; rather, it also guarantees that the possibilities for a defense are not constrained by any arbitrary restriction of the proposed means of proof or the facts to be proved.[7]

The inclusion of the right to present evidence in the Spanish Constitution (article 24.2) allows this right to be viewed from a new perspective.[8] It is a fundamental right and as such, it is afforded special legal protection. However, it is not an absolute right as suggested by the language employed in the article, and thus the determination of the essential content that enjoys specific legal protection is especially important. Furthermore, the right to present evidence is specifically dealt with in article 6, paragraph 3, letter (d) of the European Convention

declarado que dicho derecho fundamental implica el de proponer los medios de prueba autorizados por el ordenamiento (…), pero no faculta, sin embargo para exigir la admisión de cualesquiera pruebas que puedan las partes proponer, sino tan solo la recepción y práctica de las que sean declaradas pertinentes por los órganos judiciales…"

[6] Montero Aroca, Ensayos de Derecho Procesal 146 (1993).

[7] Gutiérrez-Alviz and Conradi F., La valoración de la prueba penal, 4 RDP 808 (1975).

[8] Spanish Constitution, article 24.2: "Todos tienen derecho… a utilizar los medios de prueba pertinentes para su defensa..." Este derecho está "desprovisto, en la práctica, de la importancia que su enunciado daría que pensar." De la Oliva with Aragoneses Martínez, Hinojosa Segovia, Muerza Esparza and Tomé García, Derecho Procesal Penal 67 (1996).

on Human Rights,[9] article 14, paragraph 3, letter (e) of the International Covenant on Civil and Political Rights,[10] article 8, paragraph 2, letter (f) of the American Convention on Human Rights,[11] and also in several constitutions; for example, the Sixth Amendment to the Constitution of the United States of America of 1791.[12]

It is apparent even from a quick read of article 24.2 of the Spanish Constitution that the constituents had the criminal trial in mind. There are specific references to "charges," although it would be erroneous to infer that the procedural due process guarantees described in the Constitution were only intended for the criminal trial. Rather, quite the opposite is true, especially regarding the right to present

---

[9] ECHR article 6, paragraph 3: "Everyone charged with a criminal offense has the following minimum rights: (d) ... to obtain the attendance and examination of witnesses on his behalf under the same conditions as witnesses against him." See Sartorius II, Internationale Verträge Europarecht (1995).

[10] Article 14, paragraph 3: "Everyone shall be entitled to the following minimum guarantees, in full equality: (e) ... to obtain the attendance and examination of witnesses on his behalf under the same conditions as witnesses against him." II Bundesgesetzblatt 1534 (1973).

[11] Article 8, paragraph 2: "During the proceedings, every person is entitled to the following minimum guarantees: (f) the right to a defense... to obtain the appearance (als Zeugen vorladen zu lassen), as witnesses, of experts or other persons who may throw light on the facts". EuGRZ 435 (1980).

[12] "In all criminal prosecutions, the accused shall enjoy the right to a speedy and public trial, by an impartial jury of the State and district wherein the crime shall have been committed, which district shall have been previously ascertained by law, and to be informed of the nature and cause of the accusation; to be confronted with the witnesses against him; to have compulsory process for obtaining witnesses in his favor, and to have the Assistance of Counsel for his defense."

evidence. Doctrine holds that the right to present evidence is a fundamental guarantee for any type of trial.[13] This is true to such an extent that without the right to present evidence, it would be impossible to speak of a valid trial.[14] Furthermore, if we consider article 117 of the Constitution, which describes the function of the courts and provides that all courts are united to form a single judiciary power, little can be said for unity if the courts fail to observe constitutional safeguards during the trial. Nonetheless, the issue at hand is to determine what exactly is the minimal element of this right recognized by the Constitution.

The Spanish Constitution of 1978 specifically deals with the right to present evidence in the abovementioned article 24.2, which states that all persons have the right to use the means of proof relevant to their defense. This statement immediately raises the following issues: First, what is the importance and scope of the fact that this right has been taken up by the Constitution and is now considered a fundamental right? Second, just how significant is the reference to a defense? And lastly, the question that is directly related with the purpose of this work: what must be understood by the reference to using relevant means of proof?

[13] See among others STC50/22 March 1988 FJ 3 and STC97/20 June 1995 FJ 4.

[14] Paradoxically, article 2 of the 23 July 1908 anti-profiteering law provides: "los Tribunales resolverán en cada caso, formando libremente su convicción en vista de las alegaciones de las partes." But see STS 8 March 1924.

Regarding the first question, there is no doubt as to the influence[15] the Constitution has had on evidence not only for the fact that it includes a series of rights directly related to evidence, but also and primarily due to its collection of fundamental rights that, on the whole, have led to a view of the criminal trial that has more to do with protecting and guaranteeing the rights of the accused than with fervently searching for material truth. Thus, the trial may be considered a guarantee of the rights and liberty of the accused. The constitutional provisions relating to evidence may be used as a starting point for those wishing to carefully examine the Spanish Code of Criminal Procedure (CCP), to which a good portion of this work is devoted.

In reference to our second question, article 24.2 draws attention to the relationship between the right to present evidence and the right to a defense with its reference to using evidence as a means of defense. The right to present evidence is one of the primary manifestations of the right to a defense and cannot be separated from it.[16] This reference to a defense, regardless of the type of trial,[17] must not be interpreted as the exclusive right of one of the parties, as it is with good reason that the article begins with a reference to "all

---

[15] STS 22 April 1986 refers to a collapse of the Code of Criminal Procedure.

[16] According to STC147/25 September 1987 FJ 2: "... dicho derecho (el derecho a utilizar los medios de prueba pertinentes, es) inseparable del derecho mismo a la defensa..."

[17] See among others STC116/7 December 1983 and 51/10 April 1985.

persons." Taking into account the relationship between these rights and the right to effective protection by the judges and courts, decisions given by the Spanish Constitutional Court have not been completely orthodox in situations that might be interpreted as violations of the right to use relevant means of proof. Under such circumstances, the Court has declared violations of the right to effective protection by the judges and courts,[18] violations of the right to a defense in general, and other violations. Although we do not contend that they were mistaken, more specific judgments that would have avoided, if only in part, the creation of the macro concept of defenselessness would have been preferable.

Moreover, an analysis of decisions dealing with the right to effective protection by the judges and courts suggests that the essential content of this right is unclear. The Constitutional Court has found that giving adequate grounds for a judgment is part of the essential content of the right to effective protection by the judges and courts; therefore, it follows that inadequate grounds or a groundless judgment might be viewed as a violation of this right (and also of article 120.3 of the Constitution). However, the fact that these judgments might result from a lack of evidence does not necessarily mean

[18] E.g., see among others STC89/1986, 50/1988, and 357/1993, which state that the right to use relevant means of proof (article 24.2) does not mean that evidence cannot be affected or protected in accordance with the right to effective protection by the judges and courts under article 24, paragraph 1 of the Constitution. Similarly, STC40/1986 also finds that the right to effective protection by the judges and courts encompasses the right to use relevant means of proof.

that the right to present evidence has been violated.

All in all, the fact that the Constitution has raised the status of the right to present evidence to that of a fundamental right does not mean that this right is absolute as the article itself infers limitations that warrant clarification. As we mentioned above with our third point, the right to present evidence is considered the right to use relevant means of proof (which is the very foundation of this work). The concept of relevance in connection with evidence has been a bit difficult for the Constitutional Court (which has paid close attention to Supreme Court decisions) to define, if indeed it has been achieved. It has pronounced judgments if not for all tastes, than at least for quite a few. A definition included in judgment 51/1985 FJ 9 of the Constitutional Court is the most acceptable. It provides that relative to evidence, relevance is the relationship between evidence, the object of the trial, and the thema decidendi as defined by the Court. It involves the ability of the means used to shape the final opinion of the Court. According to this definition, relevance is not synonymous with admissibility as admissibility is based on a decision regarding the necessity or utility of the items of evidence.

We will now focus on the essential content of the right to present evidence with the help of the premier authority on the Spanish Constitution, taking into account, as we have previously stated, that limitations are provided under article 24.2 and also, that the way this right is exercised is regulated only by law, which must always respect its essential content (Spanish Constitution, article 53.1). Two courses, which are not divergent but parallel, may be followed to determine this "essential content." First, the Constitutional Court suggests turning to what is generally called the legal nature or way of understanding or perceiving each right. According to this concept, a relationship must be established between the language used in regulatory clauses and what some authors have called metalanguage or widespread ideas and principles that are generally accepted among jurists, judges, and on the whole, legal specialists. Many times the designation and scope of a subjective right were existent before the right was recorded and regulated by a particular lawmaker. An abstract notion of the right existed conceptually before its legislative moment. Thus, it is possible to speak of a recognizance of the abstract conception of the right within the written regulation. Legal specialists can respond as to whether or not the lawmaker's work is in line with what is generally understood as the essence of the right. The essential content of a subjective right are those powers and potential for action that are necessary in order for the essence of the right to be identified and without such powers and potential, it would no longer be considered the same kind of right and would have to be redefined in a process of denaturalization, so to speak. All of this occurs within the context of a particular point in time and with regard to the inherent conditions of democratic societies when constitutional rights are concerned. Another way to define the essential content of a right is to seek out what an important school has called the interests that are legally protected as the heart and soul of subjective rights. We may speak of the essentialness of the content of a right in reference to that part of the content that is absolutely necessary to ensure that the interests subject to legal protection, those that give life to the right, are real, precise, and indeed protected. Thus, the essential content becomes distorted or unrecognizable when the right is subjected to limitations that make it impossible or unreasonably difficult to exercise, or that strip it of the necessary protection.[19]

Although we began by defining the "abstract notion" of the right to present evidence referenced by the Constitutional Court, we acknowledge that this alone would not be enough to proceed with a systematic analysis of the way the right is treated in judgments. We must also create an "abstract" list of the principles and interests subject to minimum legal protection before we may make reference to the right to present evidence. Limiting ourselves in the following to the criminal trial, we refer first to the work of Alsberg, who notes that before considering the right to present evidence, one must take into account the ex officio duty to clarify the facts relevant to the decision. The author considers this activity (Ermittlungsgrundsatz) the prevailing principle of not only the right to present evidence in the criminal trial, but also of the entire criminal proceedings in general.[20] This "principle

[19] STC11/8 April 1981 FJ 8.

of investigation" (Ermittlungsgrundsatz) requires the Court (Gericht), free from any proposals, requests, or clarifications made by the parties, to ascertain the facts for itself.[21]

It must be taken into account, as is well known, that the pre-trial investigative proceedings carried out by examining judges in Spain (instrucción) do not exist as such in Germany. The German investigative proceedings (Ermittlungsverfahren) are under the exclusive control of the Public Prosecutor.

Going back to our literal translation of Alsberg, the statement "the Court ascertains for itself" can be properly explained by referring to the Spanish principle governing investigation, which states that what the parties allege and may later prove could aid in the investigative and evidentiary processes; however, it never limits the investigative powers of the Judge or Court (E.g., see the Code of Criminal Procedure, article 729.1). This is referred to as material or complete defense in legal doctrine. It is a public activity in which all of the authorities and officials involved with the criminal trial are participants. The objective is to verify and evaluate the circumstances, which might be either adverse or favorable for

---

20 "... nicht das Recht der Prozessbeteiligten, Beweisanträge zu stellen, sondern die Pflicht des Gerichts, alle, für die Enstscheidung erheblichen Tatsachen von Amts wegen aufzuklären, der Ermittlungsgrundsatz, ist das alles beherrschende Prinzip des Beweisrechts der Strafprozessordnung und darüber hinaus des ganzen Strafverfahrens." Alsberg/Nüse/Meyer, Der Beweisantrag im Strafprozess 19 (5th ed. 1983).

21 "Der Ermittlungsgrundsatz bedeutet, dass das Gericht den Sachverhalt selber ermittelt (sich selbst, instruiert`) und dabei an Anträge und Erklärungen der Prozessbeteiligten nicht gebunden ist." Roxin, Strafverfahrensrecht 76 (20th ed. 1987).

the accused.

The right to present evidence as described above aids in the "search for the truth" by providing the decision maker with the items of evidence necessary for him or her to form an opinion that is as much in accordance as possible with the truth of the facts to be judged. This activity is directly connected to the duty to judge as prudently as possible. Anything that stands in the way of this search (Ermittlung) for the truth or clarification of the facts (Sachaufklärungs) is damaging to the essential content of the right to present evidence. Thus, denying a witness for the defense the opportunity to testify to what he or she witnessed would clearly at the same time obstruct the search for the truth. The same would hold true if the witness in question were to testify for the prosecution.

Nevertheless, although the right to present evidence implies that the parties are able to "demonstrate the truth" or more preferably, help to clarify the facts, it does not mean that they may do this in any and all circumstances, but rather only during the trial, when an additional set of equally protected principles and interests is involved.[22]

Thus, it is apparent that the right to present evidence is actually the right to a certain procedural activity and as such, it is subject to the same set of generally advocated principles pertaining to the trial and to criminal procedure. The following principles are of particular interest: relating to

---

[22] See generally Schöne, A., Límites de la prueba en el Derecho procesal, Trans. Rohrbach Roji, E., RDP 374 (1955).

the trial, the right to confront and cross-examine opposing witnesses or evidence and the guarantee that both parties are on an equal footing; and with respect to procedure, the right to oral argument and the guarantee that the decision maker will be present at the trial. This procedural activity, known as evidentiary process, must not be classified as such when these rights are violated.

Although we are aware of the terminological difficulties arising from the doctrine and jurisprudence dealing with this very important issue, and we acknowledge that any attempt at systematization is difficult, with the help of the doctrine and jurisprudence in question, we shall briefly expand upon the abovementioned principles relating to evidence.[23]

---

[23] To introduce, though summarily, the principles governing the criminal trial, we refer to the work of Montero, who notes: "...el principio de legalidad no ha sido recogido en la Constitución con la suficiente claridad. La fórmula del art. 25.1... es cuando menos insatisfactoria... Del principio de necesidad procesal puede decirse lo mismo. Exige una labor minuciosa de análisis incardinar las dos notas del principio en la Constitución. La primera de ellas, la relativa a que la pena sólo puede ser impuesta por los Tribunales mediante el proceso, puede rastrearse en los arts. 24, 25, 53.2 y 106.1... La segunda nota, la necesidad de poner en marcha el proceso penal cuando aparezca un hecho presuntamente delictivo, todavía es de más difícil incardinación en la Constitución. Efectivamente el art. 124 sujeta al Ministerio Fiscal al principio de legalidad en su actuación, pero ¿dónde se dice que todos los delitos deben originar un proceso?" Regarding the "principle of investigation," which developed from the principle of compulsory prosecution, the following are important elements:
(1) Court proceedings are not brought per the will of a private party.
(2) It must not be left to private parties to establish the object of the trial. In a criminal trial the object is not a claim on a criminal act, but the act itself, which is considered either a crime or a minor offense.
(3) The fact that the parties may not decide the object of the trial leads to

It is important to remember that before the Constitution entered into force in 1978, Law 42/28 November 1974 provided that as a guarantee of court procedure, the principle of legality and the right to confront and cross-examine opposing witnesses or evidence (audiatur et altera pars does not refer to direct debate between the prosecution and the defense, but rather to the opportunity to set off evidence for the prosecution with evidence in response to the charges in any suitable way that might bring the real truth to light for the judge)[24] would be recognized under all circumstances. The right to a public trial is observed (except in those instances provided under the law), and the principle governing motions and the right to oral argument is respected.

It is quite obvious from article 24 of the Spanish Constitution that there is a difference between generic guarantees (for example, defenselessness is not permitted under article 24.1) and the specific rights listed in paragraph 2 of the same article. As we have mentioned, the right to a defense and the right to present evidence are included among these specific rights.

Regarding this topic, it is necessary to clarify several issues. First, disregarding the "supposed" categories of defenselessness

---

diverse consequences in terms of congruence: the Court is not bound by the positions that the parties might maintain.
(4) Private parties do not have control over the collective interests at stake in the trial and they may not decide to conclude the trial. Montero Aroca with Ortells Ramos and Gómez Colomer, Derecho Jurisdiccional I 511, 512, 515, 516 (2d ed. 1991).

[24] Viada López-Puigcerver, C., La ausencia del acusado en el proceso penal, 3 RDP 578 (1962).

asserted by the Constitutional Court,[25] on the basis of the decisions of this Court, one might contend that the type of defenselessness mentioned in article 24 is the violation of the right to confront opposing witnesses or evidence. However, it is patently clear that every limitation placed on this right (the law itself restricts it for obvious procedural reasons) does not amount to a violation of the right. If the right to present evidence is nothing more or less than one specific aspect of the right to a defense, which in turn is found to be connected to the "right to be heard" during the trial (right to confront opposing witnesses or evidence), it follows that denying a party the opportunity to exercise a legally envisaged right to present evidence cannot always be construed as a violation of the right to be heard. Moreover, we must not suppose that the law fails to take account of the right to be heard from the fact that it does not give the party a specific opportunity to present evidence when thought appropriate.[26] On the contrary, in order to declare a violation of the right to be heard for infringement of the right to present evidence, the party must have been denied the opportunity to present any evidence

---

[25] See Gesto Alonso, G., Precisiones sobre el concepto de indefensión desde el punto de vista procesal, 2 RDP 301+ (1991), which deals with the supposed difference between procedural defenselessness and constitutional defenselessness.

[26] For example, in the German criminal trial right to evidence may be exercised until the moment in which judgment is intimated (Beginn der Urteilsverkündung) (3 Gollwitzer, Löwe-Rosenberg, Großkommentar section 244, note 100 (24th ed. 1989)), while in Spanish proceedings this is not legally envisaged. This does not mean that the right to be heard does not govern Spanish proceedings.

whatsoever or encountered obstacles or limitations that prevented the evidence from being presented appropriately.

All things considered, not every restriction on the right to present evidence violates the right to be heard. Also, as we will have the opportunity to thoroughly analyze in the next chapter with an examination of the right to a hearing (Anspruch auf rechtliches Gehör) under article 103.1 of the German Constitution (Grundgesetz), the view that the right to a defense is closely connected to the right to be heard during the trial means that the parties are entitled not only to make allegations and to use relevant means of proof, but also to know the accusations made against them and to examine documents pertaining to their case. Thus, they are prepared to argue and may eventually prove their case on the basis of accurate knowledge of the matter.[27][28]

The right to be heard is such an integral part of the trial (not only the criminal trial, but all trials in general) that the latter would not exist without the former. This point is indisputable — so much so that we might say that in a hierarchical pyramid of procedural guarantees, the right to be heard would be found at the very top.[29]

This right involves preventing a conviction if the accused has

---

[27] So held the Constitutional Court in STC13/22 April 1981 FJ 6 in fine.

[28] This point has led doctrine to treat the concept of defense not only as a right, but also as a duty. See Viada López-Puigcerver, C., La ausencia del acusado en el proceso penal, 3 RDP 137 (1962).

[29] According to STS 23 November 1950, the right to be heard is one of the pillars of procedural law.

not been given the opportunity to argue and prove a case, as is his or her right. However, this does not suggest that the right to present evidence is an absolute right, as the law may impose restrictions, so long as such restrictions are reasonable.

Article 120.2 of the Constitution provides that procedure shall be predominantly oral, especially in criminal matters. This provision has been criticized, and with good reason, in legal doctrine. The reference to criminal matters must be due to the lawmakers' realization that in precisely such matters, we are dealing with a guarantee that suggests that it is only possible to speak of evidence in the context of a plenary session[30] or that only what happens during oral proceedings may serve as grounds for a decision (Goldschmidt). Today, this guarantee might be questioned, as we will later see, not only relative to documentary evidence, but also with regard to the importance that should be given to the pre-trial investigation in criminal proceedings, which is governed by a Code of Criminal Procedure that has yielded under the influence of the Constitution. Any reference to the principle requiring oral argument refers at the same time to the following concepts: the decision maker must be present during the proceedings (article 205.3 of the Organic Law of the Judiciary and articles 746 and 749 of the Code of Criminal Procedure), all items of evidence must be examined in succession, and the trial

---

[30] Exposición de Motivos of the Code of Criminal Procedure underscores the fundamental idea that evidence should be thoroughly dealt with during public oral proceedings.

must be public. In fact, many have likened the right to oral argument or the requisite to be heard to the concept of "equal footing."[31] Along these lines, as is well known, a general statement relating to the principle of equality can be found in article 14 of the Spanish Constitution, which provides that all Spaniards are equal in the eyes of the law. This clause makes one wonder if we are truly able to speak of equality for all Spaniards in court proceedings when the truth is that justice is no where near free of charge,[32] which many times is reason enough for citizens to forego exercising their rights in court. This is especially true in the criminal trial, where it is even more likely that individuals will be unable to raise an appropriate defense due to a lack of economic means, not to mention those who are unable to appropriately exercise their right to present evidence because their economic situation does not allow them, for example, to obtain the services of a particular expert witness as such witnesses are generally unwilling to work ex officio (see CCP, article 121).

Returning to the idea of procedural equality in connection with evidence, we shall define this concept as the absence of privilege, or the fact that neither party finds itself in an advantaged position relative to the right to prove their case. This guarantee can be deduced from article 24, paragraph 2

---

[31] Goldschmidt, IV abril-mayo-junio 2 RDP 190 (1950).

[32] Article 119 of the Constitution provides that Justice shall be free of charge when the law so provides and, under all circumstances, for those who have insufficient means to litigate. Regarding this matter, the enactment of Law 1/10 January 1996 of Free Legal Assistance is significant.

of the Constitution, which states that if all persons have the right to use the means of proof relevant to their defense, then the principle of equality relative to evidence suggests that all persons are "equally" entitled to use these means of proof.

The right to equality relative to evidence is infringed when due to the existence of "inequality" of any kind, whether it is attributed to the lawmaker or different situations that might arise in practice, one party enjoys an unjustifiably privileged position that is damaging to the other party's right to present evidence. Specifically, parties are entitled to present evidence for the prosecution and evidence for the defense under equal conditions.[33] Immediately, the question arises as to whether or not this right applies to all stages of the criminal trial. It seems that the during the investigative or pre-trial proceedings, we cannot refer to a right to present evidence for the accused, at least not with the same conditions that would be afforded during the trial.

While we have said that all persons are "equally" entitled to use relevant means of proof, it is also true that in the investigative stage of the criminal trial, it is not always possible to make reference to "parties" and therefore to "equality". However, a case for equality can be found in the fact that the accused may propose inquiries, procedures, and practices (see article 311 of the Code of Criminal Procedure), and thus any possible kind of "inequality" that might be inferred, either

[33] This statement from Exposición de Motivos of the Code of Criminal Procedure refers to the trial.

from the law or in certain circumstances as a result of the actions of the judge overseeing the investigative proceedings, might be justified, according to Alonso Martínez, by the calculated introduction of inequality by the perpetrator (at the beginning of the proceedings). We will later have the opportunity to examine these evidence requests referenced in the Code of Criminal Procedure. However, at this point, it seems opportune to refer to the work of this celebrated jurist, who addresses the matter in the well-known Exposición de Motivos. He notes that all concessions, which might seem excessive to some Judges and Senior Judges, will probably still not satisfy certain radical schools that are trying to extend the right to a public trial, the right to confront and cross-examine opposing witnesses or evidence, and the principle of equality (which the proposed code provided from the time the trial is opened until final judgment is given) to the accused at the beginning of the investigative or pre-trial proceedings. Alonso Martínez notes that the provision does not suggest that he and the other distinguished authors do not ardently and faithfully support the theory maintained by the radical schools; however, they believed that at that time it could not be considered anything more than an "ideal" of the science of law to which the positive legislation of modern times was progressively coming closer to capturing. Would it someday be achieved? The authors sincerely doubted it. It is difficult to establish absolute equality of legal conditions between the individual and the State at the very start of proceedings because of the real inequality that in that critical moment exists between the two; a calculated introduction of inequality has been carried out by the perpetrator, and for this he or she is solely responsible. From the moment in which the offense is conceived, or at least from the time that his or her conscience is corrupted and the deliberate intention to commit the offense is formed, the perpetrator carefully formulates a number of precautions to elude justice and to put official authorities in a position analogous to that of the victim, who, defenseless and unprepared, is caught by surprise. Therefore, in order to reestablish equal conditions in the fight, as the aforementioned authors liken criminal proceedings to a noble duel between two opponents, the State must wield some sort of advantage at the start, if only to collect evidence of the crime and clues the suggest perpetrator's guilt. But be that as it may, only time will tell if the ideal will be achieved. In the mean time, the authors note that those who have the honor of affecting the destiny of a people must be prudent. They must not use codes to naturalize ideas that are still in a period of propaganda, concepts that have not developed in the public opinion, much less worked their way into Spanish customs or proved themselves through the true test of experience.

After more than a century, it seems that we might say that we are almost at the point of absolute equality, or at least there is a lesser degree of inequality, and it is accepted that the right to equality, at least relative to the parties' right to present evidence, should not be violated at any stage of the proceedings. It is one thing that under certain circumstances the situation favors the Public Prosecutor (although the institution of the Prosecutor has been called ambiguous, according to Carnelutti,[34] or hybrid[35]), and it is quite another to observe that because the accused is at a disadvantage, he or she is unable to exercise the right to present evidence at any stage of the proceedings to prevent the matter from going to trial or to obtain an acquittal.

In certain situations, the sub judice rule or other measures taken to preserve evidence or otherwise protect the investigation deny the accused the right to present evidence, therefore putting him or her in a situation of apparent disadvantage. In such cases, this right should be restored immediately after there is a change in the circumstances causing the situation. During investigative proceedings, it is also important to provide the accused access to the materials that are gathered so that he or she has the opportunity to conduct a defense, in keeping with the rights afforded the accused.

Therefore, the reasons for any "inequality" in evidentiary matters that might come about during the investigative stage of the proceedings must be valid, and they should never deny the accused the opportunity to exercise the right to present evidence when appropriate. The trial, nevertheless, is the time when all aspects of the principle of equality must be carefully

[34] Doctrine has pointed out that the Public Prosecutor is dealt with in an ambiguous manner in the Constitution (marzo RGD 1747 (1994)).

[35] Vives Antón, T., Comentarios a la Ley de Medidas Urgentes de Reforma Procesal, La reforma del proceso penal 116 (1992).

observed.

The Constitution, which has the tendency to include as much as possible within a single clause, also makes reference in article 24.2 to the principle of presumption of innocence. This principle is of critical importance in criminal proceedings, although it is not exclusive to these circumstances. It is important to underscore that the right to be presumed innocent is solely procedural (it has no bearing on the specification of charges) according to STC1441/12 November 1986. If something is presumed, the presumption should be logically based on a particular true fact. As someone is "the accused," it seems illogical to presume that he or she is innocent. For this reason, the expression seems inaccurate.

Perhaps the best way to conceive the misnamed principle of presumption of innocence is to think of it not as a presumption, but as the situation or state enjoyed by the accused until it is destroyed through the evidentiary process carried out during the course of the proceedings. It is equally challenging to attempt to determine the content of the so-called right to be presumed innocent. This principle is vitally important in, although not exclusive to, evidentiary matters, and might be defined in criminal proceedings as having the following characteristics:

(1) All convictions must be based on incriminating evidence or evidence for the prosecution.

(2) The examination of evidence must take place in accordance with the law and the right to be heard, the

principle of equality, and the right to oral proceedings (which covers the right to a public trial, the right to have the decision maker present during the proceedings, and the guarantee that all items of evidence will be examined successively).

(3) All items of evidence must be presented and examined during the trial in order to be considered evidence (except in those cases in which evidence is examined beforehand in accordance with all due process guarantees).

(4) Following the examination of evidence, the decision maker must give reasons to explain his or her overall assessment (STC183/1992 and 76/1990). The Constitutional Court might focus its deliberations on the first three characteristics mentioned above when a violation of the right to be presumed innocent relative to evidentiary matters is alleged. The decision maker is free to impartially assess the evidence that is produced (CCP, article 741), and therefore the Court may not take into account the trial court's assessment of evidence in any appeal founded on a violation of this fundamental right. In other words, the Court may not consider the influence the evidence may have had on the decision maker in shaping his or her opinion or as a determining factor in the judgment.

Regarding inappropriately admitting evidence or failing to admit "relevant" means of proof, anyone who takes note of an infringement of the right to be presumed innocent should draw attention to the violation as soon as he or she realizes that it has occurred. All judicial means should be exercised at the appropriate time and exhausted before an appeal on the ground of a violation of constitutional rights is brought before the Constitutional Court.

Lastly, it is clear that our conception of criminal proceedings shapes our idea of suitable ways to handle the evidence stage and the "parties" right to evidence. The Spanish Constitution and its influence on the Code of Criminal Procedure allow us to think of criminal proceedings as more than a set of guarantees relating to what is to be judged. On the basis of the Code of Criminal Procedure itself, we might contend that criminal proceedings are not a means through which to attain punishment for the guilty, but a model instrument designed so that the State might carry out an investigation of the truth and specifically apply criminal laws. This suggests that both the police officers and the Public Prosecutor have their respective duties to discover and collect or to propose or offer evidence for both the prosecution and the defense (CCP, article 2).[36]

In conclusion, we have good reason (this cannot be found in the Code of Criminal Procedure, although it may be identified upon a close examination of the Constitution) to give a better explanation of the accused's right to present evidence throughout the entire proceedings. We must also specify clear criteria to guide those deciding whether or not to allow inquiries, procedures and practices during the investigative or pre-trial proceedings and whether or not to

[36] Vélez Mariconde, A., La función judicial en lo penal, 2 RDP 302 (1968).

admit items in evidence during the trial. This endeavor is not at odds with the desire to conduct proceedings speedily, proposed since years past.

A3. Beweisantragsrecht

The German Constitution (Grundgesetz) does not make specific reference to the right to present evidence;[37] however, it is inferred from a set of general principles of procedural law. This is proved by the fact that German Constitutional Court (Bundesverfassungsgericht) judgments have recognized the right as a constitutional guarantee. There are some who classify it as the most important right afforded the "participants" (Prozessbeteiligten)[38] in oral proceedings

[37] In Germany, the term "Beweisantragsrecht" refers to the right to present evidence.

[38] Kleinknecht prefers to refer to "participants" (Prozessbeteiligten) rather than parties (Parteien) in the context of criminal proceedings. He contends that criminal proceedings do not involve parties in the same way as civil proceedings. Kleinknecht/Meyer-Gossner, Strafprozeßordnung note 9 (41st ed. 1993). Montero is not mistaken in his explanation of the difference between material and formal parties when he contends that in the criminal trial it is appropriate to speak of parties. The following definition for a formal party is given: "quien actúa en el proceso pidiendo del órgano jurisdiccional una resolución judicial, esto es, quien promueve la actuación del órgano jurisdiccional aportando, por medio de sus alegaciones y pruebas, el material para la resolución de contenido determinado que postula, quien en síntesis participa de la contradicción en que se resuelve todo el proceso." Montero Aroca, Derecho Jurisdiccional

(Hauptverhandlung).[39] It should be taken into account that up until the present day doctrine and jurisprudence based on article 14, paragraph 3, letter (e) of the International Covenant on Civil and Political Rights and article 8, paragraph 2, letter (f) of the American Convention on Human Rights have seen very little development, and there are some who contend that United States Supreme Court decisions grounded on the Sixth Amendment of the U.S. Constitution, which also refers to this fundamental right in the context of the jury trial, are the only ones that can be compared with German Supreme Court judgments.[40]

Article 103, paragraph 1 of the German Constitution guarantees the right to a hearing (Anspruch auf rechtliches Gehör). Decisions based on this guarantee that have also interpreted it as grounds for the right to request evidence (Beweisantragsrecht), which is the focus of our analysis, are singularly important.[41] However, this right has been applied

---

III 35, 52-53 (1991). To read more about different positions taken on this issue, see Muerza Esparza with De la Oliva, Aragoneses Martínez, Hinojosa Segovia, Tomé García, Derecho Procesal Penal 130-131 (1996) and 2 Clariá Olmedo, J., Tratado de Derecho Procesal Penal 28+. According to Gómez Orbaneja: "El concepto de parte es un puro concepto formal del Derecho procesal." Gómez Orbaneja-Herce Quemada, Lecciones de Derecho Procesal 96 (1946). For a view opposing the use of the term "parties" in reference to the criminal trial, see Zafra, J., Posición del Ministerio Fiscal en el futuro proceso penal, 4 RDP 818 (1961).

[39] Cf. Alsberg/Nüse/Meyer, Der Beweisantrag im Strafprozess 371 (5th ed. 1983).

[40] See Perron, Das Beweisantragsrecht des Beschuldigten im deutschen Strafprozess 28 (1995).

[41] See Schmidt-Bleibtreu, Klein Kommentar zum Grundgesetz 1310 (8th

in recent years in different ways, with differing degrees of intensity, and obviously in matters other than the criminal trial.

Before pronouncing (Erlass) judgment (Entscheidung), the Courts must ensure that the participants (Verfahrensbeteiligten) right to a hearing has been observed.[42] With regard to civil actions, the German Supreme Court (Erste Senat) delivered judgment on this right to a public hearing under article 103.1 of the Constitution in the late 1970s. Later, other decisions dealing with this fundamental procedural right were given, underscoring that denying an evidence request because the grounds on which it is based have no merit in procedural law[43] amounts to a violation of that right.

Although the right to evidence (Beweisrecht) has received constitutional backing, this does not mean that the content and limits of this right have been clearly defined. According to Perron, the praxis of the Civil Courts still differs considerably from the example set with the abovementioned judgments. This is evidenced by the fact that recently a considerable number of appeals to the Constitutional Court

ed. 1995).

[42] BVerfGE 36 88: "Für das Gericht erwächst aus Art. 103 Abs. 1 GG (Grundgesetz) die Pflicht, vor dem Erlass seiner Entscheidung zu prüfen, ob dem Verfahrensbeteiligten das rechtliche Gehör gewährt wurde."

[43] "... dann als verletzt an, wenn ein Beweisantrag abgelehnt wird aus Gründen, die ` im Prozessrecht keine Stütze finden." BVerfGE 50, 32, 35+, BVerfGE 25, 137, 140+ cited by Perron, Das Beweisantragsrecht des Beschuldigten im deutschen Strafprozess 28 (1995).

(Verfassungsbeschwerden) allege an infringement of the right to evidence on the grounds that motions have been erroneously and wrongfully denied (Nichtberücksichtigungen).

Regarding criminal proceedings, the right to a public hearing under article 103.1 of the German Constitution suggests that the accused should be given the opportunity to demonstrate the facts and lead evidence (Beweismaterial),[44] although we must not dismiss the opinion of those who believe that the right to a hearing has nothing to do with the right to evidence (Beweisantragsrecht) in criminal proceedings.[45][46] They contend that laws dealing with evidence already contain provisions that specifically guarantee this right.[47]

Perron suggests that judgments from criminal proceedings similar to the abovementioned judgments given in civil actions are scarce. However, there are strict controls resulting from

---

[44] See Schönke Bahnsen, Das Akteneinsichtsrecht der Verteidigung im Strafverfahren 15 (1996).

[45] See Werner on page 145, who contends that the right to evidence cannot be inferred from the right to a public hearing; cited by Alsberg/Nüse/Meyer, Der Beweisantrag im Strafprozess, 372 (5th ed).

[46] It is interesting to refer to the work of Roxin, who distinguishes between parties' active and passive rights (Beteiligter) and classifies those rights in "rechtliches Gehör," which does not include any rights related to evidence. Under the "activen Beteilungsrechten" of the accused (Beschuldigten), distinctions are made between those rights related to "Anspruch auf rechtliches Gehör" and the "other procedural rights" ("weitere Verfahrensrechte") that "sind im Vorverfahren noch verhältnismässig gering und schwach ausgebildet, im Zwischen- und Hauptverfahren dagegen zahlreich und vielfältig. I. e. sind zu nennen: (g) das Recht auf Stellung von Beweisanträgen" (sections 219, 244-246). Roxin, Strafverfahrensrecht 107-108 (24th ed. 1995).

[47] See StPO, sections 257 and 244, paragraphs 3-6.

decisions given by the Supreme Court (Bundesgerichtshof) and the High Courts of Ländern (Oberlandesgerichte). In a few isolated cases, the Criminal Division of the German Constitutional Court (Bundesverfassungsgericht), in appeals for judicial review, has objected to the fact that evidence requests were denied (Wiederaufnahmeverfahren), declaring a violation of the Constitution, article 103, paragraphs 1 and 3. In monetary fine proceedings (Bussgeldsache), the Second Chamber of this Criminal Division (zweite Kammer des zweiten Senats) found that denying a request for evidence amounted to a violation of the right to a public hearing.[48] According to Gollwitzer, it should be noted that the principle governing the right to a public hearing (Grundsatz des rechtlichen Gehörs) also provides for fact clarification by allowing those who participate in the proceedings (Prozessbeteiligten) to present to the Court those facts that are relevant to the decision (entscheidungsrelevanter Tatsachen). Accordingly, this duty to clarify facts (Aufklärungspflicht) is not fulfilled when the Court fails to uphold its responsibility to ensure that the accused is fully informed (Kenntnis) of the matters to be addressed during the proceedings (Mündlichen Verhandlung). This being the case, the accused will be taken by surprise with facts that he or she was not given the opportunity after indictment (Anklageschrift) or during the

[48] See BVerfGE NJW 3191-3192 (1990) and BVerfGE StV 307-308 (1992), cited by Perron, Das Beweisantragsrecht des Beschuldigten im deutschen Strafprozess 29 (1995).

course (Gang) of the proceedings (Hauptverhandlung) to adequately prepare to answer.[49]

Although up until this point it has not been necessary to carefully analyze the constitutional base for the right to present evidence,[50] such analysis would be important for those wishing to review the precepts governing the admissibility of evidence. There may be some who would like to do just that, considering that presently there are many "blockades" (to use a term similar to the German one) in German trials. These are instigated by the defense, which claims the "right to present evidence" as a tactic for holding up the proceedings and preventing justice from being done (according to Jeschek).

While it is not the purpose of this work to deal with the constitutional grounds for the right to present evidence in Germany, we found it fitting to refer to the work of Perron and devote a few lines to this task in an effort to contribute to the future work of those focusing their efforts on this important matter.

Although reference has been made to a second set of judgments that focus on the right to a hearing (Anspruch auf rechtliches Gehör) and its relationship with the right

[49] 3 Gollwitzer, Löwe-Rosenberg, Großkommentar, section 244, note 54 (24th ed. 1989).

[50] See generally Köhler, Inquisitionsprinzip und autonome Beweisführung (1979); Kühl, Prozessgegenstand und Beweisthema; and Perron, Das Beweisantragsrecht des Beschuldigten im deutschen Strafprozess (1995).

to evidence,[51] the truth of the matter is that under certain circumstances its limitations are difficult to discern, and in any case we are still unable to clearly describe the overall concept, as other principles must be considered. One such principle is Fairnessverfahren,[52][53] which is based on the guarantee of equal

---

[51] We refer to BVerfGE 57 250 (1981), which deals with a conviction based on written reports (Stellungsnahme) and police records of interrogation of witnesses (Vernehmungsprotokolle von Zeugen) who could not be personally examined or heard. Judgment was pronounced in accordance with StPO, section 251, paragraph 2, which provides that reading the record of a previous interrogation may substitute for witness interrogation during the trial under certain circumstances (such as illness, etc). that need not be described in further detail at this point. The Court confirmed that although the accused's right to a hearing guarantees the right to evidence, it does not, however, entitle the accused to any particular means of proof, and despite this restriction on a fundamental procedural right (Verfahrensgrundrecht) under article 103, paragraph 1 of the Constitution (Grundgesetz), in a criminal trial, the accused is entitled to a search for the truth that is not encumbered at any time during the proceedings (Verfahr ensgestaltungen). Therefore, in the end, section 251, paragraph 2 of StPO is not an impediment, as in light of other guarantees (under sections 244, 245, and 246, paragraph 1), the accused is afforded ample opportunity to exercise the right to evidence. Other judgments given by BVerfGE are in keeping with this line of reasoning. In accordance with these judgments, the sections of StPO that deal with the right to evidence would be revised so that reasonable requests for evidence (Bestimmtheitsanforderungen) submitted by the accused are given adequate opportunity to influence the clarification of the truth as the Court conducts its own investigation of the facts (Ermittlungsverfahren). See Perron, Das Beweisantragsrecht des Beschuldigten im deutschen Strafprozess 29+ (1995).

[52] The idea of a "fair hearing" does not have an exact equivalent in German; therefore, in law, generally reference is made to "faires Verfahren". See Miehsler/Vogler, Internationaler Kommentar zur EMRK article 6, note 341 (1986).

[53] The principle comes from article 6, paragraph 1 of the European Convention on Human Rights. See Roxin, Strafverfahrensrecht 69 (24th ed. 1995). Cf. articles 1, 20, and 28 of the Constitution (Grundgesetz).

footing (Waffengleichheit) between the prosecution and the defense,[54] and is the premise of article 6, paragraph 3 of the European Convention on Human Rights. Although some might contend that grounds for the right to evidence can be seen in the principle requiring equal footing (Grundsatz der Waffengleichheit)[55] (principio de paridad de armas),[56] this seems to be more closely related to English procedure than to the ex officio investigative procedure characteristic of the continental European system, although the highest authorities on the Convention have not found this to be true in view of article 6, paragraph 3, letter (d).[57]

As though the abovementioned concepts related to the right to a hearing weren't enough to consider, we must also take into account the principle governing the search for the truth (Ermittlungsgrundsatz), which requires the Court to ascertain the facts for itself, not being bound by the proposals and clarifications made by those participating in the proceedings (Prozessbeteiligten).[58] Moreover, we must consider the duty to clarify these facts (Aufklärungspflicht), which entitles the participants to the examination of all evidence that is expected

[54] See Frowein/Peukert, EMRK article 6, note 60 (1985).
[55] Sandermann, Waffengleihheit im Strafprozess 179 (1975).
[56] Bandrés, J.M., Eficacia y garantismo en el proceso penal, junio 1999 RGD 6374.
[57] This provision guarantees, as we noted earlier, the right of the accused to obtain the attendance and examination of witnesses on his or her behalf under the same conditions as witnesses against him or her.
[58] See Roxin, Strafverfahrensrecht 87 (24th ed). and StPO, sections 155.2 and 244.2.

to result in further clarification of the facts.[59]

We must mention the most recent judgments relating to asylum proceedings given by the German Constitutional Court (BVerfGe) for the effect they have had on the right to present evidence. These judgments were based on a former law governing asylum proceedings (Asylverfahrensgesetz) from 1982, which provided that if grounds were clearly lacking ("offensichtlich unbegründeten"), appeals (Rechtsmittel) challenging decisions given by the Administrative Court of Law (Verwaltungsgerichte) could not be lodged. The Constitutional Court found this provision constitutional in view of article 16, paragraph 2, sentence 2 of an earlier version of the Constitution. During the course (ausgestaltung) of asylum proceedings, a detailed and complete clarification of the facts surrounding the situation was contrary to correct procedure. Later, the Constitutional Court found that due to the importance of an ex officio clarification of the facts (Sachverhaltsaufklärung) in asylum proceedings, strict requirements should be established.

Thus, despite the fact that requests could be denied in accordance with the law, evidence requests submitted by those seeking asylum should only have been denied if there

[59] Aufklärungspflicht might be translated as "the duty to clarify the facts." Aufklärungspflicht des Gerichts refers to the Court's ex officio duty to clarify the facts. See Alsberg/Nüse/Myer, Der Beweisantrag im Strafprozess 372 (5th ed. 1983). "Die Amtsaufklärungspflicht des Gerichts begründet für die Prozessbeteiligten einen Anspruch auf Erhebung aller Beweise, von denen vernünftigerweise eine weitere Aufklärung der Sache zu erwarten ist."

was a legal reason for denying the request (Ablehnungsgrund) and furthermore, no special circumstance arose on which the request (Beweiserhebung) could be based. This decision would result in more appeals to the Constitutional Court (Verfassungsbeschwerden) defending the right to present evidence in response to unacceptable rulings that did not allow evidence to be presented in asylum proceedings.[60]

In conclusion, the right to evidence (Beweisrecht) is a right that is guaranteed under the Constitution in Germany, although the scope of this right is not always clear. Also, the right to a public hearing is generally recognized as grounds for the right to evidence,[61] and both rights contribute to fact-finding (Sachverhaltsfeststellung). We should also draw attention to the fact that judgments given by the German Constitutional Court are limited to special cases, as neither the laws nor the Supreme Court's interpretation of these laws have been challenged. Perhaps this is because the right to evidence is better defined than the concepts of a public hearing, fair trial (fairen Verfahren) and equal footing.[62]

---

[60] Perron, Das Beweisantragsrecht des Beschuldigten im deutschen Strafprozess 31+ (1995). See generally EuGRZ 271+ (1996) for a 14 May 1996 judgment given by BVerfGE dealing with a situation involving a violation of the right to a public hearing.

[61] "So wird die Garantie des Rechtlichen Gehörs allgemein als Basis des Beweisantragsrechts anerkannt." Perron, Das Beweisantragsrecht des Beschuldigten im deutschen Strafprozess 31 (1995).

[62] In Strasbourg, measures for defining evidentiary process (Beweiserhebung) and requests (Beweisführungsanspruchs) submitted by the accused have not been accepted. See Perron, Das Beweisantragsrecht des Beschuldigten im deutschen Strafrecht 35-36 (1995). See also Pieth,

B. Evidence in the Criminal Trial

B1. Analysis of the Stages of Evidentiary Process in the Criminal Trial

a) Evidence Proposals and Requests

Referring exclusively to the "parties" in proceedings, it must be taken into account that there are different ways to adduce means of proof (instruments). This may be done through proceedings involving either motions or proposals. The first proceeding is what is known as evidence request (Beweisantrag) in the strict sense of the term. A party initiates this proceeding, which specifically amounts to a motion that specifies both the fact that the party intends to prove and the means of proof they will attempt to use. In contrast, a proposal is made when the parties simply "offer" the Court the means of proof they believe beneficial as the Court has expressly or implicitly recognized their importance. They might also offer straightforward factual statements to be proved without specifying any particular means of proof. Under these circumstances, the only obligation that falls upon the Court

who states that both the European Commission and the European Supreme Courts demonstrate an almost immeasurable amount of judicial discretion when determining whether or not a particular witness or expert witness might contribute to the clarification of the facts. In many situations, they allow evidence to be pre-assessed (Beweiswürdigung).

relates to its duty to clarify the facts (Amtsaufklärungspflicht) or to ensure that a thorough search for the truth is conducted (CCP, article 726).

a1) History of Evidence Requests in the Criminal Trial

The principle that the purpose of evidence is to shape the opinion of the Judge was accepted in Rome. It was also widely recognized that the mind of a Roman judge was free and irrepressible. This belief was expressed through the judge's right to relieve himself of the duty to judge by claiming not to have understood any of the facts of the case.[63]

Among the different ways parties could interject knowledge of the facts into the proceedings, already in ancient times a distinction was made between oath and confession. While oath came about as a result of evidentiary process, the early idea of confession was a spontaneous announcement made by one of the parties of unfavorable facts (confessio in iure). This was similar to an oath or statement on the facts in that they both resolved the dispute. Later, the concept of confession implied a connection between the judge and what was confessed (confessio apud iudicem), taking into account that to consider confession an authentic means of proof it must be subject to the same process as all other means of proof,

[63] 1 Chiovenda, Ensayos de Derecho Procesal Civil 359 (1949). Cited by R. Valcárcel, VI octubre-noviembre-diciembre 4 RDP 584 (1950).

and above all, the Judge must freely assess it. The end result of how the concept has developed through the years is that confession is considered a means of proof (Prieto Castro).

The evidence of witnesses was of such importance in Rome that certain legal acts (testamentary instruments, conveyances, and changes in patria potestas, etc). were not valid unless witnesses were present.[64]

Germanic proceedings were modified as a result of Christianization in Germany in the High Middle Ages. Evidentiary formalism grew weaker as judges began to investigate the true relationship between what was proved and what was under debate. There were fewer opportunities for parties to take the initiative as judges stepped up and directed more of the proceedings. This tendency became stronger, bolstered by the king's power to give orders (bannus and bannitio) that was exercised through the lower court judges or implemented directly in certain cases heard by royal courts.[65]

Regarding confession, Prieto Castro notes that historically Spanish laws were more absolute than German ones, and although under the German system the oath was labeled a means of proof, this was not the case. It stayed on a merely formal plane, and the judge was not required to make any kind of personal assessment.[66]

[64] 1 Paul Ourliac and J. de Malafosse, Derecho romano y francés histórico, Tran. Fairén, Derecho de Obligaciones 111-112 (1960).
[65] Pérez-Prendes Muñoz-Arraco, Breviario de Derecho Germánico 94 (1993).
[66] See also French Code of Procedure, article 120; 1885 Italian Civil

In article 1.354 and those that follow, Napoleon's Civil Code distinguishes between two types of confession: judicial and extrajudicial. Article 1.358 and those that follow deal with the oath as a separate activity, classified as decisory.[67]

In the Spanish Code of Criminal Procedure, given the concept of evidence requests, it is necessary to first make reference to those means of proof customary under Spanish law so that later we might examine them from the perspective of litigants who would like to make use of these means during the trial. The laws compiled by Alfonso X (Las Siete Partidas) refer to certain means of proof in a limited way. For example, Partida Tercera, Law 12, Title 14 states that a criminal action that is brought against somebody should be openly proved by means of witnesses or letters, or by the knowledge of the accused and not only by suspicions. It goes on to say that an action brought against a man or his standing must be proved and verified through evidence that is crystal clear, leaving no room for doubt.

The reference made to proving something "openly" might be interpreted as one of the principles currently governing the criminal trial: the principle that requires a public hearing.

Code, article 1.372; 1865 Italian Code of Procedure, article 222; 1940 Italian Code of Procedure, article 237. Prieto Castro, Claves para la reconstrucción histórica y práctica del derecho español sobre confesión judicial civil, V julio-agosto-septiembre 3 RDP 490 (1949).

[67] Prieto Castro, Claves para la reconstrucción histórica y práctica del derecho español sobre confesión judicial civil V julio-agosto-septiembre 3 RDP 486 (1949).

Preventing whispered closed-door sessions and actions based on mere suspicion could also be deduced from the text with its reference to "crystal clear evidence." Even more pertinent to our study is the fact that the Partidas mention specific means of proof and that in modern language these have been reduced to three: witnesses, documents (from the reference to letters), and the "confession" of the accused (knowledge of the accused).[68]

In the second book of the collection of laws Fuero Real, Law XXI, Title VIII, which deals with testimony and evidence, states that if one has a thought during his hearing and says that he wishes to prove it, and regardless of the reasons he might give, if the evidence is of no use to his case or fails to discredit the other against whom it is adduced, the decision maker will not admit the evidence, and if in some way it is received, it shall not be taken into consideration.

We can draw a clear distinction between a "thought" to be proved (allegation one would like to prove), the oral statement

---

[68] We liken the term "knowledge" to the idea of "confession" in keeping with the work of Prieto Castro, who contends that the rules governing judicial confession in Spanish law today are more flawed than those from the thirteenth century. Claves para la reconstrucción histórica y práctica del derecho español sobre confesión judicial civil, V julio-agosto-septiembre 3 RDP 484, 483 (1949). However, the author concludes by saying: "Una consecuente evolución histórica de nuestro derecho procesal debería habernos puesto hace tiempo en posesión de un medio investigatorio-probatorio semejante a la Parteivernehmung del derecho austriaco y del alemán, según la Novela de 1933... o al interrogatorio non formale delle parti del derecho italiano." Fuero Real, Title VII deals with the concept of knowledge.

that makes the desire to prove known, and the criteria for ruling evidence inadmissible, which focus exclusively on what one would like to prove. Thus, when the thought in question (whether or not proved) has no bearing on the object of the proceedings (appropriate connection between what one would like to prove and thema decidendi) or fails to discredit the other against whom evidence was adduced, the judge will not admit the evidence, and if it were to be admitted, it would have no effect on the proceedings.

According to Title XV of the third book of Usages de Barcelona, evidence is led by means of witnesses, documents, reasoned statements, or credible clues. Oath is not evidence.[69]

This provision clearly sets out several specific means for presenting evidence, and consequently a reason to deny an "evidence request" when it is made by way of means that are not recognized in law or means that are specifically excluded (in this case, for example, oaths are excluded).

A precursor to evidence requests in the criminal trial in Spanish law can be identified from the way to move forward with criminal proceedings described in the oldest of Spanish texts. Information is given on "royal evidentiary process" or the examination of witnesses before the Escribano del Crimen, who was named by the King and Queen to receive complaints and take down the first reports of offenses in order

[69] Usages de Barcelona, Book III, Title XVI deals exclusively with witnesses; Book III, Title XVII refers to instruments; and Book IV, Title I deals with the concept of oath.

to apprehend those who, in light of the information, might be found guilty. This text also notes that criminal proceedings were to take place in the prison, where there were coffers in which the records were kept.[70]

If someone fell victim to a crime, common practice was to alert the head government official (Alcalde Mayor) so that he would send his court officials (Alguaciles, Merinos or Escribanos) to attend to matters. Once the guilty parties (culpantes)[71] had been apprehended and information had been taken, which included the examination of witnesses when appropriate, this information was sent to court officials.[72] If we take into account that it was necessary to "request" that the Alcalde send a court official so that he would, among other things, record witness testimony (because this was always found to be proper),[73] we might say that we are dealing with an evidence request that furthermore was reviewed[74] in order to make decisions on whether or not witnesses would be allowed to testify. Our source states that this was done

[70] Instrucción de Corregidores Chapter 35 (1500).

[71] Ley 25 de Toro (1369).

[72] We can infer that this is the way it was intended to happen in practice from a description of a different type of case in Instrucción para los Alcaldes mayores de los Adelantamientos (3 March 1543) which states: "que sobre delitos livianos no envien Alguaciles ni Escribanos, aunque sea a costa de la parte que lo pide, dentro de las cinco leguas ni fuera de ellas" (See Novísima Recopilación, Law V, Title XXXII).

[73] Instrucción de Corregidores Chapter 36 (1500).

[74] "... y asimismo mandamos, que á las personas, que los dichos Alcaldes mayores enviaren á hacer las dichas informaciones y prisiones, les tasen los testigos que han de tomar para la sumaria información... ." Instrucción para los Alcaldes mayores de los Adelantamientos (3 March 1543).

because not following this practice had resulted in many problems and expenses for the parties.[75] Furthermore, it notes that when witnesses were called, they were reminded to say what the litigant hoped to prove.[76]

The texts from this period that we have been able to examine do not provide criteria that must be observed when deciding whether or not to allow a witness to testify. However, the reference mentioned above suggests admitting only those witnesses thought adequate (or necessary) in order to avoid problems and expenses. The interpretation of the term "adequate" was left to the discretion of the Alcalde mayor.[77/78]

Later texts do specifically refer to criteria for admitting evidence; however, the references are quite general. They remained unchanged until current times and cannot be considered scientific. A 1788 text states that in criminal cases the Corregidores and Alcaldes mayores shall proceed readily and with the utmost care, both during the examination of evidence and in promptly fixing an appropriate punishment

---

[75] Instrucción para los Alcaldes mayores de los Adelantamientos (3 March 1543).

[76] Libelos del Doctor Infante VII enero-febrero-marzo 1 RDP (1951).

[77] Id.

[78] An interesting reference to the "relevance" of evidence is made in a civil action brought by Diego Colón (1512-1515). The records of evidence for the prosecution state: "devian resçibir e resçibieron a ambas las dichas partes e a cada vna dellas conjuntamente a la prueva de todo lo por ellas e por cada vna dellos antellos dicho y alegado e a que de derecho devian ser resçibidos a prueva e provado les podia aprovechar "saluo jure ynpertinençivn et non amitendorum" para la cual prueba hazer e la traer e presentar antellos les dieron e asynaron vn año de plazo" See Pleitos Colombinos, IV Probanzas del Fiscal 6 (1989).

for an offense. They must act in such a way as to ensure that unnecessary or ill-intentioned evidence is not admitted and that those items of evidence that are fair and necessary are not overlooked so that offenses do not go unpunished and the accused is not prevented from mounting a fair defense.[79]

First, we will concentrate on the two criteria for ruling evidence inadmissible set out in the text mentioned above. They have not been conserved up to the present in the Spanish legal system, although the "prolific" expression "relevant evidence," with the help of doctrine, has been used in an attempt to encompass the two concepts. However, the term fails to achieve the level of accuracy necessary for technical-legal terms. In an attempt to relate these criteria with the new term, we can say that those items of evidence that, according to the decision maker, are of no use in the case would be deemed unnecessary and consequently could be ruled inadmissible. This could be the result of incongruence between what "could" be proved and what the decision maker views as what "should" be proved in order to give judgment, regardless of whether the judgment would be for the prosecution or for the defense. In this respect, the criteria are covered by the current conception of the term "relevance."

The second criteria, which relates to "ill will", does not rule out the possibility that the requested evidence might be "unnecessary", but adds another factor that lawmakers

[79] Instrucción de Corregidores Chapter 4 (15 May 1788).

wished to recognize: evidence might be introduced with the intention of doing more than unnecessarily delaying the trial. It might be an attempt to prevent the conclusion of the trial or damage the good name of others, for example. It is difficult to imagine how such an intention might have been identified when we take into account that it would have been clothed in appropriate legal attire. It seems that the decision of whether or not to admit evidence was subject to the considerable discretion of the Corregidor or Alcalde mayor, who could have been influenced by his experience, his knowledge of the issue in question, the testimony given by the accused, the pleas and defenses raised by the accused during the hearing, etc.[80] Finally, we would like to point out that "ill-intentioned evidence" is a concept from the past that has been left out of the Spanish laws presently in force relating to admissibility of evidence. However, the German Prozessversleppungsabsicht covers a similar (but not identical) concept.[81]

Another important aspect of the text mentioned above is the way in which lawmakers addressed the topic of admissibility of evidence, which has not been conserved under the system currently in force. The text does not just provide criteria for ruling evidence inadmissible (insignificance and ill will) but, with a duel purpose statement, also provides criteria for admitting evidence by requiring those items of evidence

[80] Decision rendered by Charles IV on 18 September 1796.

[81] We say similar but not identical because Prozessversleppungsabsicht recognizes one of several instances that were considered ill will according to clear criteria set out by Spanish lawmakers of yesteryear.

considered "fair and necessary." Once again we can see how these adjectives appear (and introduce inexactness) among the criteria for admitting evidence, which means that even then there was a considerable amount of discretion involved in deciding such an important issue.

Legal references to using certain means of proof are of particular interest to our discussion on evidence requests. A precursor to this concept can be found in a 1796 decision stating that an offense should be proved by those means of proof provided under the law. It establishes that any practices or procedures not in line with the law are grounds for ruling evidence inadmissible.[82] We must consider that this reference to admissibility is not related to the criteria that we examined earlier (insignificance, ill will, fairness, necessity); rather, it refers to the way to proceed or the procedural aspect of the trial. In this respect and relative to witnesses, the legally envisaged way to examine evidence expressly forbid Escribanos from acting alone when taking statements from witnesses and from later reading them before the Judge on pain of punishment for contravention and annulment of proceedings.[83] Earlier, the Spanish Catholic Monarchs had already issued a pragmatic sanction in 1500 stating that in criminal trials and in civil cases that are particularly demanding and important, Judges must always question and examine witnesses for themselves before the Escribano. Each

[82] Decision rendered by Charles IV on 18 September 1796.
[83] Instrucción de Corregidores Chapter 5 (15 May 1788).

witness had to be examined in this fashion, and Judges could not assign this task to the Escribano or any other. The first time that the Judge or Escribano did not comply with this requirement they would be fined. The second time, the fine would be doubled, and after the third, they would be stripped of their titles and positions. This ensured that Escribanos would not act alone in the examination of witnesses and later read their testimony before the Judge.[84]

Such provisions were precursors to article 710 of the Code of Criminal Procedure (which is subject to considerable criticism) in that the decision maker had to be present during the examination for it to have value as evidence. Laws provided that in ordinary proceedings the Escribano would approve witnesses before the decision maker (Alcalde) during a hearing and the testimony of witnesses who were received in any other way would not be given credence or considered evidence.[85]

On the fringes of established legal procedure requiring the presence of a judge during the examination of evidence of witnesses was the possibility that the early formality of testifying before the Escribano might have been a filter to avoid admitting witnesses whose testimony was either "insignificant" or "ill-intentioned." A related statement is found in Book III, Title XIV of Usage I, which provides that witnesses shall not be admitted before they are examined.

[84] Pragmática de los Reyes Católicos Chapter 37 (9 June 1500).
[85] Leyes de Madrid Chapter 17 (1502).

Jacobo de Montejudaico correctly observed that there are two ways to examine witnesses. First, there is an examination of the person, which is done before he is required to make any statements on oath, and the other is an examination of what should be the object of his testimony.[86] This establishes an important argument favoring the concept of evidence request that requires, as we affirmed earlier, indicating what is to be proved. This must also be done in cases involving witnesses. Accordingly, during the first examination mentioned by this jurist, aspects such as a relationship of friendship or enmity,[87] the aptness of the witness,[88] and his or her age,[89] social position, and kinship,[90] etc. were taken into account. The second examination involved evaluating the congruence between what the witness could say[91] and what should be the object of his testimony (relevance).

---

[86] See 1 Textos Jurídics Catalans, Usages y demás Derechos de Cataluña 217 infra (1989).

[87] Usage III, Título XVI, Libro III.

[88] Id. "No se reputan idóneos testigos aquellos á quienes se puede mandar que declaren como testigos." This refers to circumstances involving minors, slaves, etc.

[89] Usage VI, Título XVI, Libro III: "Ningún hombre ni muger pueda declarar como testigo hasta haber cumplido catorce años."

[90] Usage VII, Título XVI, Libro III: "Homicidas, malhechores, ladrones, hechiceros, sacrílegos, incestuosos y todos los criminales de ningún modo sean recibidos como testigos. Además los anatematizados, excomulgados y herejes, sarracenos y judíos sean en todos tiempos excluidos de todo testimonio contra cristianos. Los primos tampoco pueden testificar contra extraños, pero si se quieren presentar, y juntos conviene en ello, hagan testimonio entre sí y no entre otros."

[91] In the event of incongruence: "no sea en adelante recibido como testigo." Usage VIII, Título XVI, Libro III.

A precursor to limiting the number of witnesses, which was undoubtedly intended to prevent unnecessary delays, can be found in a law adopted by Philip II in 1575 in Monzon, which provided that the maximum number of witnesses allowed was ten, although this law applied in civil actions and not criminal proceedings (Fontanella).[92] This allows us to conclude that even then Spanish lawmakers were aware of the importance of establishing criteria for admitting "requested" evidence, although in this case admission was subject to a numeric criterion that would be difficult to justify under the law. It is also interesting to note that during the reign of Philip II, laws dealing with motions made by the defendant for evidence of witnesses were enacted. He noted that this was due to the fact that the defendants were usually so poor that they were unable to pay the costs involved with bringing in witnesses, and many times the witnesses themselves were prevented from appearing for other reasons and were fearful that they might incur some punishment or misfortune if they were to testify for the defense.[93] This specifically brought about the examination of witnesses by the advisor to the senior judge presiding over the jurisdiction[94] for the purpose of evaluating whether or not an

[92] Later, Law 2, Title 14, Book 11 of Novísima Recopilación fixed the number at thirty, which corresponded with the 1835 provisional rules. This limitation on the number of witnesses has not been carried over to the present (see CCP, article 314.2). 1 Textos Jurídics Catalans, Usages y demás Derechos de Cataluña 228 infra 228 (1989).

[93] Philip II in the first Catalonian Parliament in Barcelona Chapter 14 (1559).

[94] Ibid.

individual should testify before the judges.

However, given what we have already seen, the lawmakers of former times did not just establish methods and criteria for admitting evidence of witnesses; rather, they also set out methods and criteria for admitting documents. The general production of records, instruments, or documents from another case was expressly forbidden. The parties were required to designate the documents that they intended to produce and the reason for the display so that the judge who had to examine the documents clearly understood their intent or the reason they had been produced. Thus, any attorney who inappropriately advised or organized (completely or in part) a production or display would be punished.[95] These important guidelines clearly refer to using a particular means of proof (documentary) and indicating what the means of proof is intended to demonstrate. Hence, it is a legal precedent for evidence requests.

a2) Investigative Proceedings under the Rome Statute of the ICC

Part 5 of the Rome Statute of the ICC is entitled "Investigation and Prosecution." We are going to examine this investigative stage of the proceedings from the perspective of the accused and his or her right to present evidence. The Statute envisages

[95] Philip II in the Parliament in Monzon Chapter 60 (1585).

an investigation under the direction of the Prosecutor subject to decisions given by the Pre-Trial Chamber, which has the power to order, when appropriate, a warrant of arrest or a summons to appear for the accused (article 58). The investigative stage of the proceedings concludes with a hearing ("to confirm the charges on which the Prosecutor intends to seek trial") during which the accused is entitled, among other things, to present evidence (article 61.6). However, the articles dealing with the investigation fail to mention any rights related to evidence afforded anyone who is detained or anyone who appears before the Court prior to the hearing.

Furthermore, while article 55 (which deals with the rights of persons during the investigation) does mention, among other rights, the right to legal assistance, it fails to address the possibility of presenting evidence for the defense at that time. Thus, counsel for the defense may find his or her hands tied.[96] The only possibility for a defense at the time of arrest or court appearance lies in requesting that the Pre-Trial Chamber issue orders "required for the purposes of an investigation" (article 57.3 (a) relative to article 56.2 (f))[97] or seek the "cooperation (of the Court) as may be necessary to assist the person in the preparation of his or her defense" (article 57.3 (b)).

This investigative stage and the "intermediate" stage preceding the trial demonstrate that the Statute recognizes the principle governing accusatorial procedure, which allows

[97] "Taking such other action as may be necessary to collect or preserve evidence."

the accused to freely put forward his or her arguments in court. If this principle is to be properly observed, clearly the same judge cannot both direct the investigation and preside at the trial[98] as that would be characteristic of inquisitorial procedure. In Spain the abovementioned principle was violated, and consequently the impartiality of the decision maker[99] was adversely affected in "emergency procedures."[100] This situation that was put to an end by the Constitutional Court with judgment 145/12 July 1988 that found Organic Law 10/11 November 1980 unconstitutional. This law, which regulated oral procedure for deliberate, summary, and flagrant crimes, was certainly surprising considering that at the time it was enacted, the Spanish Constitution had been in force for nearly two years. If advances have indeed been made in this respect, the situation becomes more complicated by taking into account, as is well known, that the Spanish legal system provides more than one criminal procedure.[101]

---

[98] This measure was identified years ago as a condition for achieving justice. Molina Pascual, E., En defensa de la Ley de Enjuiciamiento Criminal, 3 RDP 627 (1970).

[99] See generally an interesting article by Werner Goldschmidt, IV abril-mayo-junio 2 RDP 183+ (1950).

[100] The Code of Criminal Procedure, article 799 and following already originally regulated a procedure for flagrant crimes, which was followed by an 8 June 1957 law on emergency procedure for offenses under the jurisdiction of the high courts (Audiencias). Later, an 8 April 1967 law created an emergency procedure for offenses under the jurisdiction of the courts responsible for investigative proceedings (Juzgados de Instrucción), reprehensibly entrusting the investigation and adjudication of certain offenses to these courts.

[101] The Code of Criminal Procedure describes a general procedure for

Furthermore, a set of laws, which includes, for example, a law protecting witnesses and expert witnesses (Ley de Protección de peritos y testigos),[102] has had and continues to have an effect on proceedings.

Technically, it is incorrect to refer to "evidence" during the investigative stage of the proceedings, despite the fact that the Rome Statute makes specific reference to the term throughout most of its articles dealing with the topic. The Statute itself affirms the contention that evidence exists only during the trial in article 74.2. While there are many ways to approach the concept of evidence, we are most interested in evidence as a procedural activity[103] that in criminal proceedings aims to demonstrate that certain facts are true or to convince[104] the

offenses (Libros II and III) and special procedures (Libro IV), which include a summary procedure (articles 779 and 799) in accordance with Organic Law 7/28 December 1988.

[102] See, Del Cacho, Sobre la prueba de testigos y su protección en el proceso penal español, Revista Brasileira de Ciencias Criminais, núm. 26, 1999. Other examples include: a 26 December 1978 law protecting fundamental rights (Ley de Protección Jurisdiccional de los Derechos Fundamentales de la persona); Organic Law 4/1 June 1981 regulating situations of unrest, siege, and other extraordinary circumstances; Organic Law 6/24 May 1984 on habeas corpus proceeding; a 21 March 1985 law on passive extradition (Ley de Extradición Pasiva); Organic Law 4/25 May 1988 on terrorism; etc.

[103] See Silva Melero, IV julio-agosto-septiembre 3 RDP 397 (1950).

[104] According to Guasp, "El régimen de la prueba ha de ser definido en función de la producción de esta convicción psicológica del Juez y si bien es cierto que en los derechos positivos existen todavía en abundancia catalogados como pruebas determinados mecanismos de producción de resultados meramente lógico formales, ello puede explicarse como un residuo histórico de viejas concepciones en trance de continua superación." Transcripts of conferences held on 31 August and 1-2 September 1944 at

decision maker of the reality of these facts.[105] In contrast to what occurs in civil actions, the decision maker in criminal proceedings is not so much concerned with what the parties "allege" as he or she is with the belief that acts punishable under the law have occurred. Differences that might exist in the scope of evidence requests and examination of evidence in civil and criminal proceedings are also of interest. While the allegations of the parties to a civil action, acknowledged by both parties, may limit evidence requests and examinations of evidence, in criminal proceedings the parties are unable to place restrictions on "the discovery of the truth" (Erforschung der Wahrheit),[106] and the burden of proof rests exclusively on the accuser.[107] Thus, while in criminal proceedings the statements of the accuser are actually a design of the judgment that is sought, in a civil action the claim is the only design of the judgment that is sought.[108]

From this perspective, in order to make proper reference

---

the University of Oviedo in Estudios Jurídicos 393 (Ed. Pedro Aragoneses 1996).

[105] See Mittermaier, Tratado de la prueba en material criminal 39 (10th ed. 1979). Serra defines evidence as "una actividad de comparación entre una afirmación sobre unos hechos y la realidad de los mismos encaminada a formar la convicción de una persona" in Estudios de Derecho Procesal 356 (1969).

[106] This statement is in accordance with well-established German doctrine on the topic. There is a well-known distinction between "material truth" and "formal truth." This highlights one of the marked differences between criminal and civil proceedings. See Vélez Mariconde, A., La función judicial en lo penal, 2 RDP 301 footnote 12 (1968).

[107] See Silva Melero, IV julio-agosto-septiembre 3 RDP 398 (1950).

[108] Gómez Orbaneja, IV julio-agosto-septiembre 3 RDP 493 (1950).

to evidence as a procedural activity, an understanding of the difference between a source of evidence and a means of proof is required. Moreover, an understanding of the legal force of the principles guiding the proceedings and procedures is also required. For the matter at the heart of our discussion, we must have an especially clear understanding of the following principles: the right to confront and cross-examine opposing witnesses or evidence, the right to oral argument, the guarantee that both parties are on an equal footing (principle of equality), and the guarantee that the decision maker will be present at the trial. In light of these principles, we may only use the term "evidence" to refer to an activity that takes place during the trial or in special situations before the trial under conditions in which all due process rights and guarantees are observed.

Although we will later continue with an examination of the principles and rights mentioned above, we would first like to establish certain limits inherent to the concept of evidence as an activity.

All things considered and technically speaking, evidence refers to an activity that involves introducing a source of evidence into the proceedings through an examination of a means of proof that was presented in accordance with all due process guarantees. If even one right or guarantee is not observed, the activity can no longer be classified as evidence. In the investigative stage of the proceedings analyzed above, the participants, understandably, are not afforded the rights and guarantees that govern the trial. Therefore, the activity carried out during the investigative stage is not evidence from a procedural point of view. Rather, when appropriate, we should refer to "procedural steps" or "judicial inquiries," which are the focus of the next section of this work.

a3) Investigative Requests

In the Spanish Code of Criminal Procedure, the expression diligencia, which means "procedural steps" or "judicial inquiries," is frequently used in a general fashion. It is employed to express ways of confirming facts (article 336) with references to making inquiries (article 498) or making statements based on inquiries (article 79), etc. In other contexts, these inquiries and procedural steps refer to notifications, citations, and summons (articles 207-208). Lastly, there are also numerous references in the Code of Criminal Procedure that use the term in a general way to mean procedure or practice. For example, article 292 requires that criminal investigators issue a report describing the practices and procedures they have followed. Other provisions use the term to make reference to a wide variety of topics including processes for verifying offenses and identifying offenders (article 282), interrogation (article 441), statements (article 329), examinations (article 369), expert testimony (article 506), etc. This suggests that "taking procedural steps" can cover a number of markedly different activities. Even lawmakers seem to be working with this wide definition when they state that in summary procedure, all court practices related to offenses described under article 789.2 shall be classified as preliminary procedural steps. Certainly, the reference to "preliminary" adds yet another shade of meaning, but for the purposes of our discussion, what has been said up to this point shall suffice.[109]

Therefore, we can conclude that the terms "judicial inquiries" and "procedural steps" in the general sense of procedure or practice cover a large range of activities. Thus, before tackling an examination of investigative proposals in Spanish criminal proceedings, it is necessary to start from the following premises:

(1) Article 311, paragraph 1 provides that the examining judge shall take the procedural steps that are proposed by the Prosecutor or either of the parties represented in the action if he or she does not view them as pointless or damaging.[110] This provision makes specific reference to investigative proposals, and therefore to an entire series of possible procedures and practices that could be investigative in nature or might refer to orders for protective measures, bringing motions or pleas, etc. However, we shall direct our attention exclusively to proposals relating to investigation; namely, those procedures aimed at

[109] When used in connection with summary proceedings, the expression "preliminary procedural steps" refers to the preliminary investigation or pre-trial stage of the proceedings.

[110] This article is criticized in El Ministerio Fiscal en la instrucción de los delitos, marzo RDP 1757 (1994).

ascertaining and verifying punishable acts and determining the persons responsible. Furthermore, the fact that parties do not request any particular procedure or practice does not mean that the Judge should not carry them out, as suggested by a number of articles in the Code of Criminal Procedure (articles 326, 334, 336, etc).

(2) Thus, we shall now focus on the investigation of the incident and the persons responsible. In Spanish ordinary proceedings, a judge is responsible for the preliminary proceedings, which means that the investigations carried out by the police and the Public Prosecutor either prior to or during the preliminary proceedings may not in and of themselves make up the preliminary proceedings; rather, the examining judge must make inquires and take procedural steps (Ortells). However, in summary proceedings, the investigations led by the police and Prosecutor are considered part of the preliminary proceedings according to what is inferred from articles 789.3 and 785 bis.1. Thus, in summary proceedings, reference is made to the Prosecutor's preliminary proceedings and the quasi pre-trial investigation because the range of possible procedures is limited, thus preventing various practices; for example, inquires that might restrict rights (except preventive detention) (EOMF, article 5).

(3) There is no need to make any special mention at this time of adjectives used in the Code of Criminal Procedure in connection with inquiries and procedural steps, such as "necessary" (article 311), "urgent" (article 61), etc. Rather,

we prefer to focus our attention on steps and inquiries carried out during preliminary proceedings that are described in article 299 of the abovementioned Code. These include any procedure or practice aimed at preparing the trial. The purpose of carrying out these measures is to ascertain and state the commission of crimes along with all circumstances that might influence the specification of charges and the guilt of the offenders, to identify the offenders, and to indicate how they might be financially liable. In spite of what is set out in the Code, the final purpose of preliminary proceedings is not only to prepare the trial, but also to order stay of proceedings when appropriate. The Code of Criminal Procedure envisages that the Court will first examine the complaint or action and in accordance with legal doctrine, it will shelve the case when there are not sufficient grounds for proceeding with the investigation.

Article 61.7 of the Rome Statute provides: "The Pre-Trial Chamber shall, on the basis of the hearing, determine whether there is sufficient evidence to establish substantial grounds to believe that the person committed each of the crimes charged." The question at hand is if there is a set of matching criteria for determining whether or not to order a stay of proceedings or to shelve the case. Another issue is that some criteria might be relevant beforehand, while other criteria might be significant after the investigation, but in any case it serves as a guideline for determining the legitimacy of the inquiries and procedures requested by the parties during the investigative stage of the proceedings.

In practice, orders to shelve a case that are appealed to a high court (such is the case with the Provincial Courts in Spain) are often cancelled. The Court orders investigative proceedings to continue in the interest of further clarification of facts that relate to the supposedly punishable acts. This gives an idea of the fragile nature of the grounds for shelving a case that are used in most situations. In this respect, stay of proceedings differs in practice from shelving a case as it tends to take place after an activity that, while it may not have been adequate, at least it might be said: "something has been done." Criteria are used that do not match the criteria for shelving a case; for example: the identity of the person charged with the criminal acts is unknown (keeping in mind that a charge can be made in incertam personae). In theory, when shelving a case the possible defendants are not a consideration, given the fact that the original charge may be made in incertam personae. Thus, the only element to consider is the proposed cause of action, which might be rejected on the ground of its inability to convince the court that the case has merit.

Moreover, there doesn't seem to be anything in article 299 of the Code of Criminal Procedure to prevent carrying out procedures or practices involving evidence during the pre-trial proceedings; in fact, the examination of evidence of witnesses frequently occurs before the examining judge. This practice is carried out in exactly the same fashion both in the pre-trial proceedings and the actual trial. Although, we must bear in mind the purpose of the pre-trial investigative proceedings and the underlying intent of the Code's statement of purpose, which is that evidence is presented during the trial and it is there that the Court forms an opinion on the matter.[111] Consequently, doctrine distinguishes between investigative practices and practices that involve evidence, and investigative practices are further classified into those that are judicial and those that are not. The two kinds of investigative practice produce overall two separate sets of evidence that are gathered according to different systems. They have distinct purposes and different legal value.

If investigative practices are aimed (not exclusively, but primarily) at providing grounds for an order for the trial to commence or stay of proceedings as the case may be, then practices involving evidence are unequivocally required for conviction. In their absence, judgment must be given for the defendant in accordance with the principle of presumption

[111] Ortells distinguishes between "dos concepciones diferentes sobre las relaciones entre material de investigación del sumario y prueba del juicio. Según una postura, la práctica de la prueba en el juicio tiene la función propia y autónoma de convencer al Tribunal de los hechos aportados por la acusación y la defensa; reservándose al sumario una función subordinada en el doble sentido de proporcionar los datos para la aportación de hechos e indicación de las fuentes de prueba y de servir, en supuestos excepcionales, para sustituir la práctica imposible de un medio de prueba. Según la otra posición, la práctica de la prueba en el juicio tiene una función correctora y complementaria de la investigación sumarial, de lo que deriva que ésta es, por principio, apreciable junto a la prueba del juicio para dictar la sentencia". Ortells Ramos, Eficacia del acto de investigación sumarial. Estudio de los artículos 730 y 714 de la Ley de Enjuiciamiento Criminal, 2-3 RDPI 375-376 (1982).

of innocence. Furthermore, during the pre-trial proceedings the mere probability that a punishable act has occurred and that there is a responsible party is reason enough for the judge to open the trial. On the contrary, mere probability is not sufficient grounds for conviction; rather, the Court must form its opinion on the basis of an examination of evidence during the trial. This has special significance relative to evidence proposals.

(4) As we have seen, in preliminary proceedings the right to make investigative requests and proposals is expressly recognized (CCP, article 311, paragraph 1), as is the right to have investigative practices carried out. Also, parties have the right to join in and to be informed of the inquiries, procedures, and practices (CCP, article 320, paragraph 1). In the case of summary proceedings and supposing that the preliminary proceedings are under the direction of the Public Prosecutor, participation is not well regulated and for this reason the Code of Criminal Procedure, articles 297 III and 785 bis 2 tend to be applied.

(5) Regarding judicial inquiries and procedural steps, another distinction can be made relative to the fact that the procedures and practices might amount to either an examination of sources of evidence or to the search for and acquisition of these sources. In the first scenario, we would be dealing with direct measures, while the second scenario would be a case of indirect measures. Thus, entering and searching a residence, for example, would be an indirect investigative

measure, as the intent is not to directly ascertain what has occurred and who has committed the act. Rather, the purpose is to obtain another means of investigation, search out and acquire information and clues related to the crime, or bring the possible suspect in for questioning if it is believed that he or she is at the residence that is the object of the search, or if it is possible that he or she might be there.

Moreover, doctrine frequently makes reference to pre-trial inquiries according to whether they relate to the allegedly punishable act (inquiries to verify a crime) or to the person who is allegedly responsible for the crime (inquiries to identify the perpetrator). This practice can be problematic as it is not always possible to identify procedures that tend to serve only one of the two purposes: verify the crime or identify the perpetrator. Once again we are faced with a terminological issue, which is at the heart of any analysis of procedural law. In any case, any reference to "verification" suggests that it falls to the examining judge to weigh the matter and facts at issue. This activity of weighing facts and information is precisely what precedes any decisions that are made during the investigative stage of the proceedings, such as committing the accused for trial. All such decisions suggest the act of "judging." However, when the same examining judge limits himself (or herself) to looking for clues, evidence and possible sources of evidence and to making inquiries (Forschung), we might say that these practices are no different than those carried out by the police, and the act involved is "investigating." The fact that the judge both judges and investigates is at the heart of the debate over whether the preliminary proceedings are administrative or jurisdictional in nature. There is an interesting terminological distinction between the Spanish terms "averiguación" and "averiguamiento," which may not refer exclusively to the alleged offender. The first term makes reference to the action of inquiring or ascertaining, while the second is suggestive of the effect or finding.[112]

Although it is possible to employ various terms, for the purpose of this study we shall refer to the distinction made by Ortells dealing with types of sources and means used. These are judicial examination (examination of relevant objects, places, etc., articles 326-333), questioning/testimony of the accused (articles 486-488, 385-409), witness testimony (articles 410-450), statements from expert witnesses (article 456-485), and documents.[113] We shall specifically exclude confrontations as described in articles 451-455 from this

[112] This distinction is suggested by the German terms Wahrheitsforschung ("search" or "inquiry," which is the action) and Wahrheitsfindung ("finding" or "discovery," which is the effect). From Döhring, La prueba, su práctica y apreciación, Introducción, Trans. Tomás A. Banzhaf (1972).

[113] Furthermore, other investigative practices regulated by the Code of Criminal Procedure under the headings "Del cuerpo del delito" (articles 334-367) and "De la identidad del delincuente y de sus circunstancias personales" (articles 368-383) may also be classified with those listed above. Under these articles, the law categorizes provisions according to what is under investigation (the investigation is carried out by making use of various types of sources and means), rather than classifying according to the type of source or means of investigation.

classification as they are special investigative means that can only be used when there is no other way to prove that a crime has been committed or prove the guilt of the accused (article 455), and they are ordered at the judge's discretion (STS 16 March 1987). Such confrontations do not stand on their own (STS 12 February 1986 and 4 April 1987), but are a complementary means of investigation that aid in the discovery of the truth.

There is no need to further discuss terminological distinctions or ways to classify procedures and practices (whether they are used to ascertain or verify, whether they are direct or indirect, etc).. Carrying out a practice or procedure leads to an outcome that is "established" (CCP, article 299) when dealing with the main issues during preliminary proceedings.[114] Whether or not the outcome has value as evidence is another matter and shall be determined later. As we pointed out earlier, we must consider that the purpose of the preliminary proceedings is to prepare the trial and Ortells notes that the practice of verifying facts during these proceedings does not have the same purpose or effect as the act of examining evidence during the trial.[115] One final well-known factor to consider is that during preliminary proceedings it is also possible to request measures that are intended to ensure that the trial proceeds

---

[114] There are several stages to preliminary proceedings and each stage addresses one of the following matters: main issues, personal circumstances, civil liability, and vicarious liability.

[115] Ortells Ramos with Montero Aroca, Gómez Colomer and Montón Redondo, Derecho Jurisdiccional III 123 (1991).

or that judgment is enforced, when appropriate. These are known as precautionary or protective measures (detention, bond, injunction).

Now that the concept of investigative procedures and inquiries has been defined, and considering the indisputable fact that there are persons who may be considered "parties"[116] during these proceedings, we shall now consider the issue of requesting inquires and procedures. The examining judge orders these measures during preliminary proceedings either de officio (CCP, article 622)[117] or at the request of the Public Prosecutor or the "parties" represented in the action (CCP, article 311). It is important to note the difference between an investigative request and proposal. These are two distinct measures: while the motion or request (or action) solicits a certain decision[118] from the Judge, the proposal is an "offering."

Investigative requests and proposals are classified as different investigative practices. The investigative request solicits a decision from the Judge (in this case the examining judge) to carry out the requested inquiries and steps. An order must be

[116] Silva Melero, IV julio-agosto-septiembre RDP 407 (1950).

[117] See CCP, article 785 bis for summary proceedings in which the Public Prosecutor either takes it upon himself (herself) to carry out the appropriate steps or orders the Criminal Investigation Department to take these steps.

[118] Remember that article 141 of the Code of Criminal Procedure provides: "Las resoluciones de carácter judicial que dicten los Juzgados y Tribunales se denominarán: [...] Autos, cuando decidan... la admisión o denegación de prueba."

given to deny a request, which can be challenged by appeal without stay of execution (CCP, article 311). The proposal, whether it deals with ascertainment or verification, is simply an offering. It does not solicit a decision from the Judge on taking procedural steps; rather, it is intended to help with the investigation, and thus an order is not required to deny a proposal. However, given the fact that the Code of Criminal Procedure fails to recognize this distinction, the same process (mentioned above) is followed for denying a proposal as for denying a request.

It is clear that neither the Code of Criminal Procedure nor doctrine and judgments dealing with these articles make these kinds of distinctions; thus, investigative requests (article 314) and proposals (article 312) are addressed in the same way, to say nothing of the wide variety of contexts in which the phrase "procedural steps and inquiries" is employed. Although clarifying these terms might seem unnecessary, clear processes and procedures always help the decision maker, who often deals with ambiguities in texts, which are the result of unclear terms. Judges then deny requests for inquiries with orders (as required by law) that are even more ambiguous.

Keeping the classification mentioned above in mind, and in connection with motions for inquiries and procedures, it is appropriate to deal with each type of motion separately due to the different circumstances envisaged by the Code of Criminal Procedure for different types of motions made during preliminary proceedings.

Regarding the preliminary investigation, Spanish doctrine on procedure and practice is divided over the legal nature of this stage of the proceedings. While some have maintained that it is jurisdictional in nature (Fenech, Gómez, Orbaneja), others have contended that it is administrative (Serra, Viada). Still others affirm that it is both jurisdictional and administrative (Fairén, Gimeno).[119] It might be simpler to explain preliminary proceedings if we disregard their jurisdictional nature, given the complexities of analyzing this element. However, if we are not to confuse investigations with preliminary proceedings, which according to De la Oliva, involve not only investigations, but also their direction and control and the determination of legal consequences from their outcome, we must affirm the jurisdictional nature of this preliminary stage of ordinary proceedings, without prejudice to the fact that in the context of summary proceedings, in certain cases we may refer to the preliminary proceedings of the Public Prosecutor (according to CCP, articles 785 bis and 789.3, as interpreted by Ortells). Ortells suggests that in the present day from the point of view of positive law (save the novelties first introduced by Organic Law 10/11 November 1980 and Organic Law 7/28 December 1988) the jurisdictional nature of the preliminary stage of the proceedings must be affirmed.[120] Affirming the procedural

[119] Alcalá-Zamora, En torno a la noción de proceso preliminar, I Estudios de Teoría General 491.

[120] Ortells Ramos, M., Nuevos poderes para el Ministerio Fiscal en el

nature of preliminary proceedings (Fenech), while recognizing that certain activities are merely administrative or police work, means referring to this stage as truly independent proceedings, and consequently recognizing that it has its own purposes that range from preparing the trial to eliminating the possibility of going to trial. The need to impartially investigate all notitia criminis combines nicely with the necessity of preventing the weight of a charge in a trial from falling on a particular person if there are not sufficient grounds to support it.[121] This would obviously not be feasible if the accused was not allowed to join in and effectively exercise his or her right to a defense, and consequently the constitutional right to present evidence. This cannot be done as long as the law does not regulate the right to present evidence by providing clear criteria (which at the present are nonexistent) for refusing to carry out proposed inquiries and procedures.

Affirming the procedural nature of preliminary proceedings goes even further as it is essential in distinguishing the factual circumstances that support an indictment from those that support an accusation. It is inappropriate to contend that the trial puts everything right or that the purpose of the indictment is to bring a particular person up for trial for any fact that was considered proved during the hearing. In addition to infringing the right to join in ex origine in the

---

proceso penal: Límites constitucionales y valoración político-jurídica, 2 RDP 233-234 (1990).

[121] Soto Vázquez, R., El auto de procesamiento y algunos de sus problemas, 1 RDP 116 (1966).

investigation of a new charge, it would mean practically denying the procedural nature of preliminary proceedings and the purpose of these proceedings, which is to prepare the trial.

In any case, the preliminary stage of the proceedings, which is known by many names in the Spanish Code of Criminal Procedure, (sumario, instrucción, diligencias previas, etc). does not involve evidence.[122]

As a result of the "principle of investigation,"[123] as a general rule in Spanish criminal procedure the judge must commence proceedings when any apparently criminal act has occurred. During the preliminary investigation, the only limits set down are that all fundamental rights must be respected, the proceedings are subject to the "principle of legality," and under no circumstances is an inquisitio generalis[124] allowed. However, during the trial the "parties" influence the proceedings in that the decision maker is limited by the "act" adduced by the "parties" in their written pleadings as that

---

[122] De la Oliva with other authors, Derecho Procesal Penal 17 (1996).

[123] See De la Oliva with Aragoneses Martínez, Hinojosa Segovia, Muerza Esparza and Tomé García, Derecho Procesal Penal 9+ (1996).

[124] "El proceso penal no es legítimo como instrumento de una inquisitio generalis, para una pesquisa o investigación general, a no ser que esa investigación venga fundada en hechos punibles de un número y naturaleza tales que hagan racionalmente presumible el comportamiento generalmente delictivo de una persona o la índole principalmente criminal de una actividad (pretendidamente) social, económica, política, etc. La inquisitio generalis, la investigación general, en sí misma, aunque sea con laudables fines de prevención delictiva, no justifica la apertura y continuación de un proceso." De la Oliva with other authors, Derecho Procesal Penal 191 (1996).

which constitutes the crime (CCP, articles 650.1 and 790.5, sentence 1) and the "person or persons" charged with this crime (CCP, articles 650.3 and 790.5, sentence 1).

In other words, during preliminary proceedings the Spanish judge does not have to limit his or her investigation to the punishable act that has been alleged in the action, although at times this might be desirable in order to prevent real abuses in the investigation. Rather, the investigation could be extended to other acts that are somehow related and to those persons thought to have participated in these acts. In contrast, during the trial only those acts specified in the written pleadings as alleged crimes and only the defendants[125] may be judged, and judgment is given on the basis of the arguments and the evidence produced during the trial (CCP, article 741, paragraph 1).

Indeed, the steps taken during preliminary proceedings make it possible to determine the object of the action, which is constituted by certain conduct (certain facts).[126] This is particularly significant in connection with evidence. While the examining judge has considerable discretionary power during the investigation (with certain limitations), during the

[125] This is a result of the legal force of accusatorial procedure. Montero Aroca states: "En los últimos años estamos asistiendo en España a una gran confusión conceptual... confusión que se ha reflejado en la jurisprudencia de los tribunales Constitucional y Supremo y en las leyes." Montero Aroca with Ortells, Gómez Colomer and Montón Redondo, Derecho Jurisdiccional III 23 (1996).

[126] De la Oliva with Aragoneses Martínez, Hinojosa Segovia, Muerza Esparza and Tomé García, Derecho Procesal Penal 18 (1996).

trial, without prejudice to the power to examine evidence de officio, he or she should deal only with facts related to the accusation and the person or persons accused according to the pleadings. However, in situations involving a continued offense, the Court may consider particular actions that result from evidence and that are related to the arguments, even though some of these actions may not have been the object of the exact charge, as long as they are not a determining or decisive factor in fixing the sentence.[127]

Focusing now on the preliminary stage of Spanish proceedings as it relates to investigative requests or motions made before the examining judge so that he or she will order specific inquiries or procedures, it is necessary to turn to the Code of Criminal Procedure. Despite the importance of this topic, it has not been addressed by doctrine, at least regarding the right of the accused to investigative requests during preliminary proceedings. We must bear in mind that although only that which is examined during the trial can be considered evidence, preliminary proceedings still have value as evidence (STC80/17 June 1986 and STC25/23 February 1988). One thing is what "should" be considered true evidence, yet what the decision maker "might" take into account when forming an opinion is quite another. Shaping the opinion of the judge has proved to be what the "parties" should focus their efforts on (and not only with regard to evidence) if they wish to be effective, regardless of whether they are prosecuting or

[127] De la Oliva, Derecho Procesal Penal 205-206 (1996).

conducting a defense. In order to better analyze the procedure, rather than taking the perspective of the judge at the end of the proceedings, as is customary, who is in the position to "assess the evidence," we shall instead put ourselves in the position of the accused during preliminary proceedings and consider any real possibilities he or she might have for exercising the right to present evidence and also the legal criteria, which are equally limited, for ruling any evidence that might have been requested inadmissible.

Given the novelty of dealing with the right of the accused to present evidence during the investigative stage of Spanish proceedings, at this point we must also make reference to the role these proceedings play in the Spanish criminal trial for their effect on evidentiary matters. Evidentiary process depends if not entirely at least in part on the definition of preliminary proceedings. Also, a good understanding of this stage of the proceedings helps to guide participants to their true place, and therefore steers them away from roles that are undefined (or exaggerated, as is the case with those examining judges who assume the role of "police chief").

The investigative stage of the proceedings is a preliminary stage, as it is carried out before the trial. The intent, in connection with evidentiary process, is to obtain or secure sources of evidence. It is during this stage that the offenses are specified, albeit provisionally (see STC164/26 September 1988). Although doctrine makes general reference to investigative practices like those that are characteristic of this procedural stage (it is well understood that at this point in the proceedings real evidence does not exist except in those special cases in which evidence is produced before the trial in accordance with all due process guarantees), it is also true that not everything that results from the investigative practices will be placed on the record (CCP, article 315, sentence 2). Furthermore, during preliminary proceedings we are not dealing with evidence in the strict sense of the concept since the due process guarantees that govern the trial are not observed. For this reason, only that which is examined during the trial can be considered evidence. While continually affirming that evidence is only that which is examined during the trial is commendable, it is also somewhat pretentious (remember the difference between what should be evidence and what the decision maker might take into account when forming an opinion) as no one would deny the influence the preliminary proceedings continue to have on the decision maker, even though all possible efforts are made to prevent it.[128] The principle of the "uninformed judge" or that the respective stages of the proceedings (investigation and trial) are overseen

[128] Lawmakers have attempted to prevent preliminary proceedings from influencing judgment with a new organic law (Ley Orgánica del Tribunal del Jurado 5/22 May 1995), which was amended by Organic Law 8/16 November 1995. This confirms that lawmakers are aware that in other trials the jury is influenced; however, the possibility of requesting that inferences be made from evidence (article 34) has obstructed the purpose of the law. The abovementioned law, article 46.4 provides: "Las diligencias remitidas por el Juez Instructor podrán ser exhibidas a los jurados en la práctica de la prueba."

by different courts (and persons) is still in force due to the conviction that criminal justice is only administered properly with all guarantees in place if the person who is to pronounce judgment at the conclusion of the trial has not participated in the investigative proceedings and therefore has no prejudices or preconceptions.[129] However, we must consider the fact that any judge or court has access to the record of the preliminary proceedings before the trial, and it is impossible to overlook the fact that studying or having knowledge of this information will influence their opinion and does not always amount to impartiality in the trial.[130] Instead of maintaining that "only that which is examined during the trial is evidence," only to later allow the report of preliminary inquiries to be read (although there might be a requirement to respect certain conditions) and to also permit the decision maker to assess witness statements from the hearing and preliminary proceedings, the position of the accused during preliminary proceedings should be reevaluated. The articles of the Code of Criminal Procedure dealing with evidence requests seem to infer that the accused should be able to exercise the right to present evidence effectively and not be merely present during the proceedings. However, it would be quite an achievement if this were to happen in practice.

---

[129] De la Oliva with other authors, Derecho Procesal Penal 40 (1996).

[130] Studies have been done on this topic in Germany and have confirmed that studying the record of preliminary proceedings strongly influences judges. This has shown to be detrimental for the accused in the trial. See Bandilla, Informationsverarbeitung 47 (1986).

First of all, this would require carrying out a true investigation. Next, the law should be amended to include clear criteria for admissibility and provide for the possibility that the accused might exercise his or her right to present evidence when the interests at stake are weighed, which is the responsibility of the person overseeing the investigation. These interests include bringing the weight of the law to bear on punishable acts and observing the right to a defense. According to Alonso Martínez in the Exposición de Motivos, there are two divergent interests: the right of society to punish those who commit offenses and the right of the accused to a defense.[131]

We are well aware of the difficulty of possibly making any reforms relating to this issue, but in a certain way, the Code of Criminal Procedure points in that direction when it provides that every person charged with an offense is entitled to exercise the right to a defense (CCP, article 118). How else could this be done but by effectively exercising the right to present evidence during preliminary proceedings? However, we agree that this entails avoiding both a paroxysm of guarantees that end up taking procedural and fundamental precedence over the offender and an exacerbation of the intent to swiftly and openly impart justice that disregards due process, which is made up of the rights that allow us to affirm, with a clear

[131] This may be an argument for continuing to trust examining judges. See De la Oliva, El futuro del proceso penal y el papel del Ministerio Fiscal, 1 enero Tribunales de Justicia 17 (1997).

conscience, that the accused has been able to defend himself (or herself) in the areas of facts and legal reasoning.[132]

It is also true that it is common practice for counsel for the defense to adopt a passive attitude during preliminary proceedings and later go into trial wielding "all possible weapons." It is contended that in this way the approach that the prosecution intends to employ is known, while the defense has not given away their strategy, and thus has an advantage. However, no one mentions the fact that the accused also has the right to avoid being put in the dock for prisoners (with the sometimes unforeseen counterproductive consequences that might bring upon him or her) and that no criminal code covers the punishment of enduring prosecution,[133] sometimes for years, which is inflicted not only on those who should be convicted, but even more unfairly, on those who never should have been accused. Also, it is always advisable to avoid going to trial and prevent overloading the courts with unnecessary work and economic expense. Furthermore, behind all of this, it should be taken into account that it is always more noble of counsel for the defense to present arguments and lead evidence when he or she is able during preliminary proceedings. Counsel should not allow offenses to be specified after the trial has commenced in such a way that the punishment sought by the prosecution, which is often a

[132] De la Oliva with other authors, Derecho Procesal Penal 62 (1996).

[133] A report on the draft of the Spanish Criminal Code notes that the trial in itself is already punishment. This report is cited with commentary by De la Oliva with other authors, Derecho Procesal Penal 24 (1996).

matter of many years, causes the client so much worry that he or she ignorantly breathes an enormous sigh of relief when sentenced to a tenth of that punishment and all thanks to the superb representation provided by defense counsel. On the other hand, enabling the defense to present evidence during preliminary proceedings without setting out well defined limitations would result in real abuses by the aforementioned defense attorneys that would "obstruct" proceedings and consequently damage the chances of justice being done, as is the case at present in Germany.

The purpose of the investigative stage or preliminary proceedings is not only to "prepare the trial", but also to prevent the matter from going to trial if need be. This requires that the accused be given the power to not only be informed of and join in the inquiries and procedural steps that are taken (CCP, article 302), but also to request inquiries and procedures and have these measures approved. The position that the accused will be able to request procedures and practices during the trial should not be a valid argument for denying a request during preliminary proceedings (CCP, article 314). After glancing at the Code of Criminal Procedure, it seems that the prospects for achieving our goal are slim as we are dealing with the most critical and complex aspect of investigative requests that are submitted by the accused: grounds for denying these requests. It is a question of determining up to what point the examining judge is required to make the inquiries and take the steps proposed to clarify the facts and identifying the criteria that is in place, working from the principle that there is no legal limit for taking those steps that are found necessary to clarify the facts. Note also the difference between investigative requests submitted by a private prosecutor, which are optional, and those submitted by the Public Prosecutor, who is obligated to do so under EOMF, article 3.4 and CCP, articles 311, 781, and 790.

The right of the accused to submit investigative requests during preliminary proceedings is not only backed by the Spanish Constitution, as we have seen in preceding chapters, but it is also covered in law under article 311 of the Code of Criminal Procedure, which requires the examining judge to carry out the procedures and inquiries proposed by the parties as long as the judge does not find them unnecessary or damaging (CCP, article 311). For more on this topic as it relates to the accused after indictment, see article 396 in connection with articles 520 and 118. Continuing with an analysis of the procedural steps and judicial inquiries involved in investigations, we shall expand upon the following matters:

(1) Requirements for requests: time, method or means, capacity, etc.

(2) Carrying out the investigative means that the accused might request during this stage.

(3) Criteria for denying this type of request.

a4) Requirements for Investigative Requests

According to Spanish law, making investigative requests during preliminary proceedings requires the following: (a) Status of "imputado" (Suspect). The Code of Criminal Procedure, article 188, paragraph 2 provides that any person or persons charged with an offense shall be informed immediately of the admission of the complaint or action or any other court proceeding that resulted in a charge being brought. The "imputado" is defined as any person to whom a punishable act is attributed by way of an argument that is in some way substantiated (STC135/19 July 1989).

However, acquiring the status of "imputado" in the proceedings is quite meaningful and has special significance not only relative to evidentiary process, but also because until then it is impossible to refer to the presumption of innocence. In other words, it is impossible to presume the innocence of one who does not exist in the proceedings. For this reason, the abovementioned judgment given by the Spanish Constitutional Court provides that the "imputado" shall be allowed to exercise the right to a defense according to the broad sense of the term. He or she may join in the criminal proceedings (regardless of the type of proceedings they may be) either immediately after being informed of the admission of the complaint or action or any other procedural practice that resulted in the charge, or from the time he or she was taken into custody or any precautionary measure was ordered or the indictment was given, and at this time the right shall be explained.

It is essential that the "imputado" be informed "immediately" of the charge in order to refer to the right to a defense (STC141/1986) and therefore to the right to present evidence. We are dealing with "formal charges" once it is apparent, as a result of preliminary inquiries, that there is a case against a particular person (CCP, article 384, paragraph 1). At this time the examining judge, in ordinary proceedings, commits the "imputado" for trial. In summary proceedings this step is taken during the first court appearance, to which reference is made in the Code of Criminal Procedure, article 789.4, sentence 1.

In this respect, Constitutional Court judgment 277/17 October 1994 FJ 4 (b) is significant. It provides that for summary proceedings no one may be indicted without having been heard by the examining judge before the conclusion of preliminary proceedings. This guarantee means that the Judge may not close preliminary proceedings before he or she has informed the accused of the punishable act that is the object of the investigation, explained to the "imputado" his or her rights with special emphasis on procedures for appointing defense counsel, and allowed for the possibility of dismissal of charges during the imputado's first court appearance.

Furthermore, it is important to distinguish between a general definition of "charge," which unfortunately is frequently employed, and the concept of a "judicial charge."

The general definition of the term refers to attributing a presumably criminal act or acts to a person or persons. A judicial charge infers that only the examining judge may assess the situation and that his or her assessment is grounded on probability (based on the outcome of the preliminary inquiries) rather than conviction. According to the first definition, a mere complaint, action, or police report enables us to make reference (incorrectly) to the "accused", although this individual is actually a suspect. The term is employed correctly when it is done in accordance with the second definition. The law adds to the confusion by referring, for example, to "charging" people with crimes (CCP, article 188, sentence 1) when it should provide that crimes are "attributed" to particular individuals. This confusion, which is apparent not only in doctrine, but also in law, goes much further than what has been previously mentioned. In Spain there are different terms used to refer to the suspect and the accused depending upon the point in the proceedings (sospechoso, implicado, encartado, inculpado, acusado), and it is necessary to clarify these situations in law.[134]

The law provides another requirement that enables the accused to exercise the right to a defense under the Code of

---

[134] De la Oliva, *El futuro del proceso penal y el papel del Ministerio Fiscal*, 1 enero Tribunales de Justicia 15 (1997). Others have made reference to the term "indiciado." Ruiz Gutiérrez, U., *El auto de procesamiento debe desaparecer*, RDP 273 (1965): "no puede existir la cualidad de indiciado sin que sea el juez quien la otorgue, porque a él sólo es dado valorar qué ha de considerarse indicio y por ende él sólo puede crear el indiciado."

Criminal Procedure, article 188, paragraph 3, which states that to exercise the right to a defense, and therefore the right to present evidence, the persons concerned must be represented and defended by a solicitor. Article 302 provides that the "parties" represented in an action must be informed of and participate in all proceedings. Law 53/4 December 1978 amended articles 118 and 520, among others, and adapted them to constitutional requirements. Prior to these changes, during preliminary proceedings the examining judge could question the suspect without ensuring that legal assistance was provided or informing the suspect of the accusation.

At this point, it is worthwhile to consider (as we stressed earlier) that the right to present evidence is an expression of the right to a defense, and it is thought that legal representatives facilitate the exercise of this right. Perhaps for this reason the Code of Criminal Procedure, article 118, paragraph 4 requires legal representation when the case has reached the point that legal advice is necessary or some action must be taken that requires solicitor involvement. In any case, the imputado's right to a defense is not merely "legal aid and assistance" or the formal or technical defense that is typically court appointed and frequently fails to provide "aid and assistance" until it comes time to file provisional pleadings, a procedure that is also often a mere formality. Rather, the right to a defense goes or must go much further so that it makes it possible to not only participate in all inquiries and procedures that are carried out (see article 333), but also to request measures that might prevent the matter from going to trial. Lawmakers have echoed this idea of the right to a defense with new jury proceedings, providing under article 25.3, sentence 3 of new Organic Law 5/1995 that when the parties join in the proceedings, they may request any inquiries or steps[135] that they consider fitting.

In any case, for the purpose of our analysis we shall focus on the fact that the accused must be represented and defended by counsel under the Code of Criminal Procedure, article 188, paragraph 3 in order to make investigative requests. A closer look at article 188 shows that paragraph 3 provides that the Court shall appoint counsel if the person concerned requests this measure (or does not have the legal capacity to make such a request). In contrast, paragraph 4 states that the Court shall appoint counsel if the person concerned does not do so when required and the case has reached the point that legal advice is necessary or some action must be taken that requires solicitor involvement. This suggests that while any person charged with an offense has the right to a defense after being informed of the charge or from the time he or she was taken into custody or any precautionary measure was ordered or the indictment was given (article 118, paragraph 1), this right is not always exercised from this time forward, as legal representation is required (article 188, paragraph 3).

Objections might be raised to the fact that lawmakers failed

[135] See our earlier discussion on how the term "diligencia," meaning "inquiries" or "procedural steps," is used.

to envisage circumstances in which the "imputado" might act alone to make investigative requests, although it is understood that this is not necessarily feasible in those situations in which the case has reached the point that legal advice is necessary and legal assistance is required (article 118, paragraph 4). If the abovementioned situation were possible, we would have to distinguish between the following two concepts: competence as a party and legal capacity to sue or plead. The first concept refers to individuals, not corporations (Spanish Criminal Code, article 15 bis), who were involved with the offense in question (CCP, article 115). Legal capacity requires that an individual is physically and mentally able to follow the proceedings (see Spanish Criminal Code, article 8). Clearly legal capacity would be required for the "imputado" to submit a request as it could not done under any other circumstance. Thus, assuming the legal capacity of the "imputado", he or she would also be able to request inquiries or procedural steps relating to his or her incompetence as a party (under legal age for criminal matters). Although a situation like the one mentioned above might arise and legal assistance in preliminary proceedings might be unnecessary (article 118, paragraph 4),[136] it is legally required for the trial (article 652,

[136] The Code of Criminal Procedure, article 788 makes an interesting reference relative to summary proceedings when it states that the Court shall appoint counsel when legal assistance is necessary. The language in this provision is similar to the language employed in article 118, paragraph 4, which makes reference to the case reaching the point that legal advice becomes necessary and provides that some action must be taken. In any case, doubts may be raised. The provisions suggest that the law also

paragraph 2 and for summary proceedings, article 793.1). Article 25.1 of Organic Law 5/22 May 1995 (Tribunal del Jurado) has echoed this requirement by providing that once proceedings commence before the abovementioned court, the examining judge shall inform the accused of that fact and that he or she shall be summoned and must be assisted by a solicitor of his or her choosing, or if he or she fails to appoint one, by court appointed counsel.

For any person in custody or prison, Law 52/1978 amended article 520;[137] the list of rights provided is an attempt to

---

envisages situations in which legal assistance in the preliminary stage is not mandatory in summary proceedings. This is openly stated in article 791.1, which provides: "Abierto el juicio oral, si los acusados no hubieren hecho uso de su derecho a nombrar Abogado ni se les hubiera nombrado de oficio." In contrast, during the trial, the assistance provided by counsel for the defense is required (article 793.1).

[137] The rights of any person in custody or prison under the Code of Criminal Procedure, article 520.2 (see the Spanish Constitution, article 17.3) are as follows:

(a) Right to remain silent and not testify if he or she does not so choose, to refuse to answer one or several questions that are posed, or to declare that he or she will only testify before the Judge.

(b) Right to avoid self-incrimination and to not plead guilty.

(c) Right to appoint an attorney and to request that he or she be present when any statements are made before the police or the Court and join in any identification procedures. If the person in custody or prison fails to appoint an attorney, the Court shall appoint one.

(d) Guarantee that a family member or other person of the prisoner's choosing shall be informed of the arrest and the place where the prisoner is being held at all times. Foreigners have the right for the abovementioned information to be sent to their consulate.

(e) Right to the assistance of an interpreter free of charge for foreigners who do not understand or speak Spanish.

(f) Right to be examined by the specialist in forensic medicine or his or her legally recognized substitute or, in their absence, by the specialist at the further define the right to a defense. This list does not mention motions for "evidence" made in defense of the "accused", as it is well understood that at this point we are dealing with preliminary proceedings and not with evidence, as we have already commented. However, it is interesting to note that the Code of Criminal Procedure devotes several articles to "proposals for evidence" made during preliminary proceedings by third parties who may be civilly liable (articles 616-618).

All things considered, whether or not the "imputado" exercises the right to a defense and submits investigative requests during preliminary proceedings depends on the concurrence of two requirements:

(a) The individual must be informed of the punishable act of which he or she is accused, unless the individual is already in custody, in prison, accused or committed for trial, in which case this right shall be explained (compare CCP, article 118, paragraph 1 (b) with the Rome Statute, article 55.2).

(b) The individual must be represented and defended by legal counsel (article 118, paragraph 3). Silvo Melero has defended the view advocating greater participation of counsel for the defense in preliminary proceedings in keeping with the principle that a legal representative must assist every person accused of a crime. Under any other circumstances, this principle, the right to bring all kinds of motions, requests,

---

institution where the prisoner is held, or by any other that is dependent on the State or other government institutions.

and arguments[138] before the Judge, and the right to request inquiries and steps to help clarify the facts would be seriously violated.[139]

Time requirements for the accused to make investigative requests dictate that the person concerned must acquire the status of "imputado" according to the definition stated earlier and that there must not be any legal barriers to submitting requests during preliminary proceedings other than the sub judice rule. In the Code of Criminal Procedure, article 301 states the general rule in its first paragraph, while article 302 provides exceptions and limits this measure for the parties represented in the action (with the obvious exception of the Public Prosecutor) to a maximum of one month. The sub judice rule is no longer applicable ten days prior to the conclusion of preliminary proceedings (CCP, article 302, paragraph 2) so that the parties might be informed of all proceedings and be able to exercise their rights. This rule implies that there are certain restrictions on the right to a defense, although these restrictions are certainly justified being that they are intended to protect the investigation and gathering of evidence carried out during preliminary proceedings from any possible interference that might not only create problems, but also unjustly prevent the investigation from coming to a close.

Despite the aforementioned, the sub judice rule must never be an arbitrary measure; rather, it must be justified or better

[138] IV julio-agosto-septiembre 3 RDP 409 (1950).
[139] IV julio-agosto-septiembre 3 RDP 407-408 (1950).

yet, considered essential (see STC13/31 January 1985) and applicable only for the necessary period of time. If it were applied in any other way, any resulting limitation placed on the fundamental right to a defense would be inconceivable. Although lawmakers have established a limit of one month, this period of time might not correspond with the period of time deemed necessary. Accordingly, it is understood that this maximum period of one month might be extended, although this expressly contradicts legal provisions (see article 324 on extending preliminary proceedings). Providing a time limit for applying the sub judice rule might be interpreted as an expression of the lawmakers' desire for the examining judge to work diligently, and it truly does help to promote efficiency.

From the perspective of those bringing complaints, certain aspects of making investigative requests merit further comment. A 26 April 1913 decision given by the Spanish Supreme Court upheld the right of the complainant to bring an appeal even though he was not yet represented by counsel and thus could not be considered a "party" in the proceedings. This right was upheld on the grounds that under article 969 of the Code of Criminal Procedure, the complainant or accuser has the right to propose evidence. While this was an isolated decision, it must be affirmed that it is one thing to say that anyone who is party to an action has the right to propose evidence (complainant, etc). and quite another to state that to propose evidence, one must be party to an action. In any case, we must always abide by what is established by lawmakers.

Regarding the way in which investigative requests must be submitted during preliminary proceedings, we shall focus on actions that arise out of civil wrongs that under Spanish law are also offenses (querellas) as other actions are brought with a simple statement, either oral or written, of allegedly criminal acts.[140] In contrast, article 277 of the Code of Criminal Procedure, which lists the requirements that must be met when bringing this type of action, provides that the measures that should be carried out to prove that a criminal act occurred must be stated and that a request for these measures must be made. Despite these provisions, doctrine holds that investigative requests are not an essential element of an action. We must take into account that this does not refer to the way the examining judge orders practices and procedures (see CCP, article 186), which is legally envisaged (see CCP, Book I, Title VIII), but rather to the way these measures are requested by the parties. In principle, it appears that the possibility of making oral requests has not been excluded in advance.

With regard to carrying out the means of investigation that

[140] Another situation involves dealing with an action that is brought before the Public Prosecutor, who might refer the action to a judge with decision-making powers either as it was originally presented to him or her, together with statements describing the inquiries and steps to be carried out, or even as a querella, resorting to remedies under CCP, articles 105 and 271 and EOMF, article 3.4. According to the Spanish Prosecution Service, Consulta 1/1982: "Destino que deba darse a las denuncias transformadas en querellas por el Ministerio Fiscal" cited by Aragoneses Martínez with De la Oliva Santos, Hinojosa Segovia, Muerza Esparza and Tomé García, Derecho Procesal Penal 322 (1996).

might be requested by the "imputado" during preliminary proceedings, it bears repeating that when a witness testifies during these proceedings, the testimony is not considered evidence because the due process guarantees that are in place during the trial are not observed during the pre-trial proceedings. However, sources of evidence have certainly been incorporated into the proceedings once inquiries have been made and procedural steps have been taken. Moreover, a source of evidence does more than confirm the existence of a means of investigation; it has the potential to influence the opinion of the decision maker.

In theory, there are no formal limitations on the types of investigative means that the "imputado" might request during preliminary proceedings. Nonetheless, observing related precepts from the Code of Criminal Procedure, these means might be summarized as the following: judicial examination, confrontation, documents, witnesses, and expert witnesses. Doctrine holds that "investigative means" do not differ significantly from "evidentiary means," except in a formal sense, as they have different purposes. Investigative means tend to identify the facts necessary for supporting an accusation or justifying a defense, while evidentiary means are aimed at influencing the Court that is deciding the case.[141] Nevertheless, in keeping with our earlier discussion, it would be more precise in this respect to refer to investigative practices or evidentiary practices, regardless of the fact that they are

[141] 2 Almagro, Derecho Procesal (3d ed. 1990).

carried out with the "means of proof" or instruments found appropriate. There are many means or instruments used in the investigation of an offense, and it would be pointless to list them all. However, the means used to demonstrate the commission of an offense (means of proof) are fewer and are regulated by the Code of Criminal Procedure, which devotes a fair number of provisions to the topic (see Title V). We must also bear in mind that both types of practices (investigative and evidentiary) are possible during preliminary proceedings (in a general sense) for the different purposes noted above. However, evidentiary practices are intended to first influence the individual overseeing the investigation and then the decision maker. So, we are dealing with an investigative request when a source of evidence is incorporated into the proceedings during the investigation through a particular means of proof (judicial examination, expert witness, witness, document), and the due process guarantees governing the trial are not observed. The aforementioned suggests that among the inquiries and procedures carried out during preliminary proceedings, we can differentiate between an investigative practice and an evidentiary practice, although neither one in and of itself is "evidence" for the prosecution or for the defense (see STC101/1985).

a5) Criteria for Denying Investigative Requests

First, it is important to take into account that the following deals with denying investigative requests and not with ruling evidence inadmissible (CCP, article 311, paragraph 2). We shall deal with that topic when we analyze admissibility of evidence in the trial in connection with articles 659 and 792 from the Code of Criminal Procedure, which deal with admitting proposed evidence rather than granting investigative requests. Article 311 provides a general rule for carrying out measures that the Public Prosecutor or any of the parties represented in the action might propose (CCP, article 311). This rule applies to the "imputado", if he or she meets the requirements examined earlier. The examining judge shall therefore carry out the measures proposed by the parties represented in the action unless he or she finds that they are uncalled for or damaging (CCP, article 311, paragraph 1). There is nothing particularly novel about this criterion for denying requests employed by lawmakers in a Code of Criminal Procedure given to the use of adjectives. Similarly, few decisions have clarified these terms, which only serve to further inflate the macro concept of relevance.

Likewise, the only criteria for admissibility from other articles of the Code of Criminal Procedure that relate to allowing inquiries and procedures, such as article 312, which deals with investigative requests in actions arising out of civil wrongs that are also offenses (querellas), require the decision maker to find that the requested measures are not unlawful, unnecessary, or damaging to the object of the action. Furthermore, while the record will show all measures carried out at the request of a party, only those measures carried out by the Court on its own motion that lead to the object of the preliminary proceedings (CCP, article 315) will be placed on the record. If the object of preliminary proceedings is each act that is suggestive of a crime, the question arises as to what should be understood by "leading to the object of the proceedings." It would be more appropriate to say that the measures that lead to the object of preliminary proceedings are those aimed at ascertaining and verifying prima facie criminal acts or acts that are likely criminal. Practices aimed at ascertaining whether or not an act is criminal do not lead to the object of the proceedings[142] (see article 300 in connection with article 299). From the foregoing, the following criteria for denying investigative requests may be deduced:

(a) Practice is unlawful. According to this criterion, the fundamental rights of the "imputado" must be observed, keeping in mind that any restriction on these rights must be legally envisaged. Also, the measure requested in connection with its purpose must be borne in mind ("principle of proportionality").

(b) Practice is needless. It does not lead to the object of the preliminary proceedings or is not aimed at ascertaining and

[142] Molina Pascual, E., En defensa de la Ley de Enjuiciamiento Criminal, 3 RDP 632 (1970).

verifying the punishable act attributed to the "imputado" and his or her involvement in this act.[143]

(c) Practice is damaging. Carrying out the measure would obstruct or hinder the proceedings.

(d) Practice is unnecessary. Carrying out the measure would confirm a fact that, although significant, has already been verified. New Organic Law 5/1995 (Tribunal del Jurado), which recognizes the "parties" right to request practices they consider appropriate (CCP, article 25.3, sentence 3), uses a criterion for denying requests that deserves mention. The criterion states that the requested measures must be absolutely necessary to decide whether or not to proceed to trial and furthermore, the parties must be unable to carry out their request directly during the preliminary hearing (LOTJ, article 27.1).

However (and this goes to show that the abovementioned law also lacks clear guidelines for denying requests), this law does not stray very far from the requirement of "relevance" as it makes reference to a "statement of relevance" pertaining to the practices requested by counsel for the defense (LOTJ, article 30). Also, Constitutional Court Judgment 191/16 November 1989[144] provides that the complainants' right to make use of proposed investigative means is subject to restriction. It depends upon whether or not the means

---

[143] Molina Pascual, E., En defensa de la Ley de Enjuiciamiento Criminal, 3 RDP 637 (1970).

[144] BOE 291 (5 December 1989).

are considered relevant, which is for the pre-trial court to decide. The judgment goes on to say that the Constitutional Court will not review such decisions unless they appear to be completely groundless, not supported by court practices, or due to a decision that arbitrarily forbade necessary investigative practices.

Later, we shall have the opportunity to further analyze requirements for admitting evidence, and our discussion will complement what we briefly outline here. Rather than establishing a systematic procedure, it seems that lawmakers opted for "catch-all" criteria for denying requests that allow the examining judge to exercise a considerable amount of discretion and attempt to prevent a defense that could unnecessarily prolong this stage of the proceedings. Along these lines, article 6 of a 23 May 1932 order provides that the prosecution must refrain from requesting the cancellation of any orders that mark the end of preliminary proceedings in order to carry out pointless or unnecessary inquiries or procedures. Furthermore, such orders cannot be cancelled even in the event that the requested practices are considered sound if, in the opinion of the Court, they might be carried out during the trial without posing any threat to justice being done. This final criterion used by lawmakers came about as a result of the criterion mentioned earlier relative to "necessity" in connection with the intent to carry out preliminary inquiries and procedures without delay (see CCP, article 324, paragraph 2) and is also inferred from the one month time limit for the sub judice rule. Regarding summary proceedings, which aim to resolve matters quickly (or at least more quickly than ordinary proceedings), we should consider that although the cases heard involve offenses that carry sentences that are less severe than those heard in ordinary proceedings, this does not mean that the investigation into these offenses is necessarily easier and that preliminary proceedings can therefore proceed more quickly.

Now then, it is one thing to conclude that an investigative measure is unnecessary, but it is quite another to find that a request should be denied due to criteria that state that the measure can be carried out during the trial (CCP, article 314). As we have already seen, an inquiry or procedure requested by the "imputado" might have the specific purpose of preventing the matter from going to trial. This would be a justifiable request, and it would not be fitting to invoke reasons for denying the request other than those addressed earlier.

Article 315 of the Code of Criminal Procedure bears special mention regarding the practice of differentiating on the court record between inquiries and practices that are carried out at the request of the parties and those that are ordered by the Court on its own motion. Only those practices ordered by the Court on its own motion whose results lead to the object of the proceedings are placed on the record. Article 1 of a 21 March 1932 Order provides that any inquiries and procedures that cannot be used to clarify the facts will not be included on the record, even those that the Court orders on its own motion. It goes on to say that the reason for proceeding in this manner should be given. This provision seems to contradict article 315 in that it makes reference to "even" those practices that the Court orders on its own motion. This might suggest that due to the simple fact that the practices were ordered de officio, they should be placed on the record. Note that the general reference in article 315 to recording practices and procedures makes no mention of recording their outcome. (The abovementioned procedures and practices are those used for confirming or verifying).

Regarding the distinction that is made between practices requested by the parties and practices that the Court orders on its own motion, lawmakers gave examining judges a considerable amount of discretion to grant or deny requests, and in doing so they created a situation that favors judges. If it were any other way, judges' authority might be questioned if the court record showed that they ordered measures that failed to aid in the discovery of the truth and consequently, although they are deserving of our trust, we might become wary. However, the situation is different when practices are requested by one of the parties. If the request proves unwise, the other party has the opportunity to use it to their advantage either during preliminary proceedings or the trial (depending upon multiple factors that we need not mention).

A general criterion for granting investigative requests is suggested by the provisions discussed above. We might say that those requests that do not lead to the object of the proceedings, or in other words, do not help to clarify the facts should be denied. However, as this cannot always be determined ahead of time, it seems appropriate to grant requests.

The provision from the order mentioned above that stipulates providing a reason as to why a practice or procedure whose outcome is not useful is not included on the court record of preliminary proceedings is unnecessary. (This refers to practices requested by the parties and "even" those that the Court orders on its own motion). The fact that the outcome of a particular practice is of no use seems reason enough not to place it on the record. Although, a practice may only appear unhelpful because, as we noted earlier, one of the parties could use the information that was gathered against the other and expose the weak grounds on which the opposing party based his or her claims.

Another legal criterion for granting and carrying out investigative requests has to do with whether or not the requested measures will lead to "successful" proceedings in connection with article 320 of the Code of Criminal Procedure, which deals with civil petitioners. However, as this article refers to one very specific situation, we cannot generalize and affirm that one criterion for granting investigative requests is that they will lead to "successful" proceedings.

To sum up, one general criterion for granting and carrying out investigative requests submitted by the "parties" stipulates that the requests must help to clarify the facts. The facts in question might be those that are directly linked to the charges or those pertaining to other information that might help to explain what occurred, and the interested "party" would make these facts known. In the event that it is not possible to determine from the start whether or not a requested measure would be helpful, it should be allowed under the general rule (which tends toward leniency or generosity) that is observed by the Spanish Constitutional Court when evaluating "relevance."

In any case, if an examining judge opts to deny an investigative request, he or she must do so with an order (see CCP, article 311, paragraph 2) that gives reasons for the decision (CCP, article 141) and is challengeable by appeal without stay of execution (CCP, article 311).

In conclusion, a proper investigation balances public interest in criminal prosecution with the rights of the "imputado" in such a way that the right to present evidence (in a general sense) is not an obstacle to the criminal courts and their freedom to direct proceedings (Bewegungsfreiheit). Furthermore, we should not overlook the fact that the investigation is still an important aspect of criminal proceedings today, even though it does not resemble practices under the former inquisitorial system.[145]

[145] However, Silva Melero states: "aun en los días en que este sistema era el que informaba el proceso penal, se admitía la posibilidad de que el defensor, después del estudio de los autos, pudiera solicitar se completara la instrucción con ulteriores investigaciones, e incluso podía provocar un nuevo examen de testigos ya interrogados, con el fin de obtener

a6) German Investigative Proceedings (Ermittlungsverfahren)

Although the right to request evidence (Beweisantragsrecht) during investigative proceedings (Ermittlungsverfahren) in Germany is not very well developed,[146] by way of introduction, it seems fitting to summarize the doctrine and jurisprudence dealing with this topic.

Regarding the investigative stage of German proceedings and the right of the accused to request evidence, it is necessary to refer to three sections of the German Code of Criminal Procedure (Strafprozessordnung or StPO), which we shall briefly discuss in the following few pages. However, we must take into account, as Peters noted in 1984, that the right of the accused to submit investigative requests during the investigation (Ermittlungsverfahren), in contrast to what happens during the trial (Hauptverhandlung), has been given little attention in doctrine (Literatur) and jurisprudence or even by lawmakers.[147]

(1) According to StPO, section 163a, paragraph 2, if the "Beschuldigte" (or suspect) submits a request for evidence in

rectificaciones y aclaraciones, y también, ofrecer nuevos testimonios en lo que se calificó proceso convencional ad repulsam", julio-agosto-septiembre RDP 408 (1950). See also Vélez Mariconde, A., La función judicial en lo penal, 2 RDP 303 (1968).

[146] Perron, Das Beweisantragsrecht des Beschuldigten im deutschen Strafrecht 171 (1995).

[147] See Quedenfeld, Peters-Festschrift II 216 (1984).

his or her defense, the request shall be granted if the evidence is "important" (von Bedeutung). Therefore, the condition for granting the Beschuldigte's request is subject to what is understood by the term "important." The statement is reminiscent of the language employed by Spanish lawmakers when specifying that inquiries and procedures shall only be placed on the record when their outcome leads to the object of the preliminary proceedings (CCP, article 315, paragraph 2). However, the Spanish Code deals with the issue from a different perspective than that of StPO from the position of the "imputado". It is important to note that in the event that the request (Beweisantrag) is denied, the Beschuldigte does not have any recourse (Rechtsbehelf).[148] Neither doctrine nor jurisprudence expound on the subject, except for Krekeler's attempt to address the application (Übertragbarkeit) of StPO, section 244, paragraphs 3 and 5. However, even in that case, the Beschuldigte is still unable to apply for cassation of judgment (appeal before the Supreme Court) on the ground of an error (Fehler).[149] This gives the judge considerable discretionary power considering the "clash" between conflicting interests. Although the suspect is entitled to conduct a defense and seek acquittal, he or she might also use this right to abuse the system and impair the investigative proceedings (Ermittlungsverfahren). With this in mind,

[148] For the correct use of the term "Rechtsbehelf," see Gómez Colomer, El proceso penal alemán, Introducción y normas básicas 598 (1st ed. 1985).
[149] Perron, Das Beweisantragsrecht des Beschuldigten im deutschen Strafrecht 168 (1995).

the abovementioned section of StPO appears to grant the Beschuldigte the power to contribute to the clarification of the facts, without prejudice to those who declare that it is a "dangerous weapon" in the possession of the defense, who might use it during the next stage of the proceedings to claim that evidence was lost and to establish grounds for cassation of judgment (based on Aufklärungsrüge or "appeal for clarification").[150]

(2) Under section 166, paragraph 1 of StPO, if the Beschuldigte submits a request for evidence in his or her defense during questioning, the judge should grant the request if he or she finds it important and fears that evidence might be lost, and if it might be used as grounds for releasing the Beschuldigte (Freilassung). Kleinknecht and Meyer contend that the precept provides that the judge (Richter) has a duty to examine evidence requested by the Beschuldigte ("Notbeweisaufnahme zu Gunsten des Beschuldigtens") if there is a danger of losing evidence or if it might be used as grounds for releasing the Beschuldigte.[151] Although under these circumstances the decision also depends upon the examining judge (Ermittlungsrichter), the criteria for granting or denying requests are more objective than the requirement relating to "importance" mentioned earlier. First, the request must be "significant" ("erheblichkeit") and second, two different, but

[150] See Perron, Das Beweisantragsrecht des Beschuldigten im deutschen Strafrecht 168-169 (1995).

[151] Borowsky, Zum Beweisantragsrecht im Ermittlungsverfahren, 10 Strafverteidiger 455 (1986).

not opposing circumstances must come into play: it is possible that evidence might be lost and likely that the Beschuldigte could be released. The possible strength of a request for evidence must be measured by the possibility that it might be challenged if it is denied, and on this subject German doctrine is divided. Borowsky contends that if the examining judge (Ermittlungsrichter) denies a request, a complaint may be made to the Court (Beschwerde) based on StPO, section 304, although this section does not specifically address the matter. He goes on to criticize doctrine that takes an opposing view (Alsberg-Nüse-Meyer, among others), contending that those who believe that the accused has no recourse when a request is denied have no grounds for their opinion and lack legal backing.[152] The question remains whether or not a complaint (Beschwerde) may be lodged under StPO, section 166 when requests are denied, as section 304, paragraph 1, sentence 2 does not seem to expressly prohibit it.[153]

Majority opinion holds that complaints cannot be lodged under StPO, section 166, paragraph 1 in the event that a request is denied.[154] There is parallelism in the foregoing and those circumstances that in Spain result in the examination of evidence during preliminary proceedings in accordance with

---

[152] Borowsky, Zum Beweisantragsrecht im Ermittlungsverfahren, 10 Strafverteidiger 455 (1986).

[153] See 2 Riess, Die Strafprozessordnung und das Gerichtsverfassungsgeset z, Grosskommentar section 166 note 13 (24th ed).

[154] See Perron, Das Beweisantragsrecht des Beschuldigten im deutschen Strafprozess 169 (1995).

due process guarantees (prueba anticipada). This is relative to situations in which it would be impossible to reproduce or repeat evidence during the trial, and consequently in a certain sense evidence would be lost. This is the only case outside of the trial that involves "evidence" in the technical sense of the word, and we will later have the opportunity to return to this topic.

(3) Under section 168d, paragraph 2 of StPO, when expert witnesses join in the judicial inspection of evidence, the Beschuldigte may request that the experts that he or she intends to put forward for the trial be summoned. If this request is denied, the suspect, acting alone, may summon the expert witnesses. The experts designated by the suspect may join in the examination of evidence and all necessary investigations as long as their participation does not stand in the way of the experts called by the Judge. Under this provision, the Judge's possibilities for denying a request are even more limited, although actually we should differentiate between two different positions: first, we might say that StPO fails to provide any criteria for denying requests (sentence 1) and second, in view of the possibility that the suspect might summon experts, their participation in the examination of evidence and investigations might be forbidden if they stand in the way of the experts called by the Judge. It seems that requests should also be denied under StPO, section 34 if the expert witnesses named by the accused fail to behave appropriately. Complaints to the Court are admissible,

according to prevailing doctrine, under section 307, paragraph 1 without stay of execution (aufschiebende Wirkung).[155] This is another topic on which the high courts (obergerichtliche Entscheidungen) have pronounced few judgments.

a7) Intermediate Stage in Spanish and German Proceedings

The intermediate stage of ordinary proceedings in Spain is covered in Book II, Title IX of the Spanish Code of Criminal Procedure, whose title ("De la conclusión del sumario y del sobreseimiento") reflects that it deals with the close of preliminary proceedings and stay of proceedings. When the examining judge decides to bring the investigative proceedings to a close, he or she gives an order and refers the court record and evidence gathered to the appropriate court (CCP, article 622, paragraph 1).

The purpose of the intermediate stage is to avoid an incorrect decision to go to trial either due to the fact that the investigation was not carried out appropriately, in which case article 627 covers the possibility of conducting another investigation, or because a stay of proceedings is the proper course to take. The existence of this stage is justified not only

---

[155] See Perron, Das Beweisantragsrecht des Beschuldigten im deutschen Strafrecht 170 (1995).

by the specific outcome legally envisaged for the proceedings, but also in large part by the variety of courts that are involved.[156]

Lawmakers chose to entitle the legislation covering summary proceedings (Book IV, Title III, Chapter II) "Preparing the Trial" ("De la preparación del juicio oral"). The Constitutional Court seems to justify this choice of wording by contending that at that point in the proceedings, parties are not afforded opportunities to complete the investigation as initiating the preparatory stage for the trial necessarily requires that preliminary proceedings have been closed and will be not subject to review at a later time (STC66/17 April 1989). However, this does not justify the way motions for practices essential for a committal for trial are treated differently in summary proceedings under article 790. For example, when the Public Prosecutor requests certain measures, the examining judge should grant the request; however, when measures are requested by the Private Prosecutor, the judge grants what he or she finds fitting (CCP, article 790.2, paragraph 2). (See Circular 1/89 of the Spanish Prosecution Service). This distinction is not recognized in ordinary Spanish proceedings (CCP, article 627, paragraph 3).

The Spanish Code of Criminal Procedure, in contrast to the German StPO, does not include any provisions that allow

[156] Claría Olemedo, J., Del avocamiento al procesamiento, 2 RDP 213 (1968).

the suspect to request inquiries or procedures while preparing for the trial in summary proceedings. Rather, it only covers motions to carry out those measures (CCP, article 790.2, paragraph 3) that are considered essential for indictment. (See STC66/17 April 1989, which provides that the suspect must be heard to avoid inequalities between "parties" and defenselessness, which is forbidden by the Spanish Constitution, article 24). It is at this point in the proceedings that both parties (prosecution and defense) may make motions for evidence that they intend to adduce during the trial (CCP, articles 790.5, paragraph 2 and 791.2), which we shall discuss at a later point. Note that while in ordinary proceedings this stage is overseen by the trial court, in summary proceedings trial preparation is the responsibility of the examining judge.

Regarding the possibility of submitting requests at this point in the proceedings, the only situation recognized by lawmakers involves circumstances in which there is not sufficient information to specify the charges (article 622, paragraph 2). (Article 627, paragraph 3 fails to provide any criteria for such circumstances). In other words, the circumstances are such that it is impossible to issue a bill of indictment due to a lack of elements essential for specifying the offense. Thus, this is a valid reason for requesting measures that are necessary for indictment (CCP, article 790.2). The fact that the law does not provide opportunity for the suspect to submit requests during this stage of the proceedings cannot be justified[157] as the fundamental right to present evidence should not be sacrificed for efficiency, rapidity, and economic savings (STC15 February 1990). Furthermore, if one of the purposes of this stage is to avoid wrongfully proceeding to trial, shouldn't the suspect at this point be allowed to request steps that might turn out to support a stay of proceedings? Just as both the Public and Private Prosecutor may submit requests for new inquiries or procedures when they lack the information necessary to issue a bill of indictment, the defense should also be allowed to submit requests, not to prepare a plea, but rather to avoid going to trial. It is unfeasible to contend that the suspect already had this opportunity during preliminary proceedings or that the Public Prosecutor, who is subject to the "principle of legality" and impartiality, will recognize this fact or that allowing the suspect to make additional requests would hinder the proceedings. Quite the opposite, this only happens when the case actually goes to trial, and furthermore a case could also be made for violation of the principle of equality.

Clearly, under certain circumstances allowing the suspect to submit requests during this stage might mean that he or she might possibly influence the decision maker (in ordinary proceedings), even knowing full well that the request will be

[157] This position is supported by STC66/17 April 1989 (ordinary proceedings) and opposed in STC186/15 November 1990 (for summary proceedings). We share the opinion of Tomé García, who disagrees with the reasoning of the opposing judgment, which includes a discussion of the different purposes of this stage for ordinary and summary proceedings. Tomé García with De la Oliva, Aragoneses Martínez, Hinojosa Segovia and Muerza Esparza, Derecho Procesal Penal 304 (1996).

denied. We must take into account that during this stage the Judge or Court are in a better position to decide whether or not to allow the requested measures because they were the ones who oversaw the investigation. For this reason, the fact that the possibility for the suspect to submit requests is not addressed in law is inexcusable. Similarly, criteria mentioned earlier pertaining to "what the Judge finds fitting" relative to requests submitted by the Private Prosecutor (CCP, article 790.2, paragraph 2) are unclear and give the judge considerable discretionary powers for making a decision.

However, after studying the abovementioned articles (disregarding the differences between ordinary and summary proceedings)[158], it does seem possible to come away with some type of criteria on which the Judge or Court might base a decision on whether or not to grant an investigative request. If measures that are considered necessary for indictment may indeed be requested when it proves impossible to issue the bill of indictment for lack of the elements essential for specifying the charges (CCP, article 790.2), then it would be possible to deny a request for those measures unrelated to identification, participation in criminal acts, or other aspects of criminal activity. It therefore follows that the Judge or Court might deny requests when the proposed measures are

[158] In ordinary proceedings, when the Public Prosecutor oppose the order to close preliminary proceedings and request new investigative procedures or practices, they are actually doing so to prepare their case. Therefore, the purpose of this stage, which incidentally is a bit contrived, is the same in both types of proceedings.

directed at determining extenuating circumstances, the extent to which the accused was involved in the offense, or other circumstances unrelated to the type of offense in issue.

It is important to keep in mind that during this stage of preparation for the trial, we are dealing with admissibility of an exceptional nature. Inquiries, practices, and procedures are carried out in special situations in which it is impossible to indict because the elements that are essential for specifying the charges are lacking (STC186/15 November 1990).

German doctrine reveals that the situation of the suspect (Beschuldigte) is not any better[159] in this stage of the proceedings than it was during preliminary proceedings. Section 201 of StPO governs the right to present evidence, and although it allows for the possibility of requesting evidence, the drawback for the suspect is that the decision given by the Court, regardless of whether the request is granted or denied, is not exceptionable (unanfechtbar).[160] Any investigative request submitted by the suspect must make reference to the means of proof (Beweismittel) to be used and the facts

---

[159] See Perron, Das Beweisantragsrecht des Beschuldigten im deutschen Strafprozess 175 (1995).

[160] StPO, section 201 provides that the Chief Justice shall read the bill of indictment to the accused (Angeschuldigte), and at this time the accused shall be invited to state, during a period of time to be determined, if he or she wishes to request the examination of particular items of evidence before any decision relating to commencing the trial is given, or to file any claim opposing the commencement of the trial. It also states that the Court shall give judgment on any requests and claims, and their decision is not exceptionable. Gómez Colomer, El proceso penal alemán, Introducción y normas básicas 346-347 (1985).

(Tatsache) that might be proved with these means.[161]

As we mentioned earlier, it is not possible to appeal against a decision to deny a request, although it is possible to do so indirectly (nicht unmittelbar).[162] But in any case, under sections 34 and 35 of StPO, the suspect is entitled to be informed if his or her request is denied and must be given an explanation as to why. We should draw attention to the fact that at this point in the proceedings, it is more feasible for the Court to decide whether or not the request should be granted as it has the record of the preliminary proceedings (Ermittlungsverfahren) at its disposal. There is no special requirement relative to the way in which the request (Antrag) should be submitted. Written requests are the most common type, although requests may also be entered into the record (Er kann schriftlich oder zu Protokoll der Geschäftsstelle angebracht werden).

When deciding whether or not to grant a request for evidence, the Judge must consider whether or not the proposed means of proof might have an effect on an assessment (Beurteilung) of the suspicious acts (Tatverdacht).[163] This situation is covered under section 219 of StPO relative to preparing the trial (Vorbereitung der Hauptverhandlung).

---

[161] According to Alsberg/Nüse/Meyer, Der Beweisantrag im Strafprozess 343 (5th ed. 1983).

[162] See Perron, Das Beweisantragsrecht des Beschuldigten im deutschen Strafprozess 175 (1995).

[163] Alsberg/Nüse/Meyer, Der Beweisantrag im Strafprozess 344 (5th ed. 1983).

This section provides that to summon witnesses or experts or bring other means of proof to the trial, the accused must submit a request to the Chief Justice of the Court, outlining the facts relating to the proposed evidence. The acussed shall be informed of the order given pertaining to his or her request, and the Prosecution shall be informed of any requests submitted by the suspect that are granted.[164] The Court has sufficient reason to deny (Ablehnung) a request if it finds that it is not necessary to examine evidence (Beweiserhebung) to come to a decision on whether or not to commence trial (Eröffnung des Hauptverfahrens). In any case, most doctrine holds that this decision is guided by the criteria for denying evidence requests provided under section 244, paragraphs 3-5 of StPO, although the Supreme Court (Bundesgerichtshof) has pronounced few judgments dealing with the subject.

However, as Perron points out, there is one important difference to take into account relative to this stage of the proceedings. The Court that is going to adjudge is that which decides whether or not to grant requests, and if the Chief Justice (Vorsitzende) denies a request (Beweisantrag) submitted under StPO, section 219 without properly basing his or her decision on criteria provided under StPO, section 244, paragraphs 3-5, it is very probable that the very same request will be resubmitted during the trial (Hauptverhandlung).[165]

[164] Gómez Colomer, El proceso penal alemán, Introducción y normas básicas 351(1st ed. 1995).

Despite the foregoing, the intermediate stage of German proceedings is subject to criticism because when all is said and done, the trial almost always commences (Eröffnung des Hauptverfahrens), and furthermore the order for opening the trial (Eröffnungsbeschluss) places the prosecution's theory at the forefront, thus threatening the decision maker's impartiality.[166]

a8) Intermediate Stage under the Rome Statute of the ICC

We can also refer to an intermediate stage in the procedures followed by the International Criminal Court, which begins when the Presidency constitutes a Trial Chamber (once the Pre-Trial Chamber has confirmed the charges). Article 61.11 provides:

> Once the charges have been confirmed in accordance with this article, the Presidency shall constitute a Trial Chamber, which subject to paragraph 9 and to article 64, paragraph 4, shall be responsible for the conduct of subsequent proceedings and

---

[165] See Perron, Das Beweisantragsrecht des Beschuldigten im deutschen Strafprozess 177 (1995).

[166] See Perron, Das Beweisantragsrecht des Beschuldigten im deutschen Strafprozess 151 (1995).

> may exercise any function of the Pre-Trial Chamber that is relevant and capable of application in those proceedings.

Under article 64.9, the Trial Chamber also has the power on application of a party or on its own motion to "rule on the admissibility or relevance of evidence."

This confirms the comparison made between what is provided under the Rome Statute and articles 656 and 659 of the Spanish Code of Criminal Procedure, which was written years ago, yet is still in force today. If the Trial Chamber has the power to rule on the admissibility or relevance of evidence, the only conclusion that can be drawn is that evidence could not have been led during investigative proceedings before the Pre-Trial Chamber. Thus, an intermediate stage can be identified from the Rome Statute. Its purpose is to prepare the trial, and consequently the Court will rule on the admissibility of the evidence that is intended for examination during the trial.

b) Admission and Examination of Evidence

b1) Introduction

The following pages devoted to this very important topic are based primarily on doctrine dealing with sections 244 and 245 of StPO, which cover reasons for denying evidence requests (Beweisantragsablehnungsgründe). There is a general tendency to evade formalities with the idea that justice can be done faster,[167] which would in some way alleviate the increasing workload that courts are forced to handle. As we have mentioned, justice involves the period of time that transpires between bringing an action and receiving judgment, and at times it takes too long.

European procedural reforms have gone in the direction of Anglo-American[168] accusatorial procedure, which put quite simply is different. While it is not the purpose of this work to pass judgment, let it be well understood that form (not formality, which has been on a crisis course for some time)[169] and rapidity are not always mutually exclusive, especially considering that they are rights of the accused. Often, the accused will have to go through appeals to exercise a right, and if this right had not been taken lightly during the first trial and clear criteria had been in place, time and money

---

[167] The following statement made by the Spanish Minister of Justice in 1950 is significant: "...el reforzamiento de los poderes del Juez y la consiguiente acentuación del carácter público del proceso, son los medios más indicados para combatir la desesperante lentitud que tan terriblemente ha dañado la fe del pueblo en las instituciones judiciales, y del que solo son responsables los litigantes de mala fe, multiplicando sus incidentes ante un Magistrado legalmente imposibilitado para impedir lo que muchas veces llega a constituir burla de la justicia."

[168] See generally Lozano-Higuero Pinto, Introducción al Derecho Procesal 197 (1990).

[169] Hernández Gil, Obras Completas, T. V., Metodología de la Ciencia del Derecho 431 (1988).

would have been saved and, all things considered, justice would have been done more efficiently. There are not clear criteria relative to admissibility of evidence, and although any intent to offer a regulatory scheme for admissibility and examination of evidence in the criminal trial would be over ambitious, it seems appropriate, with the help of Spanish and German doctrine and jurisprudence, to give at least a few guidelines that might be of use in making future reforms.

When analyzing admissibility of evidence in any type of proceeding, two separate classes of reasons or grounds for denying requests can be considered: material grounds, which extend to the proceedings themselves, and grounds that are strictly procedural. We must also consider situations in which reasons belonging to one class have an effect on reasons from the other class; or they may even simultaneously affect each other.

Material grounds for denying evidence requests relate to the facts in issue. Accordingly, the decision maker will deny requests in all situations in which these requests are not aimed at adducing evidence related to the facts in issue and in circumstances for which lawmakers have set out special procedures to settle disputes that limit debate to only certain facts (for example, an executory procedure during which the contract that led to a bill of exchange is not examined as evidence). Procedural grounds for denying requests are an entirely different matter; they apply when legally envisaged deadlines, form, etc. are not observed. Under such circumstances, the decision maker will rule that the request is contrary to correct procedure. In Spain both types of grounds for denying requests will be subject to legal review that adapts to the situation at hand, if indeed criminal proceedings are to respect the rights of the accused.

Forgoing the well-known distinction between present or absent means of proof made in StPO (sections 244.3-244.6 and 245) and with the concept of evidence requests that has already been discussed in mind, doctrine and jurisprudence based on the abovementioned sections offer one possible way to classify different grounds for denying requests.

Common sense dictates distinguishing between applicable grounds for denying requests according to whether or not the means of proof are present. Thus, attempt to delay proceedings (Prozessverschleppungsabsicht) is not used as grounds for denying a request when the expert witness or the object to be examined is present at the trial.[170] Note, at least as an apparent contradiction, concurrence between section 244.2 and section 244.3, sentence 3 of StPO: the first article limits the duty to clarify facts (Aufklärungspflicht) to those facts and means of proof important for the decision, while the second refers to denying requests when the facts to be proved are not important for the decision. Although it is true that section 244.2 makes reference to means of proof and section 244.3 does not,[171] the importance or unimportance of

[170] See Fezer, Strafprozessrecht II 74 note 160 (1986).

the facts relative to the decision does not stop problems from arising between the duty to clarify facts (Aufklärungspflicht) and the right to evidence (Beweisrecht).

One possible way to classify different grounds for denying evidence requests, keeping in mind that there are many German authors who have devoted many pages of commentary to the issue (for example, Löwe-Rosenberg), might be the following: admissibility of evidence (inadmissible evidence or request), need for evidence (insignificance of evidentiary facts, evidentiary fact or information to the contrary is common knowledge, facts are already proved, confirmed facts are accepted as true), usefulness of evidence (means of proof is completely inadequate or inaccessible), deviation from the objective of the proceedings (intent to delay proceedings, etc).[172]

b2) Concept of Evidence Requests and their Classification

German doctrine distinguishes between different types of evidence requests. First, an evidence request in the strict sense of the term (Beweisantrag) is a motion to a court for examining evidence related to a certain affirmation, whether it be on guilt or legal consequences (Schuld-oder Rechtsfolgenfrage),

[171] See Widmaier, Kritische Gedanken zur diskutierten Reform des Beweisantrags- und Revisionsrechts, NStZ 416 (1994).

[172] Compare with Fezer's classification of different grounds for denying evidence requests. Strafprozessrecht 167 note 58 (1995).

using a particular means of proof.[173]

It is enough that the facts to be proved (Beweistatsache) are generally recognizable (in ihren allgemein Umrissen) in the request.[174]. Also, the evidence request (Beweisantrag) may be submitted subject to some sort of condition,[175] which means that the requested evidence will only be examined (Beweiserhebung) if something specific occurs or a particular procedural situation arises (Sach-oder Prozesslage). In these cases, the Court is only required to examine the request and decide whether or not to grant it if the specified condition is satisfied (bei Eintritt der Bedingung). However, the Court may also deal with the request without considering the condition.[176] According to the type of condition involved,

---

[173] See Kleinknecht/Meyer, Strafprozessordnung section 244, note 18 (42d ed. 1995). "Der Antragsteller muss in dem Beweisantrag eine bestimmte Tatsache behaupten. Der Beweisantrag muss ferner die Behauptung enthalten, dass die Beweistatsache durch ein bestimmtes Beweismittel bewiesen werden kann." Alsberg/Nüse/Meyer, Der Beweisantrag im Strafprozess 39, 47 (5th ed. 1983).

[174] This may be explained with the following examples: When requesting expert testimony, saying that a certain way of measuring the speed of an automobile may result in errors (Fehlerquellen) is enough. It is not necessary to specifically describe the error in question. Similarly, when requesting to examine a witness, it is enough to indicate that the intent is to prove that the accused has suffered from an illness that has affected his or her brain (die sich auf das Gehirn auswirkten) without going into further detail on the illness. Alsberg/Nüse/Meyer, Der Beweisantrag im Strafprozess 41 (5th ed. 1983).

[175] Alsberg/Nüse/Meyer, Der Beweisantrag im Strafprozess 57 (5th ed. 1983).

[176] BGH 32 13 and Alsberg/Nüse/Meyer 59, cited by Eisenberg, Beweisrecht der StPO 103 (2d ed. 1996).

Eisenberg[177] classifies requests according to whether or not they are process-related (prozessual bedingter Beweisantrag), continent evidence requests (Eventualbeweisantrag) or requests for auxiliary evidence (Hilfsbeweisantrag).

(a) Requests that are process-related (Prozessual bedingter Antrag) are evidence requests that are dependant upon certain procedural circumstances (bestimmten prozessualen Lage), such as specific witness testimony (Zeugenaussage) on actual occurrences (tatsächlichen Geschehen), the examination of other items of evidence by the Court (Gericht), or the taking of an oath (Vornahme einer Vereidigung).

(b) Continent requests (Eventualbeweisantrag) are those that are conditional on the Court coming to a certain understanding (Auffasung). For example, the Court might find that a document is authentic (Echtheit einer Urkunde), a witness is credible (Glaubwürdigkeit eines Zeugen), or that the accused should be charged with a crime (Schuldfähigkeit des Angeklagten).

(c) Requests for auxiliary evidence (Hilfsbeweisantrag) (see CCP, article 729.3) are important in practice, especially from a tactical perspective. These requests are usually submitted in the final report (Schlussvortrag) by the defense conditional on the Court (Gericht) coming to a certain conclusive procedural decision (verfahrensabschliessenden Entscheidung), which might be related to guilt (Schuldspruch) or legal consequences

---

[177] Eisenberg, Beweisrecht der StPO 103 (2d ed. 1996).

(Rechtsfolge). Furthermore, the affirmation to be proved (Beweisbehauptung) should relate to the ruling (Ausspruch) that is sought. This does not mean, however, that all requests included in the final report are for auxiliary evidence.

Up until this point, in keeping with German doctrine, we have explored the concept of evidence requests and different types of requests according to whether or not they are subject to certain conditions. From the very definition of an evidence request, one might conclude that it is not always possible for the requester to meet its requirements (name the facts to be proved and the means of proof). Therefore, if an individual intends to prove something during the proceedings and is unable to submit an evidence request (Beweisantrag), he or she must resort to "indirect suggestions" in the broad sense of the term (Beweisanregungen).

Although there are quite a variety of classifications relating to motions for evidence in German doctrine, we would like to refer to the work of Kleinknecht-Meyer[178] and differentiate first between an evidence request (Beweisantrag) and an indirect suggestion (Beweisanregung) in the broad sense of the term. Next, within the category of indirect suggestions (Beweisanregungen), we can further distinguish between an offering of evidence (Beweiserbieten), a request for evidentiary inquiry (Beweisermittlungsantrag), and an indirect suggestion (Beweisanregung) in the strict sense of the term. First, an

[178] Kleinknecht/Meyer, Strafprozessordnung 753-754 section 244 (42d ed. 1995).

evidence request (Beweisantrag) differs from an indirect suggestion (Beweisanregung) in the broad sense of the term in that the suggestion leaves the examination of evidence (Beweiserhebung) to the discretion of the Court because the individual requesting evidence either does not wish to submit an evidence request or is unable to do so for reasons of circumstance or law. The Court rules on indirect suggestions as part of its duty to clarify facts (Aufklärungspflicht) under section 244.2 of StPO. Indirect suggestions may be further classified as the following:

(a) An offering of evidence (Beweiserbieten) is a suggestion relating to the possibility of examining evidence that a participant in the proceedings leaves to the discretion of the Court under the assumption that the duty to clarify facts requires such action.

(b) A request for evidentiary inquiry (Beweisermittlungsantr ag) is used to prepare evidence requests that are not ready to be submitted because the facts to be proved (Beweistatsache) are not known or because the means of proof cannot be specified. For example, a request of this type might be a request for a report from an expert (Sachverständigengutachten) without establishing what it should cover.

(c) An indirect suggestion in the strict sense of the term (Beweisanregung) is a request that cannot be submitted as an evidence request for legal reasons because it only makes reference to the way evidence should be examined and neglects to mention the scope of the examination. A request for confrontation (Gegenüberstellung) belongs in this category.

In Spanish criminal proceedings evidence requests have not been dealt with in law to the same extent as under sections 244 and 245 of StPO. There are no provisions in the Spanish Code of Criminal Procedure that compare with the German sections we have cited, although many judgments have been pronounced on the admissibility of evidence, especially by the Spanish Constitutional Court. However, all of these judgments have been made considering the requirement of relevance rather than the concept of evidence requests, which has not been defined in law or doctrine.

Perhaps that would be the best place to start in suggesting a new regulatory scheme for admissibility of evidence. If we have clearly defined the concept of a evidence request as a motion asking the Court to employ a means of proof to evaluate a particular affirmation, then Spanish proposals for evidence might be compared with German indirect suggestions (Beweisanregungen) in the broad sense of the term. Therefore, the Court is not required to decide whether or not to grant proposals based on criteria for denying requests. Rather, the decision relates to the duty to clarify facts, and thus the Court has more discretionary power.

As well as to failing to distinguish between evidence proposals and requests, the Spanish Code of Criminal Procedure also neglects to differentiate between ruling "proposed items of evidence" (which are actually means of proof) inadmissible and denying evidence requests. Moreover, a list of criteria for denying requests is also lacking; the only criterion included in the Code of Criminal Procedure is the well-known reference to admitting those items of evidence found relevant (CCP, article 659, sentence 1).

Requirements for a proceeding always have a bearing on the expected effect of the proceeding and, in theory, may affect any of the three main elements into which a proceeding can be broken down: subjects, object, and alteration of reality or an activity in the strict sense of the term. A series of concepts known by a variety of names (capacity, legitimation, postulation, possibility, place, time, form, etc).[179] is found within each of these categories.

A number of issues arise from evidence requests as proceedings initiated by "parties", and they must be resolved. First, the reason for a request should not be sought in its subject as the idea of separation between the motivation for a proceeding and the subject of a proceeding (capacity and will) is clear and comprehensible. This confirms that motivation is not a subjective requirement. Similarly, the requirements for an activity (place, time, and form) must not be confused with the reason for a request as it is obvious from the fact that lawmakers made the effects of any alteration of reality produced by a proceeding conditional on the coming together of certain temporal, spatial, and formal requirements that they are independent from its motive. Regarding these

[179] Guasp, IV julio-agosto-septiembre 3 RDP 403 (1948).

requirements for an activity, lawmakers seemed to have followed the maxim that the greater the significance of the subject-matter of a proceeding, the greater the time for its development, which, from our point of view, may not necessarily be the case.[180]

All things considered, the reason for a request must be sought in so-called objective requirements or the matter on which the motion is based, which must be possible (physically and morally), suitable, and must correspond to a somewhat general reason covered by the law. In other words, it must match up with legal reasons defined under objective law. The fact that the law makes no mention of the legal reason for evidence requests suggests that the reasons are not specific. Rather, they are generic and amount to the legal interest of the individual who submits the request, which is not only personal, but is also recognized either expressly or implicitly by the legal system. Lawmakers did not have to make any reference to admitting relevant evidence because the idea is included within the general objective requirement of appropriateness that is applicable to any proceeding.[181]

The appointed decision maker should be the one to pass judgment on the concurrence of reasons for an evidence

[180] But see Barrios de Angelis, D., La Teoría general del proceso…, 1 RDP 132 (1968).

[181] See also Guasp, who states: "La inadmisión de pruebas en razón a su impertinencia o inutilidad (art. 563 de la Ley de Enjuiciamiento Civil), sólo puede v.g., explicarse mediante el juego del requisito de la idoneidad." IV julio-agosto-septiembre 3 RDP 410 (1948).

request in order to grant it and to proceed to any subsequent examination of the proposed means of proof. However, at times, it might be difficult to evaluate interests without prejudging the merits of the case.

We have noted that the way in which evidentiary means are offered, gathered, adduced, and maintained in the proceedings characterizesevidentiary process as a proceeding.[182] Focusing on the first activity listed above, it follows that we would end up with different ways of offering means of proof: requests, proposals, and even indirect suggestions as defined in German doctrine.[183]

Considering the general category for evidence requests, one might conclude that we are dealing with proceedings[184] initiated by a party and more specifically, motions indicating what is to be proved and the means of proof that the party plans to use.[185] However, in the broad sense of the term, evidence requests

---

[182] Silva Melero, IV julio-agosto-septiembre 3 RDP 398 (1950).

[183] German doctrine further classifies these suggestions (Beweisantrag, Beweisermittlungsantrag, Beweisanregungen, Beweiserbieten). See, among many others, Alsberg/Nüse/Meyer, Der Beweisantrag im Strafprozess 69+ (5th ed. 1983).

[184] Ortells defines proceedings as: "actos jurídicos de las partes y del órgano jurisdiccional (fundamentalmente) mediante los cuales el proceso se realiza y que producen sus efectos principales, de modo directo e inmediato, en el proceso." He adds: "causa extrañeza que la doctrina no se refiera a los actos de los sujetos de prueba, particularmente, testigos y peritos. Tal vez ello se deba a entender que la actividad del testigo y del perito no es, por ella sola, acto procesal, sino que los actos procesales son los de las partes y los del juez mediante los que se practican los correspondientes medios de prueba." Derecho Jurisdiccional I 585 (2d ed. 1991).

[185] 1 Gómez Orbaneja, Derecho Procesal Civil, Parte General, El proceso declarativo ordinario 187 (7th ed. 1975).

might be defined as proceedings (Prozesshandlungen) used by the requester (Antragsteller) to ask (begehren) the Court to order (anordnen) that evidence be examined (die Erhebung) or to examine it (vornehmen).[186] The reason for this type of proceeding is an interest[187] in exercising the fundamental right to use relevant means of proof. Like any legal proceeding, it involves voluntary human behavior that can be externalized and that has legal value.[188]

b3) Admissibility of Evidence

Requests for evidence shall be denied under the following circumstances:

(1) The requester is not entitled to make motions (nichtberechtigter Antragsteller).

(2) The request does not meet requirements for form, time, and capacity (or a situation arises making it unfeasible to examine evidence).

(3) The request is completely incomprehensible and it cannot be clarified by asking questions.

(4) The request is aimed at satisfying some purpose unrelated to the proceedings; therefore, examining the

---

[186] Alsberg/Nüse-Meyer, Der Beweisantrag im Strafprozess, 34 (5th ed. 1983).

[187] For more on legal interest as a reason for proceedings, see Martín de la Leona, La nulidad de actuaciones en el proceso civil 54 (2d ed. 1996).

[188] De la Oliva with other authors, Derecho Procesal Penal 256 (1996).

requested evidence would not help to clarify the facts.[189]

The Spanish Code of Criminal Procedure fails to provide a regulatory scheme of reasons for denying requests of evidence; therefore, in order to study this issue, it is necessary to use doctrine and jurisprudence to construe some of the Code's provisions. First, under articles 656 and 657, the Public Prosecutor and the "parties" are entitled to request evidence. This suggests that when someone other than the abovementioned individuals makes a motion to present evidence, his or her request should be denied (see CCP, article 729.2). Requirements for time and form (in the strict sense) for requesting evidence are also derived from articles 656 and 657, at least for ordinary proceedings involving serious offenses.

Conversely, evidence is ruled inadmissible when, under certain circumstances, it is not legally permitted. The criminal trial should also protect individual and social values, which means that certain means of proof, topics, or evidentiary methods are inadmissible. Sections 244.3, sentence 1, 245.1, sentence 1, and 245.2, sentence 2 of StPO refer to inadmissibility of evidence as a reason for denying requests. Examinations involving means of proof prohibited by law or dealing with topics that should not be the focus of evidence production (such as the perceptions (Wahrnehmungen) of

---

[189] 3 Gollwitzer, Löwe-Rosenberg, Großkommentar, section 244, note 186 (24th ed. 1989). Kleinknecht/Meyer-Goßner, Strafprozeßordnung, note 48 (42d ed. 1995).

the Judge or those of any other participant involved in the proceedings or the existence and interpretation of laws) are not allowed.

The reason for denying requests addressed in section 244.3, sentence 1 of StPO is considered primarily in cases involving a means of proof or topic that is forbidden. A topic (Beweisthema) is off limits in terms of evidentiary process (Beweisverbot) when the facts to be proved (Beweistatsache) should not be clarified because they must be kept secret (Geheimhaltungsbedürftigkeit). Means of proof (Beweismittelverbote) that are not permitted are described under sections 52, 53, 53a, 54, 81c, 96, 250, and 252 of StPO. Moreover, evidence may not be examined (Beweiserhebung) when forbidden methods are employed (StPO, sections 136a and 69.3), rights are not explained (StPO, sections 52.3, sentence 1 and 81c.3, sentence 2), or any other legal precept is violated (Verstöss).[190]

Despite the fact that the provisions dealing with this issue are scattered throughout the Code of Criminal Procedure, the foregoing suggests that there are three situations to consider in which requests are denied:

(1) request deals with a matter that is excluded from evidentiary process,

(2) means of proof is prohibited, and

[190] 3 Gollwitzer, Löwe-Rosenberg, Großkommentar section 244, note 186 (24th ed. 1989). Kleinknecht/Meyer-Goßner, Strafprozeßordnung note 49 (42d ed. 1995).

(3) evidentiary method is not permitted. As we noted earlier, while the Code of Criminal Procedure does not differentiate between evidence proposals and requests, there is nothing to prevent one from submitting an evidence request that specifies the facts relating to the evidence that is to be examined (see StPO, section 219.1, sentence 2). Once this information is given, the Court is then prepared to assess whether or not the request deals with a matter that is excluded from evidentiary process. Note that the decision on whether or not a topic is off limits is made without considering the facts to be proved during the proceedings because at this point no assessment is made on the relationship between what the "parties" intend to prove and the thema decidendi; rather, the Court is only deciding whether or not a topic is excluded from evidentiary process from the start. An example of this would be requesting that a witness answer the question set out in article 418, sentence 1 of the Code of Criminal Procedure when in accordance with the Code, witnesses are not obligated to testify when (excluded topic) his or her answer might, in a direct and important way, be materially or morally damaging to the individual or the fortune of one of the relatives mentioned under article 416.

Requests are also denied when the proposed means of proof is prohibited. For example, under article 411 of the Code of Criminal Procedure (see CPP, articles 412-415), the King, Queen, Crown Prince, and Regents may not be summoned to testify. Also, under article 416.1, the relatives of the accused who are specifically mentioned in this provision are excused from the duty to testify, although this does not mean that they cannot testify; rather, they are not obligated to do so. Furthermore, lawyers (which should include other legal representatives and notaries, although they are not specifically mentioned in CCP), priests, and public officials must also refrain from testifying under articles 416.2, 417.1, and 417.2. Solicitors are excused from testifying on anything that a client might say to them while in their role of defender (CCP, article 416.2). Ecclesiastics and ministers of any type of religious order may not testify on anything revealed to them while they are performing the duties of their positions (CCP, article 417.1). Similarly, both civil and military public officials may not testify if doing so would reveal anything that they are obligated to keep confidential or (as they are expected to heed the orders of their superiors) if their hierarchical superior does not allow them to testify (CCP, article 417.2). However, this does not mean that they may not testify on those matters that are not confidential.

Finally, requests are denied if they involve evidentiary methods that are not permitted. Examples include using torture to obtain witness testimony, using coercion or threats (see StPO, section 389, sentence 3), and employing other methods that are illegal or violate fundamental rights. Spanish decisions have dealt with these types of situations; for example, using narcoanalysis was prohibited by a 22 May 1982 Spanish Supreme Court decision[191] that resolved an appeal involving a confession that was made under the effects of thiopental sodium. The opinion states that the method could not be trusted to produce reliable results, that its use might entail possible dangers, and most notably that serious objections might be raised if it were allowed to be used indiscriminately. The method violates the principles of legality and is an indirect and tortious way of obtaining a prisoner's confession. The opinion goes on to say that in the end, the practice suggests disregard for the individual as it destroys human mental and physical faculties.

The lack of significance or importance of the stated facts (Bedeutunglosigkeit der behaupteten Tatsachen)[192] is specifically mentioned in section 244.3, sentence 2 of StPO as a reason for denying evidence requests because examining evidence related to matters that are not important for the decision (Entscheidung) is unnecessary. A fact is insignificant or unimportant for the decision when it is unrelated (Zusammenhang) to the matter to be judged or despite the fact that there is some sort of connection, it is not enough (geeignet) to influence the decision.[193] This lack of significance or importance might come about from reasons of circumstance or law.

---

[191] Ar. 2702.

[192] See Fezer, who uses the term "Unerheblichkeit." Strafprozessrecht note 61 (1995). Conversely, Kleinknecht/Meyer-Goßner use the term "Bedeutunglosigkeit." Strafprozeßordnung note 54 (40th ed. 1991).

[193] Kleinknecht/Meyer-Goßner, Strafprozeßordnung note 54 (42d ed. 1995).

German doctrine has differentiated between direct and indirect (unmittelbar and mittelbar) significant evidentiary facts (beweiserhebliche Tatsachen).[194] A directly significant fact is one that is enough (geeignet) either by itself or relative to other facts to constitute a certain type of offense (Tatbestand) (oder seiner Erfüllung den Boden zu entziehen), eliminate, reduce, or increase the sentence (Strafbarkeit), establish the limits of (Zumessung) the sentence, or use as a starting point (Anknüpfungstatsache) for determining legal consequences (Rechtsfolge).[195] In contrast, facts to be proved (Beweistatsachen) are indirectly significant when either by themselves or relative to other facts, according to life experience (Lebenserfahrung) or mens legislatoris (Denkgesetzen), it is either possible or unavoidable to draw a positive or negative conclusion as to the existence of a fact that is directly significant for the decision (Indiztatsachen).[196] This group also includes auxiliary facts (Hilfstatsachen), which are used to assess means of proof, such as the credibility of a witness (StPO, section 244.4)[197] or the authenticity of a document, and maxims of experience (Erfahrungssätzen),

---

[194] 3 Gollwitzer, Löwe-Rosenberg, Großkommentar section 244, note 219 (24th ed. 1989).

[195] 3 Gollwitzer, Löwe-Rosenberg, Großkommentar section 244, note 219 (24th ed. 1989).

[196] 3 Gollwitzer, Löwe-Rosenberg, Großkommentar section 244, note 219 (24th ed. 1989).

[197] For a commentary on a 22 October 1992 BGH judgment on an exceptional case of assessing the credibility of a witness using an expert witness, see 11/93 StV 567.

which help to judge other direct or indirect significant facts.[198] Lastly, a fact is insignificant (unerheblich) when it is unrelated to the object of the proceedings (Prozessgegenstand) or although it is related, the outcome of its examination fails to influence the decision.[199] As we will later see when we discuss facts of common knowledge, this is a situation in which examining evidence is unnecessary as it can be assessed regardless of whether or not evidence has been examined or might be examined.

We shall now attempt to define what should be understood by relevance and significance, bearing in mind that they both refer to facts. A fact is relevant if it is related to what is to be judged. A fact is significant if it might in some way influence the decision that will be given. Therefore, irrelevant facts cannot be significant; however, relevant facts are not always significant.

When the Court, on the basis of the evidence examined up to that moment, is firmly convinced that the evidentiary facts (Beweistatsache) are genuine, and it does not wish to carry out subsequent examinations before pronouncing judgment, it is not necessary to proceed with any more examinations.[200]

It is unnecessary to examine evidence if the outcome of the

198 3 Gollwitzer, Löwe-Rosenberg, Großkommentar section 244, notes 219, 223 (24th ed. 1989).

199 3 Gollwitzer, Löwe-Rosenberg, Großkommentar section 244, note 219 (24th ed. 1989).

200 Kleinknecht/Meyer-Goßner, Strafprozeßordnung note 57 (41st ed. 1993).

hearing as described under section 261 of StPO[201] convinces the Court that the fact in support of which evidence is offered is true.[202] One might argue against this reason for denying evidence requests by contending that in cases such as these, evidence is assessed prematurely (Vorwegnahme der Beweiswürdigung). Here, this ban on premature assessment is only a consideration when it might be to the disadvantage of the accused.[203] Thus, facts that might be "significant" for the decision are not admitted, and this reason for denying a request applies regardless of whether the facts are for the prosecution or for the defense, but not when the Court finds satisfactorily proved the opposite of what was intended.[204] If a request is denied on the grounds that the facts are already considered proved, the Court must state this in its judgment.[205] In any case, it would be less problematic to use other reasons for denying a request; for example, the facts are insignificant (Bedeutunglosigkeit) or the facts are not accepted as true. Despite what has been said and as is the case for other reasons for denying evidence requests under section 244, paragraph 3, sentence 2 of StPO, the Court's duty to clarify facts supersedes

[201] According to section 261, the Court shall render judgment on the outcome of any examination of evidence based on its beliefs, which are unrestricted and shaped by the hearing in its entirety.

[202] 3 Gollwitzer, Löwe-Rosenberg, Großkommentar section 244, note 235 (24th ed. 1989).

[203] See "Vorwegnahme der Beweiswürdigung," Alsberg/Nüse/Meyer, Der Beweisantrag im Strafprozess 597 (5th ed. 1983).

[204] Compare 3 Gollwitzer, Löwe-Rosenberg, Großkommentar section 244, note 235 (24th ed. 1989).

[205] BGH 18 October 1988 in NStZ 83 (1989).

this reason for denying requests.[206]

This situation would be not be acceptable at the present in Spain in light of the criterion of necessity[207] (not criteria relating to relevance that, as is well known, applies at the time of admission), which applies when examining evidence. This criterion is very important in criminal court proceedings as compared with civil proceedings.

However, the foregoing situation is not the only one in which it might be said that it is unnecessary to examine evidence. It is also unnecessary in those situations in which facts of common knowledge (offenkundige Tatsachen) are involved. The theory that certain facts are common knowledge was recently associated with the idea of quick justice under the maxim brocardo notoria non egen probatione ("the obvious does not require proof"). The German StPO specifically cites this maxim as a reason for denying evidence requests (see section 244.3, sentence 2), affirming that common knowledge makes examining evidence (Beweiserhebung) unnecessary (überflüssig),[208] which is not the same as saying that evidence is inadmissible. Note that section 244.3 does not provide that

---

[206] Compare Alsberg/Nüse/Meyer, Der Beweisantrag im Strafprozess 599 (5th ed. 1983).

[207] See Díaz Cabiale, La admisión y práctica de la prueba en el proceso penal, 20 Cuadernos del CGPJ 71+ (1992) for the difference between relevance and necessity. The article also reveals how the notion of evidentiary necessity is vague, and thus the author develops his own concept.

[208] 3 Gollwitzer, Löwe-Rosenberg, Großkommentar section 244, note 227 (24th ed. 1989).

knowledge of the facts to be proved (Offenkundigkeit der Beweistatsache) is a criterion for denying evidence requests; rather, it expressly states that this knowledge makes an examination (Beweiserhebung) unnecessary (überflüssig) or excessive. Moreover, it would be inappropriate to contend that common knowledge might substitute an examination of evidence; rather, the examination might be omitted, although not entirely given that a conviction must be based on due process guarantees. Therefore, for example, even though television stations might broadcast the assassination of a public figure, and thus the circumstances of the offense and the perpetrator would be public knowledge, the Court should not dispense with an examination of evidence. Rather, the tape on which the event was recorded should be admitted as a means of proof. It has not been easy to define the concept of "common knowledge" because in doctrine the term has been used in a variety of ways, which makes the task of clarifying its meaning an arduous one.[209][210] If common knowledge is a fact or event that is publicly known, the question arises whether or not common knowledge could be erroneous. Theoretically, it could. Otherwise, common knowledge would be confused with what is evident.[211]

---

[209] See Ghisalberti, La teoria del notorio nel diritto comune 403 (1957).

[210] In fact, the term (notorio) was even used in many different contexts in earlier Spanish law, for example, to describe default. See Viada, La ausencia del acusado en el proceso penal, 3 RDP 574 (1962).

[211] However, expressions have been used employing both terms (notorio and evidente) as the fact that something is evident is grounds for it being

The source from which the Judge acquires any common knowledge is unimportant,[212] and furthermore common knowledge does not depend upon the powers of observation that might be required of certain people.[213] German doctrine differentiates with the "supra-concept" (Oberbegrif) of common knowledge (Offenkundigkeit) between common general knowledge (Allgemeinkundigkeit) and common judicial knowledge (Gerichtskundigkeit).[214] Common general knowledge (Allgemeinkundigkeit) refers to facts or maxims of experience (Erfahrungssätze)[215] that are generally known by ordinary people or that might be ascertained from reliable sources (zuverlässigen Quellen) without the need for any special expertise (Fachkunde). Examples of this type of knowledge[216] are the distance between two places, the location of a place, and information that might be acquired

---

common knowledge. See Rodríguez Valcarce, 2 RDP 255, 257 (1948). We might also point out that Spanish jurisprudence (not in connection with evidence) uses the term "common knowledge" ("lo notorio") to mean what is evident ("lo que es evidente").

[212] Vegas Torres, Dissertation, La presunción de inocencia del artículo 24.2 de la Constitución en el proceso penal español 92 (1992) addresses the fact that it is unnecessary to monitor precisely how the decision maker comes to find out about these facts.

[213] Compare 3 Gollwitzer, Löwe-Rosenberg, Großkommentar section 244, notes 227-228 (24th ed. 1989).

[214] To examine this topic in depth, consult Feuerpeil, Der Beweisablehnungsgrund der Offenkundigkeit gemäss par. 244 Abs. 3 Satz 2, 1 Var. StPO (1987).

[215] See generally Feuerpeil, Der Beweisablehnungsgrund der Offenkundigkeit gemäss par. 244 Abs. 3 Satz 2, 1 Var. StPO 46+ (1987).

[216] Feuerpeil, Der Beweisablehnungsgrund der Offenkundigkeit gemäss par. 244 Abs. 3 Satz 2, 1 Var. StPO 43 (1987).

by consulting books or pamphlets, such as the arrival and departure times of a train on a particular day. The sources that the Court might use to acquire this type of common knowledge[217] include reference books, road maps, radio and television, newspapers, history books, etc.

It is important, however, to differentiate common knowledge (although it is said to be "what the sparrows speak about on the roofs")[218] from rumor and opinion as the media can and in fact does exert a great amount of influence[219] and inexact information is often given.[220] Common judicial knowledge (Gerichtskundigkeit), however, refers to facts that the Judge considers reliable because of the activities he or she carries out without using private sources of information.[221] Here we must point out what is obvious in view of the principles that govern criminal proceedings (especially in light of the right to have the decision maker present at the trial or "Unmittelbarkeit"): the outcome of an examination of evidence that was carried out in one trial may not be considered common knowledge in later proceedings.[222] Examples of common judicial knowledge

[217] See 3 Gollwitzer, Löwe-Rosenberg, Großkommentar section 244, note 229 (24th ed. 1989).

[218] In a statement from Wach (1986 Conferences) "was sich die Spatzen auf den Dächern erzählen" in Prieto Castro, Cuestiones de Derecho Procesal 125 (1947).

[219] Incidentally, this is one of the primary problems for empanelling a jury.

[220] See Ruiz Vadillo, Estudios de Derecho procesal penal 280 (1995).

[221] Compare 3 Gollwitzer, Löwe-Rosenberg, Großkommentar section 244, note 230 (24th ed. 1989).

[222] Compare 3 Gollwitzer, Löwe-Rosenberg, Großkommentar section

include the name of the Chief Justice of the Court and the office hours of the court office.[223] German doctrine holds that the history of a political movement and the plot of a political organization are some examples of commonly known judicial facts. The possibility of denying an evidence request on the grounds that information to the contrary is common knowledge violates the principle of presumption of innocence under article 6.2 of the European Convention on Human Rights; furthermore, it is at odds with the idea that the outcome of an examination should not be predicted beforehand.[224] As we pointed out earlier, common knowledge could be erroneous. One might argue in view of section 261 of StPO that common knowledge is used in exceptional cases as the Court comes to a decision based on the hearing in its entirety and through the examination of evidence (compare with CCP, article 741).

The same terminology is not found in Spanish jurisprudence, although there have been situations in which evidence was ruled inadmissible due to common knowledge.[225] In Spain common knowledge is considered a situation in which evidence is unnecessary, and since clear criteria established through court decisions for determining necessity are

244, note 230 (24th ed. 1989).

[223] Feuerpeil, Der Beweisablehnungsgrund der Offenkundigkeit gemäss par. 244 Abs. 3 Satz 2, 1 Var. StPO 44 (1987).

[224] Feuerpeil, Der Beweisablehnungsgrund der Offenkundigkeit gemäss par. 244 Abs. 3 Satz 2, 1 Var. StPO 134 (1987).

[225] See, e.g., STS 22 January 1996, Ar. 48.

lacking,[226] it would be possible to rule evidence inadmissible on the grounds of common knowledge if an evidence request in the strict sense of the term were submitted. This means that the requester would specify the facts to be proved, and thus the Court would be able to pass judgment on the matter of common knowledge.

Furthermore, it is one thing to say that a fact of common knowledge makes the examination of evidence unnecessary and quite another to maintain that this fact does not need to be alleged. Making the allegation might be advisable, especially if we take into account that for as much as we think a fact is common knowledge, we cannot assume that everyone, including the Court, shares in this knowledge. Moreover, the allegation of a fact of common knowledge must not be confused with the consequence that the party who makes the allegation intends to prove. The consequence might be probable, but it is not true. This would be the case, for example, in a situation in which a party maintains that the fact that it was hot the day of the crime is common knowledge, intending to convince the Court that the alleged murderer was not wearing a fur coat.

Maxims of experience can also be distinguished, as is well known, from facts. They are abstract ideas or judgments (which incidentally are not given exclusively by judges) that are inferred from common facts or are in a certain way

---

[226] Díaz Cabiale, La admisión y práctica de la prueba en el proceso penal, 20 Cuadernos del CGPJ 74 (1992).

interrelated. We might also say that these maxims are a type of common knowledge, keeping in mind that they are not facts[227] (although they might be used to clarify facts). Thus, an evidence request for an expert report on a maxim of experience might be denied.[228] However, maxims of experience may be used to assess what is examined during the trial (CCP, article 741).

Under certain circumstances, it is not necessary (überflüssig) to examine evidence because the fact to be proved, under certain conditions, can be treated as though it were true (Wahrunterstellung der behaupteten Tatsache).[229] These conditions are that the fact must be significant and in defense of the accused, and the requested examination of evidence must not be suitable for clarifying the facts.[230] The only facts that should be found insignificant (unerheblich-bedeutungslos) are those that from any rational point of view are not enough to positively influence judgment in favor of the accused.[231] If these conditions are strictly observed, we might conclude that this reason for denying requests can be applied in very few

[227] See generally Stein, El conocimiento privado del juez 31+ (2d ed. 1988).

[228] See generally Alsberg/Nüse/Meyer, Der Beweisantrag im Strafprozess 555+ (5th ed. 1983).

[229] See generally 3 Gollwitzer, Löwe-Rosenberg, Großkommentar section 244, especially notes 237, 241 (24th ed. 1989).

[230] See Julius, Strafprozessordnung 881 section 244, note 33 (1997) and Schöch, Kommentar zur Strafprozessordnung section 244, note 114 (1993).

[231] Deckers, 4/1992 StV 147.

situations (Anwendungsbereich);[232] however, it is one of the most widely used reasons, according to recent studies.[233]

Obviously, any particular facts that are accepted as true should be consistent with the grounds for the ruling (Urteilsgründe) that is later given. Thus, a party might also submit a request with the intention of receiving advance information on the decision maker's thoughts. The Court shall only accept facts as true if in doing so it does not fail to perform its duty of discovering the truth (die Wahrheit zu erforschen). It is possible that the Court, after examining evidence, may find that facts it had previously accepted are not true. If that were the case, it must expressly inform the accused of its new findings at the appropriate time. This reason for denying evidence requests is valid for any type of request as long as the specific fact that should be proved is stated;[234] furthermore, this statement might be a simple supposition, hypothesis, or speculation (Annahme).[235] Making this reason for denying a request conditional on it being in defense (Entlastung) of the accused is understood as applying the principle in dubio pro reo[236] in advance, and obviously the grounds for the ruling (Urteilsgründe) must not contradict the facts that were accepted as true.

[232] See generally Fezer, Strafprozessrecht 168 (1995).
[233] See Perron, Das Beweisantragsrecht des Beschuldigten - Ursache oder Symptom der Krise des deutschen Strafprozesses?, 108 ZStW (1996). See also Herdegen, NStZ 337 (1984).
[234] Herdegen, Zum Begriff der Beweisbehauptung, 11/1990 StV 518.
[235] Herdegen, Zum Begriff der Beweisbehauptung, 11/1990 StV 519.
[236] Roxin, Strafverfahrensrecht 277 (20th ed. 1987).

It is interesting to note that the principle supporting procedural efficiency has also been recognized as one of the grounds for this reason for denying requests[237] as lawmakers have hoped to facilitate the use of statements important for the decision that might be considered true.[238] The Court can only accept stated facts as true (als wäre sie wahr) when deciding whether or not to grant an evidence request, although the accused should be informed that the Court could possibly change its assessment of the facts (Bewertungswandel unterrichtet). The Court should also inform the accused of its position relative to the facts that it accepted as true so that he or she might take this assessment into account when submitting other evidence requests.[239]

However, if examining evidence fails to corroborate that the accepted facts are true, the Court may set aside (widerrufen) the initial ruling (Wahrunterstellung) with a specific declaration (ausdrücklichen Hinweis).[240] Depending on the prevailing opinion of the Court, it is also possible to accept leading facts as true,[241] although in the event that the Court does not want to deny an evidence request for this reason,

---

[237] See generally Kommentar zur Strafprozessordnung, KMR section 244, note 442 (1993).

[238] See Herdegen, Bemerkungen zum Beweisantragsrecht, Cuaderno 8 NStZ 340 (1994).

[239] Schöch, Kommentar zur Strafprozessordnung, section 244, note 118 (1993).

[240] Schöch, Kommentar zur Strafprozessordnung, section 244, note 129 (1993).

[241] Kleinknecht/Meyer-Gossner, Strafprozeßordnung section 244, note 70 (42d ed. 1995).

it is becoming evident that it will deny it on the grounds of insignificance (Bedeutunglosigkeit), which was explored earlier.[242]

Regarding the usefulness of evidence, we must first consider complete inadequacy of a means of proof (Völlige Ungeeignetheit des Beweismittels). The Court cannot be required to consider a means of proof when it does not contribute to clarifying the facts and considering it would only cause delays (Verzögerungen).[243]

However, we should distinguish between different means of proof (Beweismittel). Some means of proof are objectively inadequate - supposing objective impossibility (objektiver Unmöglichkeit) - for proving facts declared true. This would be the case, for example, if a blind witness were to testify on the color of the jacket that the alleged murderer wore the day of the event in question. (This is in line with section 245.2 of StPO for present means of proof). The Court may find that other means of proof have little value as evidence, as would be the case if a particular witness was clearly not going to provide any useful information[244] (subjective incapacity). This is also an exception to the rule against prematurely assessing evidence (Vorwegnahme der Beweiswürdigung).[245][246]

---

[242] Schöch, Kommentar zur Strafprozessordnung section 244, note 117 (1993).

[243] Compare 3 Gollwitzer, Löwe-Rosenberg, Großkommentar section 244, note 276 (24th ed. 1989).

[244] Compare 3 Gollwitzer, Löwe-Rosenberg, Großkommentar section 244, note 280 (24th ed. 1989).

[245] See 3 Gollwitzer, Löwe-Rosenberg, Großkommentar section 244, note

Regarding witnesses, although a long period of time may pass between the events and the opportunity to testify, a witness would not be considered incompetent when the event (Vorgang) was significant for him or her or when he or she might depend upon something to help his or her memory. However, jurisprudence and some doctrine have ruled witness evidence inadmissible (Ablehnung des Zeugenbeweises) when experience suggests, considering the circumstances of the case at hand (importance of the event, period of time, personality of the witness, etc)., that it is not improbable, but impossible that the witness remember the event.[247]

Another point to consider is whether or not a means of proof is unattainable (Unerreichbarkeit des Beweismittels). When a means of proof is not present during the proceedings, and it is impossible to calculate the time it would take to acquire the means of proof, and furthermore any attempts made by the Court to obtain information on the importance and potential value of the means of proof have been futile, German doctrine holds that this means of proof is unattainable.[248] In court practice, this reason for denying evidence requests primarily applies to witness testimony (Zeugenbeweis). Situations frequently arise in which witnesses whose residence

278 (24th ed. 1989).

[246] See also CCP, articles 793.2 and 417.3 on the fact that witnesses who are incompetent are not under obligation to testify.

[247] See Schöch, Kommentar zur Strafprozessordnung section 244, note 93 (1993).

[248] Compare 3 Gollwitzer, Löwe-Rosenberg, Großkommentar section 244, note 260 (24th ed. 1989).

is unknown or in another country leave the Court with two options: denying the request or adjourning proceedings. In cases such as these, the institutions responsible for bringing the weight of the law to bear on criminal offenders face many problems. The defense has a powerful "weapon" in that it might submit evidence requests not with the intention of having them granted, but simply for the purpose of pressuring and inconveniencing the Court.[249]

Perhaps it is due to the importance this reason for denying requests has acquired that German lawmakers introduced the new section 244.5, sentence 2 with an 11 January 1993 law covering court officers' responsibilities (Gesetz zur Entlastung der Rechtspflege). It provides that evidence requests for examination of a witness who would have to be summoned in another country may be denied under the same conditions as evidence requests for judicial examination of evidence (when the examination is not necessary for discovering the truth).[250]

German doctrine has interpreted this provision to mean that evidence requests for examination of witnesses who are abroad may also be denied when the necessary information can be obtained by another way or means.[251] Generally, when

---

[249] See Perron, Das Beweisantragsrecht des Beschuldigten im deutschen Strafprozess 245-246 (1995).

[250] "Unter derselben Voraussetzung kann auch ein Beweisantrag auf Vernehmung eines Zeugen abgelehnt werden, dessen Ladung im Ausland zu bewirken ware."

[251] See Böttcher, Mayer, Änderungen des Strafverfahrensrechts durch das Entlastungsgesetz, Cuaderno 4 NStZ 155 (1993). For Spain, see Organic Law of the Judiciary (Ley Orgánica del Poder Judicial), article 276 and

requesting that a witness be examined (see StPO, section 219), it is not necessary to provide the witness's name or address; but rather, it is enough to give only the information needed for identification. However, in cases involving witnesses who are abroad the difficulty does not so much lie in acquiring this information, but in the fact that the Court does not have any way to compel (Zwangsmittel) witnesses to appear that would guarantee their presence during proceedings.[252] In spite of this fact, the Court should attempt to formally summon witnesses through judicial assistance (Rechtshilfeweg).

One special situation involves a witness detained in a foreign country who might possibly be brought in for the proceedings[253] subject to article 11 of EuRHÜ,[254] which provides that the request shall be denied under the following circumstances:

(a) The person in custody does not agree.

(b) His or her presence is required in proceedings that are already under way in the country of the party to whom the summons was served.

(c) The person might be kept in custody for a longer period of time if brought in to participate in the proceedings.

(d) Other pressing considerations advise against sending the

CCP, articles 410, 424, 440, 441, 711, and 785.1.

252 Hoffmann, Der unerreichbare Zeuge im Strafverfahren 115 (1991).

253 See 3 Gollwitzer, Löwe-Rosenberg, Großkommentar section 244, note 266 (24th ed. 1989).

254 II Bundesgesetzblatt, Herausgegeben von Bundesminister der Justiz 1390 (1964).

person to the country of the party serving the summons.

Here, the principle of reciprocity (Prinzip der Gegenseitigkeit) applies, which allows parties to seek judicial assistance (Rechtshilfe) as long as collaboration is possible. However, because of the demanding conditions that are set out in the abovementioned provision, in practice this principle is hardly significant.

Furthermore, a witness is not found to be unattainable according to section 244.3, paragraph 2 of StPO if he or she has not returned to prison following a leave.[255]

B2. Criminal Evidence Assessment

It is critical to differentiate between assessments that are made after examining evidence (which has customarily been known as the principle of free assessment or "Beweiswürdigung") and assessments that precede examination with a view to decisions on admissibility of evidence.

The principle of free assessment of evidence (FreiBeweiswürdigung) as it relates to general examinations involves making an assessment after examining evidence and giving reasons to explain the outcome of the examination. The decision maker must state the objective criteria and guidelines he or she used to form an opinion. The law does

[255] See generally 10/1933 StV 514.

not give some items of evidence precedence over others; thus, here again the decision maker has discretionary power. In international criminal law, problems might be created in connection with evidence assessment because of the different languages used by those participating in the proceedings. The spontaneity of answers, gestures, etc. that allow the Court to form its personal opinion on the truthfulness of the testimony given by participants might be lost. Lastly, criminal evidence assessment cannot be separated from the presumption of innocence.

Criteria for assessing evidence can also be found in the Draft Rules of Procedure and Evidence. Rule 140.3 provides that a witness who has heard the testimony of another witness shall not be disqualified for that reason alone; however, this fact shall "be considered by the Trial Chamber when evaluating the evidence."

Even more importantly, article 74.2 of the Rome Statute establishes, in our view, what is known as the principle of free assessment of evidence with the restrictions mentioned above. It provides: "The Trial Chamber's decision shall be based on its evaluation of the evidence and the entire proceedings. The decision shall not exceed the facts and circumstances described in the charges and any amendments to the charges."

The reference in article 74.2 to basing decisions on the Court's "evaluation" of the evidence suggests that the Statute acknowledges the principle of free assessment of evidence. We must consider the fact that very few policies make any reference to the "evaluation" of evidence in their provisions.

C. Rules of Procedure and Evidence for the New International Criminal Court

Article 51 of the Rome Statute of the International Criminal Court provides that a two-thirds majority of the members of the Assembly of States Parties must vote to adopt the Rules of Procedure and Evidence. (As we write, we are referring to the draft of the final version of the Rules of Procedure and Evidence, New York, 13-31 March and 12-30 June 2000). Article 51 states that when these Rules of Procedure and Evidence fail to provide for a particular situation, the judges may draw up and apply provisional rules that could later be rejected at a session of the Assembly of States Parties. This legitimizes possible violations of the principle of equality relative to how judging is done at one time or another in the event that the judges, facing a situation not covered by the rules, adopt a provisional rule (by a two-thirds majority), and the Assembly later adopts a different rule. This suggests that the Assembly will later approve the "provisional" rules adopted by a two-thirds majority vote of the judges. Rules are clearly lacking in connection with criteria for ruling evidence admissible or inadmissible, as we shall later see.

We shall now examine the provisions of the Rome Statute that deal with evidence and later move on to the Rules of

Procedure and Evidence. Note that the Rome Statute prevails over the Rules of Procedure and Evidence (Rome Statute, article 51.5).

Procedure dictates that charges shall be confirmed before the trial (Rome Statute, article 61) at a hearing before the Pre-Trial Chamber attended by the accused, his or her legal representative, and the Prosecutor. This hearing may also be held when the person charged is not present. Regarding the right to present evidence, during this hearing the accused shall be informed of the evidence on which "the Prosecutor intends to rely at the hearing." During the hearing, the Prosecutor shall "support each charge with sufficient evidence to establish substantial grounds to believe that the person committed the crime charged," but it is not necessary that he or she call witnesses (although calling witnesses is not prohibited under article 61.5). Therefore, the purpose of evidence in this hearing is to convince the Pre-Trial judges that "the person committed the crime charged" according to article 61.7. The right to a defense relative to evidence is covered under article 61.6, which provides that the accused is entitled to not only challenge the evidence presented by the Prosecutor, but also to present evidence in his or her defense.

Part VI of the Rome Statute is devoted to the trial (articles 62-76). Note that article 64 mentions evidence as it describes the functions and powers of the Trial Chamber. Paragraph 6 makes specific reference to the possibility of requiring the attendance and testimony of witnesses and ordering the production of documents and other evidence (article 64.6 (b)) and the power to order the production of additional items of evidence.

The Trial Chamber has the power to rule on the admissibility of evidence under article 64.9 of the Rome Statute. However, article 69 deserves special mention as it sets out the rules for examining evidence. The provision makes specific reference to the parties' right to "submit evidence relevant to the case" (article 69.3), thus restricting this right to present evidence to that which is considered relevant. Consequently, the need to discover what should understood by "relevant" arises, and a positive conclusion cannot be drawn from the jurisprudence of various countries that adopted the Statute. Article 69.4 fails to offer any clarification. It refers to relevance in connection with evidence with several diverse phrases such as "probative value" and "any prejudice that such evidence may cause to a fair trial or to a fair evaluation of the testimony of a witness." Here we should take into account the difficulties associated with assessing evidence and the fact that pre-assessing evidence is prohibited (see infra Chapter II, C).

Article 69.6 provides that facts of common "public" knowledge do not require proof; however, it seems that the article fails to cover other types of common knowledge (see supra B, b2). Furthermore, article 69.7 provides:

> Evidence obtained by means of a violation of this Statute or internationally recognized

> human rights shall not be admissible if:
> (a) The violation casts substantial doubt on the reliability of the evidence; or
> (b) The admission of the evidence would be antithetical to and would seriously damage the integrity of the proceedings.

This reference to ruling evidence inadmissible if it is acquired in these ways is incorrect in that it suggests that violating the Statute or human rights always "damages the integrity of the proceedings" or is "antithetical" to the proceedings. Instead, it would have been preferable to employ language that also prohibited obtaining evidence by means of a violation of fundamental rights. Thus, the reference to "reliability of the evidence" is not technically correct.

Chapter 4 of the Draft Rules of Procedure and Evidence of the International Criminal Court is entitled "Provisions relating to various stages of the proceedings." Section I is devoted to evidence (rules 63-75), Section II deals with disclosure (rules 76-84), and Section III covers victims and witnesses (rules 85-103).

We shall now draw attention to the following provisions, and later we shall point out how they are subject to criticism:

(1) First, rule 63.2 of the Draft Rules of Procedure and Evidence of the International Criminal Court provides: "A Chamber shall have the authority . . . to assess freely all evidence submitted in order to determine its relevance or

admissibility." The only criterion provided for ruling evidence inadmissible relates to whether or not the evidence is relevant. As we have said, this term seems to be used interchangeably with "admissibility," thus failing to distinguish between two key moments in the evidentiary process: admission and examination. Also, the language employed in this provision suggests that the Court has a considerable amount of freedom to rule proposed evidence inadmissible.

(2) Second, rule 64.2 envisages that judgments will be given on the admissibility of evidence, and it requires the Chamber to "give reasons for any ruling it makes on evidentiary matters" and place them on the record.

(3) Witness testimony is regulated under rules 65-68, which specifically refer to the possibility of using methods and instruments that have been developed through technological innovation. These methods and instruments are not covered in the older legal systems of some of the States Parties.

(4) Rule 70 sets out guidelines for evidence assessment, although Rule 71 covers a specific case in which evidence relative to the "prior or subsequent sexual conduct of a victim or witness" is not admissible.

(5) Rule 72 is more questionable. It envisages "in camera" procedure for ruling on the admissibility of evidence. Allowing the Court to find that the "evidence has a sufficient degree of probative value" (rule 72.2) without observing the due process guarantees that should govern proceedings legitimizes the premature assessment of evidence, and even

worse, the fact that the trial could turn into a charade due to a violation of the right to an "uninformed" judge or judge who has not had access to information on the matter prior to the trial (see Chapter III).

CHAPTER II
Critique

A. A Critique of Relevance as a Criterion for Ruling Evidence Inadmissible

If we take into account that Chapter 4, Section I of the Draft Rules of Procedure and Evidence makes repeated mention of relevance as a criterion for ruling evidence inadmissible, it is important, in a critique, to reflect on this matter.

Not even the Rome Statute of the International Criminal Court employs the term "relevant" exclusively in reference to criteria that should be applied when ruling evidence inadmissible. For example, article 61.11 refers to exercising "relevant" functions and article 64.6 (f) makes reference to the power to "rule on any other relevant matters."

Doctrine has criticized the lack of precision in legal language on numerous occasions, and imprecision is apparent in these and many other terms. There is an abundance of vague, undefined terms that at the very least threaten legal certainty. In matters of admissibility or inadmissibility of proceedings in general, dangers arise from unsuitable, imprecise language used by lawmakers,[256] and analyses of evidentiary process have one particular flaw: idiomatic confusion.[257]

Furthermore, we must acknowledge that it is no small task to define terms such as "admissibility"[258] and "inadmissibility."[259] To do so, it is important to underscore the critical distinction between a mere "proposal" and a "motion" for using a particular means of proof to prove a certain evidentiary statement. The "motion" is known as a evidence request. These are two distinct proceedings, and we must consider the fact that the ease with which the decision maker gives judgment on admissibility and on any resulting examination of evidence depends in large part on whether he or she is dealing with a proposal or a request.

Indeed, references by Spanish lawmakers to proposing practices and procedures (proposición de diligencias), proposed evidence (pruebas propuestas) etc., suggest that they are unfamiliar with the concept of the evidence request discussed earlier, even though this term can be found in both Spanish Supreme Court and Spanish Constitutional Court judgments. Further clarification is necessary, and we

---

256 Pérez Gordo, La admisibilidad de los actos procesales, 1 RDP 223, 219 (1980).

257 Sentís Melendo, Introducción al Derecho probatorio, 4 RDP 637 (1965).

258 See Furno, Teoría de la prueba legal 88 (1954).

259 Inadmissibility is the legal consequence that the System envisages for proceedings that are flawed because they are invalid, because they cause the "decadenza" of a right, or because they preclude subsequent proceedings. 1 Sabatini, Principi di Diritto Processuale Penale 406 (1948).

might consider, for example, a 14 December 1903[260] decision rendered by the Supreme Court (more recent judgments follow the same line; for example, STS 29 February 1988).[261] The Court ruled on whether or not to set aside judgment for a case in which proceedings were not adjourned when some of the witnesses for the defense failed to appear. Proceedings were not adjourned because the trial court ruled their testimony unnecessary. Given that the object of the means of proof was not stated, the Supreme Court held that it lacked the information necessary for assessing whether or not the testimony was relevant. This suggests that while the Supreme Court required the object of the means of proof to be identified (the statement from the evidence request) so that it could assess relevance, the trial court, strangely, did not require this information when it initially assessed "relevance." Consequently, how could the trial court have supported its finding that evidence was irrelevant?

In the Spanish Code of Criminal Procedure, the conditions for ruling "proposed" evidence inadmissible (relevance and necessity, from CCP, articles 659 and 746.3 and 6 respectively), underscore that the trial court has absolute power[262] when it comes time to render judgment on admitting and examining evidence. Furthermore, judgments on relevance and necessity

[260] No. 177, Jurisprudencia criminal 71, Biblioteca Jurídica de la Revista General de Legislación y Jurisprudencia 338.
[261] Ar. 1345.
[262] See Gutiérrez-Alviz and Conradi, La valoración de la prueba penal, 4 RDP 814 (1975).

are only subject to review under very strict conditions. The stage involving admission of evidence requires that a judgment be made, although at this point judgments are based on what is probable. This "absolute power" contributes greatly to the creation of a confusing gray area that envelopes two key terms relating to the admission and examination of evidence in the Spanish criminal trial: relevance and necessity.

If we are to critique the term "relevance," we must take into account that for many years doctrine has criticized its imprecision in connection with what should be understood by relevance[263] and how it differs from other concepts such as significance,[264] usefulness, and necessity. The usual reasons for maintaining the term cannot be used to justify having made it the key element in a supposed judicial review of evidence,[265]

263 The following publications relating to this topic are of particular interest: Zafra, La pertinencia de la prueba civil, 1 RDP 635 (1960 segunda época); Gesto Alonso, La pertinencia y utilidad de las pruebas (1991); and Díaz Cabiale, La admisión y práctica de la prueba en el proceso penal, 20 Cuadernos del CGPJ (1992). The topic is also thoroughly covered in Taruffo, Studi sulla rilevanza della prova 66 (1970), especially p. 68, where the ambiguity of the phrase "relevant evidence" is criticized and the author contends that greater clarification is needed.

264 See Gutiérrez-Alviz and Conradi, La valoración de la prueba penal, 4 RDP 815 (1975): "unas veces, distingue (la doctrina) estos conceptos incluso radicalmente respecto al campo de acción que cubren ambos juicios y, otras, los confunden equiparándolos, lo que también en la práctica suele acontecer."

265 Zafra states: "la preocupación legal por el control judicial de las pruebas… representa una clara continuidad y progresión de intenciones plasmadas en textos fundamentales de nuestro Derecho histórico." The author cites Ley VII, Título XIV, Tercera Partida, which provides: "Otro sí decimos de aquella prueva debe ser tan solamente recebida en juyzio,

which is more closely related to the "inquisitorial system" than the effective application of the right to present evidence. This does not mean that we support doing away with the term, but rather we would prefer that the context in which it should be applied be defined, as has been done with the term "erheblichkeit" in the German Code of Criminal Procedure (see StPO, section 244.3).

In Amendment number 779 to the draft of the Constitution, the Union of the Democratic Center (Unión Centro Democrático) proposed replacing the term "suitable" ("conveniente") with the term "relevant" ("pertinente"). They justified this change by contending that the right to use means of proof should be modified by the word "relevant"[266] because

que pertenece al pleito principal sobre que es fecha la demanda... non deue consentir el Juzgador que las partes despiendan su tiempo en vano, en prouando cosas de que non se puedan despues aprouechar, maquer las prouasen". Ley XXXI, Título VIII, Libro II del Fuero Real: "Si alguno razonare alguna cosa en pleyto, e dixere que la quiere probar, si la razon tal fuere, que aunque la prueba no le preste a su pleyto, ni empezca al otro contra quien la aduce, el Alcalde no resciba tal prueba; si por ventura la rescibiere, no le vala." Lastly, the author cites Novísima Recopilación, which covers word for word what was just transcribed in Ley V, Título X, Libro XI and was a precursor to the 1855 Rules of Civil Law Procedure. Zafra, La pertinencia de la prueba civil, 1 RDP 635 (1960 segunda época).

[266] Constitución española, Trabajos Parlamentarios 486-487 (1980). Article 24.2 of the Draft (BOCG 5 January 1978) provides: "Asimismo todos tienen derecho al juez natural, a la defensa y a la asistencia de letrado, a ser informados de la acusación formulada contra ellos, a un proceso público sin dilaciones indebidas y con todas las garantías, a utilizar los medios de prueba convenientes para su defensa, a no declarar contra sí mismos, a no confesarse culpables y a la presunción de inocencia." Garrido Falla (with other authors), Comentarios a la Constitución 307 (1980).

it was thought to be a strict procedural term. However, it is one thing to say that a word is a strict legal term and quite another to say that it is used strictly in legal contexts.

In any case, it is one thing to define guidelines or conditions for denying evidence requests (which has been done in German doctrine and jurisprudence) and quite another to analyze what is understood by the term "erheblichkeit." The difficulties surrounding this term have been underscored since ancient times in Germany.[267]

Spanish doctrine has also dealt with the issue of whether or not relevance must be linked to facts.[268] This has been confused in French doctrine, which makes vague references to relevance in connection with facts and evidence proposals (offres de preuve). This suggests that relevance is not only considered the relationship between what is alleged and the factual theory behind the law that is to be applied, but also the relationship between what is alleged and the way these facts enter into the proceedings.[269] Adding the two elements

[267] Samuel, Die Ablehnbarkeit von Beweisanträgen und ihr Prinzip 65 (1913).

[268] See Gesto Alonso, La pertinencia y utilidad de las pruebas (1991). Also, other authors, such as Théodor, relate relevance to facts: "Est pertinent tout fait de la cause virtuellement propre á produire des effets de droit ou á interdire cette production." L'interprétation des faits en Droit 118 (1988). Devis Echandia contends: "La pertinencia... se refiere, en realidad, al hecho objeto de prueba y... no es una cuestión de derecho, sino de hecho." Facultades y deberes del juez, 3 RDP 427 (1968). See also Sicard, La preuve en Justice 2-10 (1960).

[269] See Sicard, La preuve en Justice 33 (1960). The fact that this author also uses the term "relevance" in connection with a fair number of different reasons for ruling evidence inadmissible is interesting. The term

that tend to be discussed in connection with admissibility to the mix (facts and "proposals")[270], it is difficult to define a clear criterion for ruling evidence inadmissible from the concept of relevance. The definition of the term is extremely complicated as it refers to radically different elements.[271]. Moreover, it was unnecessary for lawmakers to provide that "relevant" evidence shall be admitted as this is covered under the general objective requirement of suitability that applies to all legal proceedings.[272]

The term "irrelevant" has also been used in Spanish jurisprudence in reference to facts that are different from those addressed in the case. Among other things, it is interesting that relevance has been an issue both in the inquiries and practices carried out during preliminary proceedings and in connection with evidence proposals for decades. For example, a 22 February 1969 Spanish Supreme

---

"irrelevant" is used to describe facts that are too vague, such as facts that do not pertain to the outcome sought with the laws that are to be applied. Reference is also made to evidence proposals that are irrelevant because the means of proof are legally inadmissible. Here, it is not really correct to refer to "irrelevance," as these cases refer more generally to "inadmissibility of evidence."

[270] See Bonet Navarro (A)., La prueba de confesión en juicio 89 (1979).

[271] Reference is even made to the relevance or irrelevance of the principle of evidence. Burgos Ladrón de Guevara, El principio de prueba en el proceso civil español 104-105 (1989).

[272] See Guasp, who states: "la inadmisión de pruebas en razón a su impertinencia o inutilidad (Ley de Enjuiciamiento Civil, artículo 563) solo puede v. gr. explicarse mediante el juego del requisito de la idoneidad." Indicaciones sobre el problema de la causa en los actos procesales, 3 RDP 410 (1948).

Court judgment[273] tried to define the concept of relevance and criticized the fact that few legal precepts explain how it should be understood. The Court noted that article 311 and others suggest that evidentiary practices should not be allowed if they are found pointless or damaging. It affirmed that generally speaking, first in preliminary proceedings and then during the trial, relevant practices are those that are likely to prove that an offense either exists or does not exist and to establish the identity of the perpetrator if the Court finds that there was criminal activity, and the next step is to identify the person responsible. Practices that are properly proposed, that are related to the facts in issue, and that might be useful for substantiating the facts are relevant, and they should be allowed and carried out. Conversely, practices that are not related to the incriminating facts or that might not be able to substantiate them should not be permitted. Requests must either be consistent with the facts established by the party that has proposed evidence (corroborating evidence) or with the facts set out in the pleadings of the opposing party (counter-evidence). Another criterion for ruling on matters of relevance is the objective that a party is trying to achieve with the evidence as compared with the problems under debate in the proceedings. Thus, anything that cannot be used to clarify the facts in issue or to influence the final judgment should not be allowed because it is markedly irrelevant.

A reference to omitting anything that is unnecessary from

[273] Ar. 1089.

preliminary proceedings was included in former article 312 of the Code of Criminal Procedure (see CCP, article 314). Regarding the trial, perhaps the judgment that came the closest to defining what should be understood by relevance was Constitutional Court judgment 51/10 April 1985.[274] It provides that relevance is the relationship between evidence, the object of the proceedings, and what the Court considers the matter in issue (thema decidendi). It reflects the power of the means used to influence the final opinion of the Court. According to this definition, whether or not evidence is relevant is different from whether or not it has the potential to be significant, which is a matter of being deemed necessary or useful.

Furthermore, using significance together with relevance as a criterion for admissibility has also created confusion[275] (Fenech,[276] Leone,[277] Devis Echandía,[278] among others) as significance is then said to only relate to facts and not to evidence once it has been examined. This has led some

---

[274] BJC 49 FJ 9 555.

[275] Taruffo criticizes the lack of precision of the expression "rilevanza della prova" when used as a requirement for admissibility evaluated beforehand; that is, before evidence is examined (and thus confusing the concept with the idea of relevance), and relative to the outcome of examinations of evidence; that is, whether or not the outcome is legally significant. Studi sulla rilevanza della prova footnote 52 bis (1970).

[276] See 2 Fenech, Derecho Procesal Penal 136 (1945).

[277] "Pertinenza della prova significa riferimento di essa all'accertamento in corso; ... Rilevanza della prova significa possibilitá di concorrere, anche mediatamente ed indirettamente, all'accertamento in corso." 2 Leone, Trattato di Diritto Processuale Penale 181 (1961).

[278] Compendio de pruebas judiciales 67 (1969).

authors to describe it erroneously.[279] Relating significance to facts has led to references to "leading facts" as facts that steer toward some practical outcome.[280] This is rather unfortunate[281] because in the end significance is confused with relevance.[282][283] Relating significance to means of proof has led some doctrine to use this term in references to amassed evidence. Thus, an item of evidence is said to be significant in view of the extent to which it allows an opinion that is based on stronger grounds than any other on the matter in issue.[284]

We can see, even with this brief discussion, that the confusion that arises is due not only to the use of the same term to convey different meanings, but is also caused by what the term is used to describe (means of proof or facts). Confusion increases when the term "significant" is used improperly

---

[279] Gutiérrez-Alviz and Conradi, La valoración de la prueba penal, 4 RDP 817 (1975). "...la relevancia alude a la valoración, esto es, juicio de valoración una vez que la prueba ha sido practicada, por lo que se encuadra en un momento procesal sucesivo."

[280] Sentís Melendo, Valoración de la prueba, 2-3 RDP 289 (1976).

[281] The author mentioned earlier in footnote no. 124 acknowledges this idea.

[282] There have been attempts to differentiate between something that is relevant and something that is leading. The former is a question of fact, while the latter is a matter of law. Devis Echandía, Compendio de pruebas judiciales 125 (1969).

[283] German doctrine has defined the concept of facts that are "doubly significant" in that they refer (erheblichkeit) not only to legal issues and guilt, but also at the same time to procedural issues, such as kinship between a witness and the accused, for example. Kleinknecht/Meyer-Gossner, Strafprozeßordnung 749 note 8 (42d. ed. 1995).

[284] Muñoz Sabaté, Jurisprudencia constitucional sobre pertinencia y relevancia de la prueba, 4 RJC 1110 (1991).

(which incidentally happens quite often with Anglo-Saxon jurists) to convey the idea of importance. According to Fairén, those who write in this fashion are unaware of the kind of maze they have wandered into.[285]

B. Necessity and Evidence Examination

The Rome Statute of the ICC is not oblivious to the difference between relevance and necessity in connection with evidence. Note that article 69.3 provides: "The parties may submit evidence relevant to the case, in accordance with article 64. The Court shall have the authority to request the submission of all evidence that it considers necessary for the determination of the truth." However, this does not mean that the Rome Statute draws a clear distinction between the time of admission and the time evidence is examined. It would be a good idea to do so with a view to setting out clear criteria for ruling evidence inadmissible; the Statute fails to provide such criteria, as we have pointed out in Chapter Two, Part A.

In Spain "necessity" is not a criterion that the Court takes into account when deciding whether or not proposed evidence is admissible. It is a consideration, however, for adjourning proceedings (see CCP, article 746 for ordinary proceedings) or denying requests to examine evidence. An

[285] Ley del Jurado de 22 de mayo de 1995 y modelo inquisitivo. Un apunte., 1 RDP footnote 36 (1996).

item of "evidence" that was previously admitted because it was "relevant" might be deemed "unnecessary," and this ruling does not violate the right to use relevant means of proof (Spanish Constitution, article 24.2). Therefore, as we noted earlier, we must differentiate between two procedural events, according to the Code of Criminal Procedure (see article 659): admission of evidence and examination of evidence, during which the criteria of relevance and necessity are applied respectively. Both are in dire need of review in order to afford the right to present evidence, which is acknowledged by the Constitution under article 24.2.

Both the Rome Statute and the Draft Rules of Procedure and Evidence fail to distinguish the time evidence is submitted from the time it is examined. Also, rule 64.1 may cause further confusion as it deals with different times for raising "issues relating to relevance."

C. A Critique of the Practice of Prematurely Assessing Evidence

It seems important to specifically address the fact that any premature assessment of evidence is forbidden as both the Rome Statute and the Draft Rules of Procedure and Evidence provide that evidence assessment is intended "to determine …relevance or admissibility" (rule 63.2). Furthermore, the reference made in the Rules of Procedure and Evidence that states: "evidence ruled irrelevant or inadmissible shall not be considered by the Chamber" is especially significant because in practice, situations might arise that make it very difficult to abide by this provision.

If evidentiary process means that a judgment is made on the certainty of a fact, and thus it formally establishes[286] that the fact is true, then granting evidence requests entails a judgment on something that appears to be real (that what is stated might be true) rather than a judgment on a fact. If the opposite were true, the decision maker would be prejudging the facts, which should be avoided according to German jurisprudence and doctrine that prohibits premature assessment of evidence. Forbidding this practice suggests the belief that the Court is not any better informed after receiving a evidence request than it was before the request was submitted.[287]

There are two ways to conceive the concept that premature evidence assessment is not allowed (Beweisantizipationsve rbot).[288] First, premature assessment (Beweisantizipation) refers to a negative assessment of the potential that an item of evidence that has not yet been examined has for succeeding. In this case, the Court is not allowed, when deciding whether or not to examine evidence, to make any negative prediction on the outcome of an examination or on

[286] Carreras (with Fenech), Estudios de Derecho procesal 342 (1962).
[287] Schulz, Die Erosion des Beweisantragsrechts, 8/1991 StV 361.
[288] See Frister, Das Verhältnis von Beweisantragsrecht und gerichtlicher Aufklärungspflicht im Strafprozess, 105 ZStW 347-348 (1993).

how the outcome might influence the Court. However, this term (Beweisantizipation) also refers to prematurely assessing evidence that has already been examined. In this respect, the Court must render a conclusive judgment only after all evidence has been examined. According to this definition of the term, the fact that premature assessment of evidence is not permitted (das Verbot der Beweisantizipation) means that the Court must not make any predictions on evidence requests (if the predictions might be detrimental for the requester)[289] on the basis of the outcome of any examinations of evidence that had been carried out up to that point.[290]

StPO does not specifically prohibit premature assessments, although section 244.2 does infer that they are not allowed. Section 244.2, as we know, addresses the Court's duty to exhaust all possibilities in its quest to clarify the facts and to find material truth. Moreover, the "parties'" right to evidence broadens the context under which the Court has a duty (provided under section 244.2 of StPO) to clarify facts.[291] This should broaden the scope of the examination to include those facts that are necessary for rendering judgment (Schuldspruch) and sentencing (Strafausspruch). Furthermore, they should not be linked to any confession of guilt (Schuldbekenntnisse), considering that trials are often held for defendants who have

[289] Predictions are only allowed when the requester stands to benefit. Alsberg/Nüse/Meyer, Karlheinz, Der Beweisantrag im Strafprozess 411 (5th ed. 1983).

[290] See Rieker, Die Ablehnung von Beweisanträgen in der Hauptverhandlung 90 (1935).

statement) is proved.[301] However, although what is stated may be proved, the true objective of the request may not necessarily be achieved. The fact that a particular evidentiary statement may be important for the Court's decision is something that can generally be determined ahead of time. However, whether or not this evidentiary statement will be proved during the trial is something that no one can predict beforehand with the same degree of certainty. Thus, prematurely assessing evidence is not permitted, which means that the Court may not predict or assess the outcome of any examination of evidence or prematurely assess the importance that any such outcome will have on the opinion of the Court.

Prematurely assessing evidence, which is not specifically prohibited under Spanish law (although the Code of Criminal Procedure, article 741 suggests that it is forbidden), should not be allowed in connection with evidentiary facts or relative to means of proof. Emphasizing the contention that evidence refers only to those items that are examined during proceedings, all of the efforts of those who render judgment, especially the Spanish Constitutional Court, are futile if it turns out that the decision maker denies an evidence request because he or she has made a premature assessment that is unjustifiable. For example, it would not be proper for the Court to deny an evidence request for documents because the document in question failed to prove the requester's

[301] Von Greyerz, Der Beweis negativer Tatsachen 54 (1963).

contention.[302] This is a "judgment" that the Court may not give at that time; it might, however, be rendered after examining evidence, at which time it would be appropriate to make an assessment.[303]

Regarding grounds for not permitting premature assessments of evidence, the well-known article 741 of the Code of Criminal Procedure, which deals with assessing evidence, is often cited. Article 741 is not the subject of this work as there is a difference between the references to assessment made in the article and the potential to pre-assess evidence with a view to ruling on admissibility. This must be kept in mind when tackling the issue of evidence proposed with the aim of delaying proceedings. The person responsible for ruling on whether or not proposed evidence will be admitted and examined does not assess "evidence" that has been examined (CCP, article 741, paragraph 1), but rather "evidence" that the "parties" set out in their respective pleadings (CCP, article 656, paragraph 1). This assessment is made prior to admitting and subsequently examining the evidence.

Now we shall differentiate between two situations relative to premature assessments of evidence. The first deals with anticipating (or predicting) the outcome of an examination

---

[302] See Alsberg/Nüse/Meyer, Karlheinz, Der Beweisantrag im Strafprozess 417 (5th ed. 1983).

[303] "En la admisión opera una calificación previa de la legalidad del medio presentado o aducido y su relación con los hechos del litigio o la causa, sin que por ello se esté valorando o apreciando su fuerza o mérito de convicción, que es una tarea propia del acto decisorio." Devis Echandía, Compendio de pruebas judiciales 105 (1969).

of proposed evidence, while the second relates to prematurely assessing this outcome in terms of how it might influence the opinion of the Court. Provisions that prohibit premature assessments state that the Court may not affirm prior to an examination of evidence that the examination will turn out a certain way as it is impossible to predict the outcome ahead of time.[304] Similarly, the Court may not affirm that a statement set out in a request will not be proved. Also, even if a statement is proved, it should not influence the Court at that time. Although the Court may exercise its exclusive power to freely form an opinion (see STC84/4 May 1990),[305] considering the Code of Criminal Procedure, article 741, paragraph 1, at that point the Court would be forming an opinion outside of the trial, which is the only point in the proceedings when evidence has true procedural importance (with the well-known exception of CCP, article 627, paragraph 3). In other words, evidence is produced and examined in the presence of the decision maker and in observance of all due process guarantees during the trial.

Nonetheless, doctrine has criticized and continues to criticize the idea that evidence is only that which is examined during the trial, and with reason. Although, perhaps it would be better to qualify that thought and say that even though (procedural) evidence is only that which is examined during

[304] See Onecha Santamaría, Los medios de prueba y la convicción judicial, 1 RDP 259 (1980).
[305] BJC 109 FJ 2 265.

the trial, the trial is not the only factor helping the decision maker to form an opinion. Rather, the Court's opinion is also influenced by circumstances that are almost unidentifiable as they are impossible to express in legal terms that have been strictly construed.[306] The reference to pre-assessing evidence under article 627 covers an issue that is different from the matter at hand. We are not dealing with assessing opportunities for examining evidence before the trial (a situation that is addressed in law), but with the practice of prematurely (before the trial) assessing evidence. These are clearly different situations that require no further explanation.

Now, it is worthwhile to consider what happens when on the basis of evidence that has already been examined during the trial, the Court rules that an item of "evidence" that was admitted will not be examined. Under such circumstances, is it possible to argue that the Court is not permitted to prematurely assess evidence? The idea that assessment was "premature" would no longer be a feasible argument as the Court, which has already formed an opinion as a result of what has occurred during the trial, might find the requested evidence "unnecessary" and decide against proceeding with the examination (in the interest of ensuring that the right to a speedy trial is observed) because proceedings might be delayed. Delaying proceedings is often the purpose of requests, especially if it would be necessary to adjourn or to

[306] Mittermaier, Tratado de la prueba en materia criminal 95 (9th ed. 1959).

continue with another session in order to be able to examine evidence. In this scenario, note that the Court has already formed its opinion; however, it did so during the trial and not beforehand.

Working from the idea that it is only possible to legitimately assess evidence after it has been examined, it is not appropriate (as it would involve determining the finding beforehand and result in a violation of the presumption of innocence) for the Court to make an assessment beforehand (prematurely) if it is reasonable to presume[307] that the assessment would cause the Court to become biased in such a way that its objective judicial impartiality would be negatively affected.[308]

The duty to clarify the facts is the backdrop of the foregoing; thus, one might also argue that when the Court believes that it has upheld its duty to clarify the facts during the trial, it is not "necessary" to examine any other items of "evidence." Conversely, if further clarification is expected, evidence should be admitted and examined. However, there are those

---

[307] Regarding presumptions: "La palabra alemana vermuten (sospechar, presumir) se diferencia del término latino praesumere en que sólo se utiliza para designar cierta actividad mental del hombre, mientras que praesumere, originariamente da a entender un movimiento corporal, y sólo en sentido figurado se aproxima al alemán vermuten, viniendo a significar algo semejante al verbo annehmen (suponer, admitir)." "Praesumere y vermuten son palabras sinónimas solamente cuando representan una de las expresiones graduales de la labor intelectual." Hedemann, Las presunciones en el Derecho, Revista de Derecho Privado 11, 12 (1931).

[308] See Oraá González, (J. and P)., El derecho a un juez imparcial y la jurisprudencia constitucional. Un decepcionante paso atrás, 26 Poder Judicial 167 (1992).

who contend that even when the Court is convinced that further examinations are not necessary, it should still examine the evidence that is requested.[309]

Thus, given that anticipating the outcome of an examination is not permitted, there are some who will call a large number of witnesses whose testimony does nothing more than corroborate the statements of others who testified previously. Consequently, the Court has to impassively endure examinations that fail to help it form an opinion and that cause delays that could be described as inappropriate. In cases such as these, due to the fact that pre-assessing evidence is forbidden, it is not proper to deny a request because the witness is going to give testimony that is similar to that of a witness who preceded him or her.[310] It is a different matter if experience dictates that the witness will not be able to affirm the facts that he or she has been called to affirm (due to objective impossibility, as in the case of the blind witness) or that his or her affirmation will have absolutely no value as evidence.[311]

In practice, solicitors will sometimes call a large number of witnesses to appear at a trial (summary proceedings) with the idea of easily reaching an agreement[312] as the Judge (and

[309] Herdegen, Die Beruhensfrage im strafprozessualen Revisionsrecht, NStZ 518-519 (1990).

[310] Alsberg/Nüse/Meyer, Karlheinz, Der Beweisantrag im Strafprozess 418 (5th ed. 1983).

[311] Compare Alsberg/Nüse/Meyer, Karlheinz, Der Beweisantrag im Strafprozess 418 (5th ed. 1983).

[312] According to Instrucción 6/1992, Spanish Prosecution Service: "...

also the Prosecutor) foresee that by holding the trial they would have to postpone subsequent trials and deal with the resulting difficulties that would arise, or they would simply have to prolong (more than they had anticipated) an already demanding work day. In cases such as these, we might say that the requester achieved his or her goal, which was not exactly related to helping to clarify facts or discover the truth. The following questions arise: When might the Court find that it has fulfilled its obligation to clarify the facts? And in the event that the facts have not yet been clarified, can the Court predict that examining an item of evidence will not be at all helpful to fact clarification? We might conclude that during the trial, the duty to clarify the facts obligates the Court to examine evidence when the outcome of an examination might be expected to influence the Court and therefore change, even in a very small way, the opinion it has held on the facts to be judged up to that moment.

Now, how might the Court deny a evidence request that does not aim to help clarify the facts or discover the truth, but instead is intended to delay proceedings if the Court has

---

ante la necesidad de flexibilizar la actuación de los poderes encargados de la investigación que permitan mejores soluciones de política criminal... se hace imprescindible considerar nuevas instituciones introducidas en países de nuestro entorno cultural... (en los que se parte) de la atribución de la investigación al Fiscal... (que posee) amplias facultades de disposición del objeto del proceso, permitiendo suspenderlo o truncarlo mediante el llamado principio de oportunidad y el acuerdo entre la acusación y la defensa con el consentimiento del acusado, que permite, mediante la imposición de una pena reducida, llegar al reconocimiento de culpabilidad."

not yet formed its opinion and hence cannot deny the request on the grounds that it is unnecessary? We have stated and given reasons to support why the Court cannot pre-assess the outcome of an evidence request (although the laws fail to address the issue). However, if the Court believes that the purpose of a request is not to clarify the facts (even though it might help in some way), but to delay proceedings, how might it deny the request? The Rome Statute also fails to provide grounds for denying requests intended to delay proceedings. Thus, the Court might deny these requests by applying an ever-accommodating criterion: relevance.

Another argument that might support prohibiting premature assessments of the outcome of a requested examination is based on the idea that often, no matter how experienced the Court may be, it is only possible to perceive the true possibilities offered by an item of evidence or any special qualities it might have that might influence the opinion of the Court by considering an overall view of all of the evidence examined during the trial. Before the trial, that is, during any kind of pre-assessment, it might not be possible to gauge the value of the evidence. Moreover, it is our belief that when a regulatory scheme for denying evidence requests is not provided, the Court judging the case is more apt to prematurely assess the evidence.[313] We ask: how can one who

[313] But see for the German Code of Procedure, "… die in 244 Abs. 3 enumerierten Ablehnungsgesichtspunkte… sichern die Beachtung des Beweisantizipationsverbotes." Engels, Beweisantizipationsverbot und Beweiserhebungsumfang im Strafprozeß 26 (1981).

is biased judge fairly?

We have seen that generally the value of a means of proof can only be perceived after examining evidence because it is impossible to make an exact calculation beforehand of the significance of an item of evidence.[314] However, there are exceptions to the general rule that pre-assessing evidence is not permitted.[315] In certain cases, it is possible to make a prediction by considering capacity or competence.[316] In this way, the Court is not compelled to use means of proof that are completely worthless; for example, such may be the case when testimony is requested from witnesses who are incompetent or clearly opposed to cooperating with the Court. (Actually, these are cases in which the means of proof are completely inadequate).[317] Pre-assessing evidence is also acceptable if the means of proof are unattainable or if a request might delay proceedings. In cases such as these, the requester may not have submitted the request with delay in mind; however, the Court is certain that he or she will not manage to prove anything with the requested means of proof.[318]

---

[314] Onecha Santamaría, Los medios de prueba y la convicción judicial, 1 RDP 260 (1980).

[315] See Alsberg/Nüse/Meyer, Karlheinz, Der Beweisantrag im Strafprozess 418-419 (5th ed. 1983).

[316] See generally Onecha Santamaría, Los medios de prueba y la convicción judicial, 1 RDP 259 (1980).

[317] See 3 Gollwitzer, Großkommentar section 244, note 278 (24th ed. 1989).

[318] Thole, Der Scheinbeweisantrag im Strafprozess 189 (1992).

CHAPTER III

CONCLUSIONS

The Rome Statute of the International Criminal Court and the Draft Rules of Procedure and Evidence do not include a list of reasons for ruling evidence inadmissible; rather, decisions are based on the concept of relevance. The concept of relevance is likened to the concept of admissibility, and this leads to legal uncertainty. Furthermore, the Court has the power to use a considerable amount of discretion when deciding whether or not to admit evidence. In fact, the Rules of Procedure and Evidence provide that the Court shall have the authority and discretion to "assess freely all evidence submitted in order to determine its relevance or admissibility."

The terminological chaos prevailing in the legal systems of many of the States Parties in connection with evidence in criminal proceedings is untenable. Thus, in order to create a scientific international regulatory scheme for evidence, it is absolutely necessary to scientifically define the concepts and terms to be used and to provide corresponding translations for different countries. Experts in criminal proceedings should translate these concepts and terms. Furthermore, vague terminology negates the fundamental right to evidence or more specifically, the right to request evidence (Beweisantragsrecht). It also leads to legal uncertainty as demonstrated by an analysis of judgments given over time by both the Spanish Supreme Court and the Spanish Constitutional Court, which have developed in a way that is subject to criticism.

Judging the admissibility of evidence in accordance with the provisions of the Rome Statute and the Rules of Procedure and Evidence is what we understand to be a ("legal") way to prematurely assess evidence that is detrimental to ensuring a fair trial with all due process guarantees. The Court is given a considerable amount of discretion to rule evidence inadmissible. Specific provisions for "closed" sessions may actually "open the door" for arbitrariness and violations of the guarantees that should govern proceedings.

Although up until this point it has not been necessary to delve into the constitutional grounds supporting the right to present evidence, it is important to do so in order to amend the precepts relating to the regulatory scheme for admissibility of evidence. A regulatory scheme that bases rulings of inadmissibility on the criterion of relevance is not acceptable. In addition to converting relevance into a macro-concept, the regulatory scheme of the Rome Statute and the Rules of Procedure and Evidence also underscores the absolute power afforded the Trial Chamber when giving judgment on the admission and examination of evidence. Furthermore, judgments on relevance and necessity of evidence are only subject to review under very strict conditions. This "absolute power" greatly contributes to the creation of a confusing gray area in which "relevance" is a criterion for ruling evidence inadmissible.

The right to present evidence is also associated with delays that are purposefully instigated during proceedings. If the States Parties are dealing with the problem of procedural delays as they attempt to ensure that justice is done in their own countries, it is foreseeable that the new International Criminal Court would face the same problem. Solutions to this problem under the Rome Statute and the Rules of Procedure and Evidence, which involve establishing time limits, have already failed many times and have been the subject of many decisions rendered by the European Court of Human Rights.

The regulatory scheme for evidentiary process set out in the Rome Statute and the Rules of Procedure and Evidence, at least in connection with the concept of admissibility, is most certainly inadequate. Striving to develop a more complete regulatory scheme for denying evidence requests would make it more difficult for the Court to deny requests; however, the parties would be able to influence evidentiary process to a greater extent. There are no magic formulas. Either the scales tip in favor of a "paternalistic" Court that decides what should be admitted and examined, or to a large extent it is in the hands of the parties to influence this decision (even though it is always the Court's job to decide). The advantage of the first situation is that few decisions have been subject to review by the Spanish Supreme and Constitutional Courts, thus alleviating some of their workload. The disadvantage lies in the fact that this solution to the problem of admitting and examining evidence in criminal proceedings has very little scientific rigor and is detrimental to the well-known right to a defense. It has even come to the absurd point of requiring those who have lodged appeals for the defense of this basic constitutional right to demonstrate that the evidence ruled inadmissible would have altered the course of proceedings. If the "parties" are to be allowed to participate more fully in decisions relating to admission and examination of evidence (which would involve the decision maker taking a more neutral stance and result overall in fairer proceedings) a new regulatory scheme or system for ruling on the admissibility of evidence must be introduced. The new system must clearly set out reasons for ruling evidence inadmissible and avoid vague concepts or adjectives that over time are incomprehensible and lead to legal uncertainty.

The novel provision included in the Rome Statute that allows decisions on admissibility to be made in closed sessions is also questionable. If the Court finds that certain items have sufficient value as evidence without observing the due process guarantees that should govern a trial, it is legitimating a premature assessment of evidence. Even worse, it legitimates turning the trial into a charade by violating the right to appear before a judge who has not had access to information on the matter prior to the trial.

In the absence of a legal definition of "relevance," the concept has been extremely difficult to explain and define through jurisprudence and doctrine, if indeed it has been done. The term has developed unacceptably through decisions rendered by both the Spanish Supreme Court and the Spanish Constitutional Court. Perhaps the answer does not lie in reconsidering terminology, but in creating a regulatory scheme for ruling on the admissibility of evidence that is based on the concept of evidence requests and that includes reasons for denying requests that are clear and provided under the law. It is not our intent to ignore the disadvantages associated with this type of system; while it would allow the parties to participate more fully in the evidentiary process, it would also lend itself to abuse by those who, finding themselves with more room to maneuver (as they would not have to depend as much on the "subjective" view of the decision maker ruling on evidence requests), would use the possibilities provided for them under the law with the singular aim of delaying proceedings. These delays are real "blockades" as the passing of time is a way to not only prevent justice from being done, but to cause it to lose all meaning. Yet above all, it is important to consider the inadequacies of the regulatory scheme provided under the Rome Statute and the Rules of Procedure and Evidence of the International Criminal Court, which bases decisions on admissibility of proposed evidence on the concept of "relevance."

BIBLIOGRAPHY

AGUILERA DE PAZ, *Comentarios a la Ley de Enjuiciamiento Criminal*, Ed. Reus S.A., Madrid, 1914-1924, Ts. I, II, III.

ALCALÁ ZAMORA Y LEVENE, *Derecho Procesal Penal*, Ts. II y III, Ed. Guillermo Kraft Ltda., Buenos Aires, 1945.

ALSBERG/NÜSE/MEYER,

Der Beweisantrag im Strafprozess, 2 Ed. Carl Heymanns, Colonia-Berlin, 1956.

Der Beweisantrag im Strafprozess, 5 Ed. Carl Heymanns, Berlin, 1983.

AMBOS, K.,

Procedimientos abreviados en el proceso penal alemán y en los proyectos de reforma sudamericanos, RDP, 1997, n. 3.

El proceso penal alemán y la reforma en América Latina, Ediciones Jurídicas Gustavo Ibáñez, Santa Fe de Bogotá D. C., 1998.

Elementos del Crimen así como reglas de procedimiento y prueba de la Corte Penal Internacional, La Ley 1998, V. 9.

Armenta Deu,

Criminalidad de bagatela y principio de oportunidad: Alemania y España, Ed. Promociones y publicaciones Universitarias S. A., Barcelona, 1991.

Principio acusatorio: realidad y utilización (lo que es y lo que no), RDP, 1996, n. 2.

El proceso penal, nuevas tendencias, nuevos problemas, Poder Judicial, ns. 41-42, 1996.

Asencio Mellado,

Principio acusatorio y derecho de defensa en el proceso penal, Ed. Trivium, Madrid, 1991.

La intervención de la defensa en la fase de instrucción, RDP, 1997, n. 1.

Bahnsen, *Das Akteneinsichtsrecht der Verteidigung im Strafverfahren*, Frankfurt, 1996.

Bajo Fernández, *Coste y eficacia de la Justicia penal en España*, Documentación Jurídica, Ministerio de Justicia, Madrid, 1983, Vol. I, 37/40.

Bandisch, *Zum Entwurf des Kriminalitätsbekämpfungsgesetzes der Fraktionen der CDU/CSU und FDP*, vom 4.1.1994, StV 3/1994.

Bandrés, *Eficacia y garantismo en el proceso penal*, RGD, 1995, n. 609.

Bano y Aracil, *El Ministerio Fiscal en la instrucción de los delitos,* RGD, 1994, págs. 1743 a 1773.

Barona Vilar, *La conformidad en el proceso penal,* Ed. Tirant lo blanch, Valencia, 1994.

Barrios de Angelis, *La teoría general del proceso,* RDP, 1968, n. 1.

Beling, *Derecho Procesal Penal,* Ed. Labor S.A., Barcelona, 1943.

Belloch Julve, *Las dilaciones indebidas,* Revista Jueces para la Democracia, n. 7, 1989.

Bonet Navarro (A)., La prueba de confesión en juicio, Ed. Bosch, Barcelona, 1979.

Borrajo Iniesta, *Tribunales de Justicia,* 7/1997, ns. mgs. 742 y sigs.

Böttcher, Mayer, *Änderungen des Strafverfahrensrechts durch das Entlastungsgesetz,* NStZ, 1993, C. 4.

Bueno Arús, *El sumario en el derecho comparado, en Jornadas de Derecho procesal,* CGPJ, Madrid, 1984.

Burgos Ladrón de Guevara, *El principio de prueba en el proceso civil español,* Ed. Montecorvo S. A., Madrid, 1989.

Calvo Sánchez, *Contribución del Secretario Judicial a la efectividad del derecho a un proceso sin dilaciones indebidas,* RGD, 1997, n.

632.

Cappelletti, *La oralidad y las pruebas en el proceso civil, Ediciones Jurídicas Europa-América*, Buenos Aires, 1972.

Carnelutti,

Lezioni sul processo penale, T. III, Edizione dell'Ateneo, Roma, 1947.

Las miserias del Proceso Penal, Ediciones Jurídicas Europa-América, Buenos Aires, 1959.

La Prova Civile, Ed. Temis, Bogotá, 1969.

La prueba civil, 2 Ed. Depalma, 1982.

Carreras (con Fenech), *Estudios de Derecho procesal*, Ed. Bosch, Barcelona, 1962.

Castejón, *Teoría y práctica del recurso de casación en lo criminal*, RDP, 1948, n. 2.

Chamorro Bernal, *La tutela judicial efectiva*, Ed. Bosch, 1994, Barcelona.

Cid Cebrián, *La regulación del Jurado ante la reforma de la Ley de Enjuiciamiento Criminal*, Poder Judicial, 1982, n. 4.

Claría Olmedo, *Del avocamiento al procesamiento en la instrucción penal*, RDP, n. 2, 1968.

Climent Durán,

Sobre las dilaciones indebidas: el descarte constitucional de una determinada solución judicial, RGD, 1994, ns. 598-599.

La fase de juicio oral en el procedimiento ante el Tribunal del Jurado, RGD, 1996, n. 627.

COSACOV, BELAUS, GORENC, NADELTICHER, *Variables interactuantes en el retardo del proceso penal en México: análisis jurídico empírico*, RDP, 1983, ns. 2-3, págs. 343 y sigs.

DAMIÁN MORENO, Sobre el derecho de defensa y prueba prohibida, Poder Judicial, 1989 (2), n. 16, págs. 151 y 152.

DE LA OLIVA SANTOS,

Sobre conceptos básicos del Derecho procesal, RDP, n. 1, 1976.

Comentario a la LECrim, Poder Judicial 1981/82, n. 4.

Disponibilidad del objeto, conformidad del imputado y vinculación del Tribunal a las pretensiones en el proceso penal, RGD, 1992, ns. 577-578.

El proyecto de Ley del Jurado, de 1994, y la estructura del proceso penal, RDP, 1994, n. 3.

Derecho Procesal Penal, (con otros autores), Ed. Centro de Estudios Ramón Areces, Madrid, 1996, pág. 67.

El futuro del proceso penal y el papel del Ministerio Fiscal, Tribunales de Justicia 1/1997.

DEL CACHO, *Sobre la prueba de testigos y su protección en el proceso penal español*, Revista Brasileira de Ciencias Criminais, abril-junio de 1999, n. 26.

Del Moral García, *Anotaciones al Proyecto de Ley Orgánica del Tribunal del Jurado*, Jueces para la Democracia, n. 22.

Delmas-Marty, *El proceso penal en Europa: perspectivas*, *Poder Judicial*, 1995, n. 37.

Devis Echandia,

Objeto, tema o necesidad, fin y resultado de la prueba judicial, RDP,1965, n. 4.

Facultades y deberes del juez, RDP, 1968, n. 3.

Compendio de pruebas judiciales, Ed. Temis, Bogotá, 1969.

Fraude procesal, sus características, configuración legal y represión, RDP, 1970, n. 4.

Principios fundamentales del derecho procesal penal, RDP, 1982, n. 4.

Díaz Cabiale, *La admisión y práctica de la prueba en el proceso penal*, Cuadernos del CGPJ, 1992, n. 20.

Díez-Picazo (L)., *Notas sobre el derecho a la tutela judicial efectiva*, Poder Judicial, 1987.

Döhring, *La prueba, su práctica y apreciación, Introducción*, Ediciones Jurídicas Europa-América, Buenos Aires, 1972.

Echávarri Casi, *El nuevo procedimiento para las causas ante el Tribunal del Jurado. Algunas cuestiones procesales*, BIMJ, n. 1770.

ELLERO, *De la certidumbre de los juicios criminales*, 5 Ed. Instituto Editorial Reus, Madrid, 1953.

ENGELS, *Beweisantizipationsverbot und Beweiserhebungsumfang im Strafprozeß*, Goltdammer's Archiv für Strafrecht, 1981.

EISENBERG,

Persönliche Beweismittel in der StPO, Ed. C. H. Beck'sche Verlagsbuchhandlung, München, 1983.

Beweisrecht der StPO, Spezialkommentar, 2 Ed. C. H. Beck'sche Verlagsbuchhandlung, München, 1996.

ESCUSOL BARRA, *El proceso penal por delitos: Estudio sistemático del procedimiento penal abreviado*, Ed. Colex, Madrid, 1990.

ESER, *Das rechtliche Gehör im Strafbefehls- und Strafverfügungsverfah ren*, JZ, 1966, págs. 660 a 669.

FAIRÉN GUILLÉN,

Temas del Ordenamiento Procesal, Ed. Tecnos, Madrid, 1969, Vol. II.

Estudios de Derecho Procesal Civil, Penal y Constitucional, Ed. Edersa, Madrid, 1992, Vol. III.

El plazo razonable y el Tribunal Europeo de Derechos Humanos (La Sentencia 2/1992/147/420, asunto Ruiz Mateos v. España), RDP, 1994, n. 1.

Proceso equitativo, plazo razonable y Tribunal Europeo de Derechos Humanos, Ed. Comares, Granada, 1996.

Ley del Jurado de 22 de mayo de 1995 y modelo inquisitivo. Un apunte, RDP, 1996, n. 1.

FENECH, *Derecho Procesal Penal*, Ed. Bosch, Barcelona, 1945, Ts. I, II, III.

FERNÁNDEZ VIAGAS, *Las dilaciones indebidas en el proceso y su incidencia sobre la orientación de las penas hacia la reeducación y reinserción social*, Poder Judicial, 1991 (2).

FEUERPEIL, *Der Beweisablehnungsgrund der Offenkundigkeit gemäss par. 244 Abs. 3 Satz 2* , Ed. Centaurus, Freiburg, 1987, 1 Var. StPO.

FEZER,

Strafprozessrecht II, Ed. C. H. Beck, München, 1986.

Strafprozessrecht, Ed. C. H. Beck, München, 1995.

FLORIÁN, *De las pruebas penales*, 2 Ed. Temis, Bogotá, 1976, Ts. I y II.

FRISTER,

Comentario a la sentencia del BGH de 3 de agosto de 1988, StV 9/1989.

Das Verhältnis von Beweisantragsrecht und gerichtlicher Aufklärungspflicht im Strafprozess, ZStW (105) 1993.

FROWEIN, *La protección europea de los Derechos Humanos como inicio de una jurisprudencia constitucional europea*, Justicia, 1988, n. IV.

FROWEIN, PEUKERT, *EMRK-Kommentar*, Kehl, 1985, artículo 6.

FURNO, *Teoría de la prueba legal*, Madrid, 1954.

GARCÍA DE ENTERRÍA, *La lucha contra el abuso de los procesos: juicios provisionales y medidas cautelares*, Poder Judicial, 1990, n. 20.

GARCÍA DE LA PUERTA LÓPEZ, *La suspensión del proceso penal por información suplementaria,* Ed. El almendro, Córdoba, 1987.

GARCÍA PONS, *Contenido esencial del derecho a un proceso dentro de un plazo razonable o sin dilaciones indebidas*, RGD, 1996, n. 627.

GARRIDO FALLA (con otros autores), *Comentarios a la Constitución*, Ed. Civitas, Madrid, 1980.

GELSI BIDART,

Indicación sobre el elemento voluntario en el acto procesal, RDP, 1957, n. 2 (segunda época).

Noción de fraude procesal, RDP, 1970, n. 1.

GESTO ALONSO (B).,

La pertinencia y utilidad de las pruebas, Servicio de Publicaciones de la Universidad de Navarra, Pamplona, 1991.

El derecho a los medios de prueba pertinentes en el texto constitucional, RGD, 1996, n. 619.

GESTO ALONSO (G)., *Precisiones sobre el concepto de indefensión desde el punto de vista procesal*, RDP, 1991, n. 2.

GHISALBERTI, *La teoria del notorio nel diritto comune, Anali di Storia del Diritto*, Ed. Giufré, Milan, 1957.

GIMENO SENDRA,

La reforma urgente y la "aceleración" del procedimiento civil, Justicia 85, n. 2.

Derecho Procesal. Proceso penal, con otros autores, Ed. Tirant lo blanch, Valencia, 1987, T. II, Vol. I.

Causas históricas de la ineficacia de la Justicia, Justicia 87, n. 3.

Algunas sugerencias sobre la atribución al M.F. de la investigación oficial, Justicia 88, n. 4.

El derecho a un proceso sin dilaciones indebidas, Poder Judicial, n. especial, 1988

Jornadas sobre Derechos Humanos, 23-25 de abril de 1986.

El derecho a un proceso sin dilaciones indebidas, Problemas actuales de la Justicia (Homenaje al Dr. D. Faustino Gutiérrez-Alviz y Armario), Ed. Tirant lo blanch, Valencia, 1988.

La reforma del proceso penal en el actual sistema democrático español, RDP, 1992, n. 3.

Las garantías constitucionales en el proceso y el Secretario Judicial dentro del marco del Consejo de Europa, Poder Judicial, 1995, n. 38.

La segunda reforma urgente de la Ley del Jurado, Poder Judicial, 1995, n. 39.

GIACOMO PRIMO, *L'onere de la prova*, Societá Editrice del "foro italiano.

Gisbert Gisbert, *El derecho a un proceso sin dilaciones indebidas en el proceso penal*, RGD, n. 571, 1992.

Gollwitzer, *Einschränkungen des Beweisantragsrechts durch Umdeutung von Beweisanträgen in Beweisanregungen*, StV 9/1990.

Gómez Colomer,

El proceso penal alemán. Introducción y normas básicas, 1 Ed. Bosch, S.A., Barcelona, 1985.

Acción particular y popular y sobrecarga de la Administración de Justicia penal, Poder Judicial, 1987, n. 8.

El nuevo proceso penal abreviado, Poder Judicial, n. 26, 1992 (1).

Concreciones en torno al registro domiciliario en el proceso penal español, RDP, 1993.

Gómez-Escolar Mazuela, *El Fiscal instructor: la experiencia portuguesa*, Poder Judicial, 1994 (1).

Gómez Orbaneja,

Comentarios a la Ley de Enjuiciamiento Criminal, Ed. Bosch, Barcelona, 1947, Ts. I y II.

Derecho Procesal, (con Herce Quemada), 2 Ed., Madrid, 1948, Vol. II.

Principio acusatorio y medida de la pena, cuestión nueva en casación, RDP, 1950, n. 3.

Derecho Procesal, 4 Ed., Madrid, 1955, Vol. I.

Derecho Procesal Civil, Parte General, El proceso declarativo ordinario, 7 Ed., Madrid, 1975, Vol. I.

GÓMEZ SANTAMARÍA, *El derecho a un proceso sin dilaciones indebidas como derecho fundamental*, Justicia 90, n. IV.

GONZÁLEZ MONTES,

La prueba obtenida ilícitamente con violación de los Derechos Fundamentales (El derecho constitucional a la prueba y sus límites), RDP, 1990, n. 1.

El inculpado en la fase intermedia. Doctrina del T. Constitucional, RDP, 1994, n. 3.

GONZÁLEZ RUS (con otros autores), *Curso de Derecho Penal español*, Ed. Marcial Pons, Madrid, 1997, Parte especial II.

GORPHE, *L'appréciation des preuves en justice, Essai d'une méthode technique*, Librairie du Recueil Sirei, París, 1947.

GÖSSEL, *Empfehlen sich Änderungen des Strafverfahrensrechts mit dem Ziel, ohne Preisgabe rechtsstaatlicher Grundsätze den Strafprozeß, insbesondere die Hauptverhandlung zu beschleunigen? Verhandlungen des 60. Deutschen Juristentages (DJT)*, Münster,Gutachten, München, 1994, T. I, págs. C 1 a C 94.

GRANADOS PÉREZ, *La individualización y ejecución de las penas*, CGPJ, 1993, págs. 191 y sigs.

GUASP,

Indicaciones sobre el problema de la causa en los actos procesales, RDP, 1948, n. 3, pág. 410.

Estudios Jurídicos, Ed. Civitas, Madrid, 1996.

GUTIÉRREZ-ALVIZ,

La valoración de la prueba penal, Escritos en homenaje al profesor Prieto-Castro, Ed. Nacional, Madrid, 1979, T. II.

La valoración de la prueba penal, RDP, 1975, n. 4.

La ley 53/1978 de 4 de diciembre y la instrucción sumaria penal, Derecho y Proceso, Estudios en honor del Profesor A. Martínez Bernal, Universidad de Murcia, Secretariado de Publicaciones, 1980.

GUTIÉRREZ DE CABIEDES, *El principio pro reo en el derecho a en el proceso penal*, RDP, 1966.

HEDEMANN, *Las presunciones en el Derecho*, Revista de Derecho Privado, Madrid, 1931.

HERDEGEN,

Bemerkungen zum Beweisantragsrecht, NStZ, 1984.

Zum Begriff der Beweisbehauptung, StV 11/1990.

Die Beruhensfrage im strafprozessualen Revisionsrecht, NStZ, 1990.

HESSE, *Grundzüge des Verfassungsrechts*, 20 Ed. Müller, Heidelberg, 1995.

HEVIA BOLAÑOS , *Curia philipica*, Madrid, 1997.

HERNÁNDEZ GIL, *Obras Completas*, Metodología de la Ciencia del Derecho, Madrid, 1988, T. V.

HIPPEL, *Der Entwurf einer Strafprozessordnung*, Ed. Carl Winter's Universitätsbuchhandlung, Heidelberg, 1909.

HIRSCH, *Der zum Zwecke der Prozessverschleppung gestellte Beweisantrag und seine strafprozessuale Behandlung*, Ed. Peter Lang, Frankfurt, 1996.

HOFFMANN, *Der unerreichbare Zeuge im Strafverfahren*, Duncker & Humblot, Berlin, 1991.

HUBER, *Möglichkeiten der Beschleunigung von Wirtschaftsstrafverfah ren*, NStZ, 1996.

HÜNERFELD, *Kleinkriminalität und Strafverfahren*, ZStW 1978, págs. 905 a 926.

IBÁÑEZ, *Cien años después. Lo que queda de la Ley de Enjuiciamiento Criminal*, Poder Judicial, 1981/82, n. 4.

JESCHECK, *Tratado de derecho Penal, Parte General*, 4 Ed. Comares, Granada, 1993.

JIMÉNEZ ASENJO, *Concepción técnico jurídica de la instrucción criminal*, RDP, 1960, n. 4.

JULIUS,

Zum Verhältnis von Aufklärungspflicht und Beweisantragsrecht im Strafprozess, NStZ, 1986, C2.

Strafprozessordnung, Heidelberg Kommentar, Ed. Müller, Heidelberg, 1997, parágrafo 244.

KLEINKNECHT, MEYER-GOSSNER,

Strafprozeßordnung, 40, 41, 42 y 43 Ed. C. H. Beck, München, 1991, 1993, 1995, 1997.

Kommentar zum Grundgesetz für die Bundesrepublick Deutschland, T. I, Luchterhand, 1989.

KREHL, *Strafprozessordnung*, Heidelberg Kommentar, Ed. Müller, Heidelberg, 1997, parágrafo 160, n. mg. 1.

KREKELER, *Der Beweiserhebungsanspruch des Beschuldigten im Ermittlungsverfahren*, NStZ, 1991, pág. 372.

KURTZE, *Die Ablehnung von Beweisanträgen im deutschen Strafprozess*, Ed. Robert Noske, Borna-Leipzig, 1926.

KÜHNE,

Strafprozesslehre, 2 Ed. Engel, Kehl am Rhein, 1982, n. mg. 452.

Der Beweiswert von Zeugenaussagen, NStZ, 1985, C. 6.

Leone, Trattato de Diritto Processuale Penale, Casa Editrice Dott. Eugenio Jovene, Nápoles, 1961, Ts. I y II.

LESSONA,

Teoría general de la prueba en el Derecho Civil, Ed. Hijos de Reus Editores, Madrid, 1907.

Teoría general de la prueba en el Derecho Civil, Ed. Hijos de Reus Editores, Madrid, 1913, T. IV.

Lluis y Navas Brusi, *El fraude de Ley ante el Derecho interno de los Estados*, Revista General de Legislación y Jurisprudencia, 1957.

López-Muñoz y Larraz, *La justicia penal por jurados*, RDP, 1980, n. 1.

Löwe-Rosenberg

Großkommentar, 24 Ed. de Gruyter, Berlin, 1989, Ts. II y III.

Grosskommentar, 25 Ed. de Gruyter, Berlin, 1997, §§ 112-136a.

Lozano-Higuero Pinto,

Apuntes sobre la preclusión y su función saneadora de las nulidades procesales, en Problemas actuales de la Justicia (Homenaje al Dr. D. Faustino Gutiérrez-Alviz y Armario), Ed. Tirant lo blanch, Valencia, 1988.

Introducción al Derecho Procesal, Ministerio de Justicia, Secretaría General Técnica de Publicaciones, Madrid, 1990.

Manzini, (V).,

Tratado de Derecho Procesal Penal, Ediciones Jurídicas Europa-América, Buenos Aires, 1951, 1952, Ts. I, II, III.

Trattato de Diritto Processuale Penale italiano, Unione Tipografico-Editrice Torinese, 4 Ed., T.I, Torino, 1952.

Marchena Gómez, *Aproximación crítica al procedimiento penal directísimo (Anteproyecto de Ley de Medidas Urgentes de Reforma*

Procesal), A. P., n. 3, 1992.

MARTÍN DE LA LEONA, *El derecho de defensa en la fase de preparación del juicio oral en el procedimiento abreviado*, Poder Judicial, 1991, n. 22.

MARTÍN REBOLLO, *Jueces y responsabilidad del Estado*, Ed. Centro de Estudios Constitucionales, Madrid, 1983.

MARTÍNEZ DEL CAMPO, *Notas al Libro Primero de la Ley de Enjuiciamiento Criminal*, Madrid, 1886, T. II.

MARTÍNEZ SILVA, *Tratado de pruebas judiciales*, Ed. Atalaya, Buenos Aires, 1947.

MARTÍNEZ VAL,

La identificación de la pretensión punitiva y derecho de defensa, RGD, 1996, n. 619.

Aporía del restablecimiento del derecho a un proceso sin dilaciones indebidas en el orden jurisdiccional penal, RGD, 1996, n. 624.

MICHALKE,

StV 6/1989.

Noch einmal: Hilfsbeweisantrag-Eventualbeweisantrag-Bedingter Beweisantrag, StV 4/1990.

MICHELI, *La carga de la prueba*, Ediciones Jurídicas Europa-América, Buenos Aires, 1961.

MIEHSLER, VOGLER, *Internationaler Kommentar zur Europäischen Menschenrechtskonvention*, Ed. Carl Heymanns, 1995.

MITTERMAIER, *Tratado de la prueba en materia criminal, 9 y 10 Ed. Instituto editorial Reus*, Madrid, 1959, 1979.

MOLINA PASCUAL, *En defensa de la Ley de Enjuiciamiento Criminal*, RDP, 1970, n. 3.

MONTERO AROCA,

Derecho Jurisdiccional III, Ed. Bosch, Barcelona, 1991.

Ensayos de Derecho Procesal, Ed. Bosch, Barcelona, 1993.

Los privilegios en el proceso penal, Poder Judicial, 1995, n. 39.

La prueba en el proceso civil, 2. Ed., Civitas, 1998.

MORENO CATENA,

La defensa en el proceso penal, Ed. Civitas, Madrid, 1982.

Garantía de los derechos fundamentales en la investigación penal, Poder Judicial, 1987, n. especial II.

MÜLLER, *Rechtsprechung im Vergleich der Länder Europas*, DRiZ (Deutsche Richterzeitung), 10/1993.

MUÑOZ SABATÉ,

La prueba de la simulación, Ed. Hispano Europea, Barcelona, 1972.

Técnica probatoria, 2 Ed. Praxis, Barcelona, 1983.

Jurisprudencia constitucional sobre pertinencia y relevancia de la prueba, RJC, 1991, n. 4.

MUÑOZ ROJAS, *Las cuestiones previas en el proceso penal*, RDP, 1964, ns. 1-2.

NARVÁEZ RODRÍGUEZ, *El jurado en España*, Ed. Comares, Granada,

1995.

NELLES, *Der Einfluss der Verteidigung auf Beweiserhebungen im Ermittlungsverfahren*, StV 2/1986.

NIETO Y GELSI BIDART, *Revista de Derecho, Jurisprudencia y Administración*, Montevideo, T. L.

NÜSSE, *Verfahrensbeschleunigung ohne Beeinträchtigung der Verteidigung aus der Sicht eines Richters*, StraFo, 1996.

ONECHA SANTAMARÍA, *Los medios de prueba y la convicción judicial*, RDP, n. 1980, n. 1.

ORAÁ GONZÁLEZ,

El derecho a un juez imparcial y la jurisprudencia constitucional. Un decepcionante paso atrás, Poder Judicial, 1992, n. 26.

El procedimiento penal ordinario por delito y la garantía de imparcialidad judicial, La Ley, 1992, n. 2981.

ORDOÑO ARTES, *La prueba de reconocimiento judicial en el proceso civil español*, Ed. Montecorvo, Madrid, 1987.

ORTEGA LORCA, *La individualización y determinación de las penas*, CGPJ, 1993, págs. 55 y sigs.

ORTELLS,

Eficacia del acto de investigación sumarial. Estudio de los artículos 730 y 714 de la LECrim, RDP, 1982, ns. 2-3.

Eficacia probatoria del sumario en el juicio ante el Jurado, Justicia, 1987, n.2.

Nuevos poderes para el Ministerio Fiscal en el proceso penal: Límites constitucionales y valoración político-jurídica, RDP, 1990, n. 2.

Derecho Jurisdiccional I, Parte General, (con otros autores), 2 Ed. Bosch, Barcelona, 1991.

Correlación entre acusación y sentencia: antiguas y nuevas orientaciones jurisprudenciales, Justicia 91, n. 3.

La adecuación del proceso en el procedimiento penal abreviado, RDP, 1994, n. 3.

Derecho Jurisdiccional III (con otros autores), Ed. Bosch, Barcelona, 1994, pág. 138.

Sobre la instrucción previa en el procedimiento ante el Jurado, Tribunales de Justicia, 2/1998.

PALLADINO, *Giustizia e Democracia*, Ed. Dot. A. Giuffré, Milano, 1969.

PASTOR LÓPEZ,

El sumario: su función y naturaleza jurídica, RDP, 1965, n. 1 (primera época).

El proceso penal especial de la ley del automóvil: examen crítico, RDP, 1966, n. 3 (primera época).

PEDRAZ PENALVA,

La Reforma procesal penal de la R. F. de Alemania de 1975, RDP,1976, ns. 2 y 3.

Sobre la crisis de la Justicia, Poder Judicial, 1988, n. 10.

El derecho a un proceso sin dilaciones indebidas, Poder Judicial, ns. 43 y 44, 1996.

PÉREZ CRUZ, *Reflexiones sobre la instrucción en el nuevo proceso penal ante el Tribunal del Jurado. Especial consideración de los artículos 24 a 33 de la Ley Orgánica 5/1995 del Tribunal del Jurado*, RGD, 1995, ns. 610-611.

PÉREZ GORDO, *La admisibilidad de los actos procesales*, RDP, 1980, n. 1.

PÉREZ MARTÍN Y SCHOLZ, *Legislación y jurisprudencia en la España del Antiguo Régimen*, Ed. Universidad de Valencia, Secretariado de Publicaciones.

PERRON,

Das Beweisantragsrecht des Beschuldigten im deutschen Strafprozess, Ed. Duncker & Humblot, Berlin, 1995.

Das Beweisantragsrecht des Beschuldigten - Ursache oder Symptom der Krise des deutschen Strafprozesses?, ZStW, 1996, T. 108.

PETERS, *Strafprozess*, Ed. Müller Juristischer Verlag, Heidelberg, 1985.

PEUKERT, *Die überlange Verfahrensdauer (Art. 6 Abs. 1 EMRK) in der Rechtsprechung der Strassburger Instanzen*, EuGRZ, 1979.

PICÓ I JUNOY, *El derecho a la prueba en el proceso civil*, Ed. Bosch, Barcelona, 1996.

PRIETO CASTRO,

Exposición de derecho procesal civil de España, 2 Ed., 1944, Zaragoza, T. I.

Cuestiones de Derecho Procesal, Instituto Editorial Reus, Madrid, 1947.

Derecho Procesal Penal (con Gutiérrez de Cabiedes), 3 Ed. Tecnos, Madrid, 1987.

PRIETO RODRÍGUEZ, *Dilaciones indebidas y Derecho penal*, Ed. Akal, 1997.

QUERALT Y JIMÉNEZ QUINTANA, *Manual de Policía Judicial, 2* Ed. Ministerio de Justicia, Secretaría General Técnica, Centro de Publicaciones, Madrid, 1989.

RAMOS MÉNDEZ,

La eficacia del proceso, Justicia, 1982, n. 2, pág. 97.

El Proceso Penal (lectura constitucional), Ed. Bosch S.A., Barcelona, 1991.

Meditación en la hora nona sobre las reformas procesales, Justicia, 1995, ns. 1 y 2, pág. 4.

RASCÓN ORTEGA, *El nuevo modelo de investigación sumarial en la Ley del Jurado y los diferentes papeles procesales que atribuye a sus protagonistas*, Poder Judicial, ns. 41-42.

REVERÓN PALENZUELA, *La contradicción procesal como garantía del derecho de defensa en la llamada "fase intermedia" del proceso penal por delito (II)*, La Ley, n. 4573, 1998.

RICCI, *Delle prove*, Torino, 1891.

RIECKER, *Die Ablehnung von Beweisanträgen in der Hauptverhandlung*, Tübingen, 1935.

ROCCO, *Trattato di diritto processuale civile*, 2 Ed., Utet, 1966, T. III.

RODRÍGUEZ LLAMOSÍ, *Las diligencias indeterminadas: a falta de una adecuada regulación de la materia*, Poder Judicial, 1995, n. 37.

ROXIN,

Strafverfahrensrecht, 20 Ed. C. H. Beck, München, 1987.

Strafverfahrensrecht, 22 Ed. C. H. Beck, München, 1991.

Strafverfahrensrecht, 24 Ed. C. H. Beck, München, 1995.

RÖMBKE, *Der Ablehnungsgrund wegen Prozessverschleppung gem. par. 244 Abs. 3 Satz 2 6.Fall StPO*, Münster, 1995.

RUIZ GUTIÉRREZ,

Algunos problemas de la instrucción en los Derechos francés, italiano y español y su crítica, RDP, 1956.

Crítica de la casación penal española, RDP, 1963, n. 1.

RUIZ VADILLO,

La actuación del Ministerio Fiscal en el proceso penal, Poder Judicial, Justicia Penal, 1987, n. especial II.

Algunas breves consideraciones sobre las dilaciones indebidas en el proceso penal español, BIMJ, 1993, n. 1690.

Estudios de Derecho procesal penal, Ed. Comares, Granada, 1995.

SABATINI, *Principi di Diritto Processuale Penale*, Ed. Casa del Libro, Catania, 1948, Vol. I.

SÁEZ JIMÉNEZ Y LÓPEZ, *Compendio de Derecho procesal, civil y penal*, Ed. Santillana, 1968, T. IV, Vol. II.

SAMUEL, *Die Ablehnbarkeit von Beweisanträgen und ihr Prinzip*, Greifswald, 1913.

SANCHÍS CRESPO,

El Ministerio Fiscal y el reconocimiento de hechos, RDP, 1996, n. 1.

El derecho fundamental a utilizar los medios de prueba pertinentes para la defensa (Un recorrido por la jurisprudencia constitucional), Tribunales de Justicia, págs. 521 y sigs.

SANDERMANN, *Waffengleihheit im Strafprozess*, Köln, 1975, págs. 179 y sigs.

SCHÄFER, *Die Praxis des Strafverfahrens*, 2 Ed. W. Kohlhammer, Stuttgart, 1980.

SCHEFFLER, *Verletzung des Beschleunigungsgebots als wesentlicher Strafmilderungsgrund*, StV 11/93.

SCHMIDT-ASSMANN, *Verfahrensgarantien im Bereich des öffentlichen Rechts* (Darstellung der Rechtslage in der Bundesrepublik Deutschland mit vergleichenden Hinweisen auf die Bundesver waltungsrechtspflege in der Schweiz im Blick auf Art. 6 Abs. 1 EMRK).

SCHMIDT-BLEIBTREU, *Klein Kommentar zum Grundgesetz,* 8 Ed. Luchterhand, Berlin, 1995.

SCHÖCH, *Kommentar zur Strafprozessordnung*, Ed. Luchterhand, Berlin, 1993, parágrafo 244.

SCHÖNKE,

Derecho Procesal civil, Barcelona, 1950.

Límites de la prueba en el derecho procesal, RDP, 1955, n. 3.

SCHULZ, *Die Erosion des Beweisantragsrechts*, StV 8/1991.

SENTÍS MELENDO,

Introducción al Derecho probatorio, RDP, 1965, n. 4.

Existencia y delimitación del derecho probatorio, RDP, 1968, n. 1.

Qué es la prueba (Naturaleza de la prueba), RDP, 1973, ns. 2-3.

La instrucción en el proceso penal, RDP, 1973, ns. 2-3.

Valoración de la prueba, RDP, 1976, ns. 2-3.

La prueba. Los grandes temas del Derecho Probatorio, Buenos Aires, 1979.

SERRA DOMÍNGUEZ, *Estudios de Derecho procesal*, Ed. Ariel, Barcelona, 1969.

SERRANO GÓMEZ,

El procedimiento abreviado y su dudosa constitucionalidad, A.P., 1990/1.

El procedimiento abreviado (Crisis de la jurisprudencia e indefensión), A. P., 1990/1.

SICARD, La preuve en Justice, Librairie du Journal des Notaires et des Avocats, Paris, 1960.

SILVA MELERO, *La prueba procesal*, Ed. Revista de Derecho Privado, Madrid, 1963, T. I.

SILVA SÁNCHEZ, *Las recomendaciones del Consejo de Europa sobre determinación judicial de la pena: algunas observaciones*, Revista de Ciencias Penales, 1988, Vol. I, n. 1, págs. 11 a 22.

SIMADER, *Die Ablehnung von Beweisanträgen in der Hauptverhandlung*, Ed. Hirschfeld, Feipzig, 1933.

SOTO VÁZQUEZ, *El auto de procesamiento y algunos de sus problemas*, RDP, 1966, n. 1.

STEIN, *El conocimiento privado del juez*, 2 Ed. Temis, Bogotá, 1988.

STINTZING Y HECKER, *Abschreckkung durch Haupverhandlungshaft?* -

Der neue Haftgrund des "vermuteten Ungehorsams", NStZ 12/1997.

STRATHMEYER HERMANN, *Die Beweisaufnahme während der Vorbereitung der Hauptverhandlung*, Disertación, 1933.

STÜTZEL, *Der Beweisantrag im Strafverfahren*, Ed. Hirschfeld, Leipzig, 1932.

TARUFFO, *Studi sulla rilevanza della prova*, Ed. Cedam, Padova, 1970.

THÉODOR, *L'interprétation des faits en Droit*, Librairie générale de droit et de jurisprudence, París, 1988.

THOLE, *Der Scheinbeweisantrag im Strafprozess*, Ed. Duncker & Humblot, Berlin, 1992.

TÖBBENS, Der Freibeweis und die Prozessvoraussetzungen im Strafprozess, NStZ, 1982, C. 5.

TOHARIA, *Cuarto Barómetro de opinión del Consejo General del Poder Judicial*, Poder Judicial, 1988, n. 12.

TEXTOS JURÍDICS CATALANS, *Usages y demás Derechos de Cataluña*, Ed. Generalitat de Catalunya, Departament de Justícia, Barcelona, 1989, Vol. I.

VÁZQUEZ SOTELO, *El principio acusatorio y su reflejo en el proceso penal español*, RJC, 1984, n. 2.

VEGAS TORRES, *La presunción de inocencia del artículo 24.2 de la Constitución en el proceso penal español (Tesis Doctoral n. 399/92)*, Ed. Universidad Complutense de Madrid, 1992.

VELAYOS MARTÍNEZ, *El derecho del imputado al silencio*, Justicia, 1995, ns. 1 y 2.

VÉLEZ MARICONDE, *La función judicial en lo penal*, RDP, 1968, n. 2.

VIADA,

Lecciones de Derecho procesal penal, Imprenta Alpe, Madrid, 1950.

La ausencia del acusado en el proceso penal, RDP, 1962, n. 3.

VIVES ANTÓN, *Doctrina constitucional y reforma del proceso penal*, Poder Judicial, n. especial II, Jornadas sobre la Justicia penal en España, 1987, págs. 93 y sigs.

VON GREYERZ, *Der Beweis negativer Tatsachen*, Ed. Stämpfli&Cie, Bern, 1963.

WIDMAIER, *Kritische Gedanken zur diskutieren Reform des Beweisantrags- und Revisionsrechts*, NStZ, 1994.

WILFINGER, *Das Gebot effektiven Rechtsschutzes in Grundgesetz und Europäischer Menschenrechtskonvention*, Ed. Peter Lang, Frankfurt, 1995.

ZAFRA,

La pertinencia de la prueba civil, RDP, 1960, (2a época), n. 1.

Posición del Ministerio Fiscal en el futuro proceso penal, RDP, 1961, n. 4.

ZUBIRI DE SALINAS, *La policía judicial*, Poder Judicial, 1990 (2), n. 19.

ZULETA, *El principio de lealtad en la prueba penal*, Revista Pretor, n. 61.

ANNEX

Finalized draft text of the Rules of Procedure and Evidence

Explanatory note

The Rules of Procedure and Evidence are an instrument for the application of the Rome Statute of the International Criminal Court, to which they are subordinate in all cases. In elaborating the Rules of Procedure and Evidence, care has been taken to avoid rephrasing and, to the extent possible, repeating the provisions of the Statute. Direct references to the Statute have been included in the Rules, where appropriate, in order to emphasize the relationship between the Rules and the Rome Statute, as provided for in article 51, in particular, paragraphs 4 and 5.

In all cases, the Rules of Procedure and Evidence should be read in conjunction with and subject to the provisions of the

Statute.

The Rules of Procedure and Evidence of the International Criminal Court do not affect the procedural rules for any national court or legal system for the purpose of national proceedings.

In connection with rule 41, the Preparatory Commission considered whether the application of the rule would be facilitated by including a provision in the Regulations of the Court that at least one of the judges of the Chamber in which the case is heard knows the official language used as a working language in a given case. The Assembly of States Parties is invited to give further consideration to this issue.

Chapter 1 General provisions

Rule 1

Use of terms

In the present document:

"article" refers to articles of the Rome Statute;

"Chamber" refers to a Chamber of the Court;

"Part" refers to the Parts of the Rome Statute;

"Presiding Judge" refers to the Presiding Judge of a Chamber;

"the President" refers to the President of the Court;

"the Regulations" refers to the Regulations of the Court;

"the Rules" refers to the Rules of Procedure and

Evidence.

Rule 2

Authentic texts

The Rules have been adopted in the official languages of the Court established by article 50, paragraph 1. All texts are equally authentic.

Rule 3

Amendments

1. Amendments to the rules that are proposed in accordance with article 51, paragraph 2, shall be forwarded to the President of the Bureau of the Assembly of States Parties.

2. The President of the Bureau of the Assembly of States Parties shall ensure that all proposed amendments are translated into the official languages of the Court and are transmitted to the States Parties.

3. The procedure described in sub-rules 1 and 2 shall also apply to the provisional rules referred to in article 51, paragraph 3.

Chapter 2 Composition and administration of the Court

Section I General provisions relating to the composition and administration of the Court

Rule 4

Plenary sessions

1. The judges shall meet in plenary session not later than two months after their election. At that first session, after having made their solemn undertaking, in conformity with rule 5, the judges shall:

(a) Elect the President and Vice-Presidents;

(b) Assign judges to divisions.

2. The judges shall meet subsequently in plenary session at least once a year to exercise their functions under the Statute, the Rules and the Regulations and, if necessary, in special plenary sessions convened by the President on his or her own motion or at the request of one half of the judges.

3. The quorum for each plenary session shall be two-thirds of the judges.

4. Unless otherwise provided in the Statute or the Rules, the decisions of the plenary sessions shall be taken by the majority of the judges present. In the event of an equality of votes, the President, or the judge acting in the place of the President, shall have a casting vote.

5. The Regulations shall be adopted as soon as possible in plenary sessions.

Rule 5

Solemn undertaking under article 45

1. As provided in article 45, before exercising their functions under the Statute, the following solemn undertakings shall be made:

(b) In the case of the Prosecutor, a Deputy Prosecutor, the Registrar and the Deputy Registrar of the Court:

"I solemnly undertake that I will perform my duties and exercise my powers as (title) of the International Criminal Court honourably, faithfully, impartially and conscientiously, and that I will respect the confidentiality of investigations and prosecutions."

2. The undertaking, signed by the person making it and witnessed by the President or a Vice-President of the Bureau of the Assembly of States Parties, shall be filed with the Registry and kept in the records of the Court.

Rule 6

Solemn undertaking by the staff of the Office of the Prosecutor, the Registry, interpreters and translators

"I solemnly undertake that I will perform my duties and exercise my powers as (title) of the International Criminal Court honourably, faithfully, impartially and conscientiously, and that I will respect the confidentiality of investigations and prosecutions.";

The undertaking, signed by the person making it and witnessed, as appropriate, by the Prosecutor, the Deputy Prosecutor, the Registrar or the Deputy Registrar, shall be filed with the Registry and kept in the records of the Court.

2. Before performing any duties, an interpreter or a translator shall make the following undertaking:

"I solemnly declare that I will perform my duties faithfully, impartially and with full respect for the duty of confidentiality.";

The undertaking, signed by the person making it and witnessed by the President of the Court or his or her representative, shall be filed with the Registry and kept in the records of the Court.

Rule 7

Single judge under article 39, paragraph 2 (b) (iii)

1. Whenever the Pre-Trial Chamber designates a judge as a single judge in accordance with article 39, paragraph 2 (b) (iii), it shall do so on the basis of objective pre-established criteria.

2. The designated judge shall make the appropriate decisions on those questions on which decision by the full Chamber is not expressly provided for in the Statute or the Rules.

3. The Pre-Trial Chamber, on its own motion or, if

appropriate, at the request of a party, may decide that the functions of the single judge be exercised by the full Chamber.

Rule 8

Code of Professional Conduct

1. The Presidency, on the basis of a proposal made by the Registrar, shall draw up a draft Code of Professional Conduct for counsel, after having consulted the Prosecutor. In the preparation of the proposal, the Registrar shall conduct the consultations in accordance with rule 20, sub-rule 3.

2. The draft Code shall then be transmitted to the Assembly of States Parties, for the purpose of adoption, according to article 112, paragraph 7.

3. The Code shall contain procedures for its amendment.

Section II

The Office of the Prosecutor

Rule 9

Operation of the Office of the Prosecutor

In discharging his or her responsibility for the management and administration of the Office of the Prosecutor, the Prosecutor shall put in place regulations to govern the operation of the Office. In preparing or amending these regulations, the Prosecutor shall consult with the Registrar on any matters that may affect the operation of the Registry.

Rule 10

Retention of information and evidence

Rule 11

Delegation of the Prosecutor's functions

Except for the inherent powers of the Prosecutor set forth in the Statute, inter alia, those described in articles 15 and 53, the Prosecutor or a Deputy Prosecutor may authorize staff members of the Office of the Prosecutor, other than those referred to in article 44, paragraph 4, to represent him or her in the exercise of his or her functions.

Section III
The Registry

Subsection 1

General provisions relating to the Registry

Rule 12

Qualifications and election of the Registrar and the Deputy Registrar

1. As soon as it is elected, the Presidency shall establish a list of candidates who satisfy the criteria laid down in article 43, paragraph 3, and shall transmit the list to the Assembly of States Parties with a request for any recommendations.

2. Upon receipt of any recommendations from the Assembly of States Parties, the President shall, without delay, transmit the list together with the recommendations to the plenary session.

3. As provided for in article 43, paragraph 4, the Court, meeting in plenary session, shall, as soon as possible, elect the Registrar by an absolute majority, taking into account any recommendations by the Assembly of States Parties. In the event that no candidate obtains an absolute majority on the first ballot, successive ballots shall be held until one candidate obtains an absolute majority.

4. If the need for a Deputy Registrar arises, the Registrar may make a recommendation to the President to that effect. The President shall convene a plenary session to decide on the matter. If the Court, meeting in plenary session, decides by an absolute majority that a Deputy Registrar is to be elected, the Registrar shall submit a list of candidates to the Court.

5. The Deputy Registrar shall be elected by the Court, meeting in plenary session, in the same manner as the Registrar.

Rule 13

Functions of the Registrar

Rule 14

Operation of the Registry

1. In discharging his or her responsibility for the organization and management of the Registry, the Registrar shall put in place regulations to govern the operation of the Registry. In preparing or amending these regulations, the Registrar shall consult with the Prosecutor on any matters which may affect the operation of the Office of the Prosecutor. The regulations shall be approved by the Presidency.

2. The regulations shall provide for defence counsel to have access to appropriate and reasonable administrative assistance from the Registry.

Rule 15

Records

1. The Registrar shall keep a database containing all the particulars of each case brought before the Court, subject to any order of a judge or Chamber providing for the non-disclosure of any document or information, and to the protection of sensitive personal data. Information on the database shall be available to the public in the working languages of the Court.

2. The Registrar shall also maintain the other records of the Court.

Subsection 2

Victims and Witnesses Unit

Rule 16

Responsibilities of the Registrar relating to victims and witnesses

1. In relation to victims, the Registrar shall be responsible for the performance of the following functions in accordance with the Statute and these Rules:

(a) Providing notice or notification to victims or their legal representatives;

(b) Assisting them in obtaining legal advice and organizing their legal representation, and providing their legal representatives with adequate support, assistance and information, including such facilities as may be necessary for the direct performance of their duty, for the purpose of protecting their rights during all stages of the proceedings in accordance with rules 89 to 91;

(c) Assisting them in participating in the different phases of the proceedings in accordance with rules 89 to 91;

(d) Taking gender-sensitive measures to facilitate the participation of victims of sexual violence at all stages of the proceedings.

2. In relation to victims, witnesses and others who are at risk on account of testimony given by such witnesses, the Registrar shall be responsible for the performance of the following functions in accordance with the Statute and these Rules:

(a) Informing them of their rights under the Statute and the Rules, and of the existence, functions and availability of the Victims and Witnesses Unit;

(b) Ensuring that they are aware, in a timely manner, of the relevant decisions of the Court that may have an impact on their interests, subject to provisions on confidentiality.

3. For the fulfilment of his or her functions, the Registrar may keep a special register for victims who have expressed their intention to participate in relation to a specific case.

4. Agreements on relocation and provision of support services on the territory of a State of traumatized or threatened victims, witnesses and others who are at risk on account of testimony given by such witnesses may be negotiated with the States by the Registrar on behalf of the Court. Such agreements may remain confidential.

Rule 17
Functions of the Unit

1. The Victims and Witnesses Unit shall exercise its functions

in accordance with article 43, paragraph 6.

2. The Victims and Witnesses Unit shall, inter alia, perform the following functions, in accordance with the Statute and the Rules, and in consultation with the Chamber, the Prosecutor and the defence, as appropriate:

(a) With respect to all witnesses, victims who appear before the Court, and others who are at risk on account of testimony given by such witnesses, in accordance with their particular needs and circumstances:

(i) Providing them with adequate protective and security measures and formulating long- and short-term plans for their protection;
(ii) Recommending to the organs of the Court the adoption of protection measures and also advising relevant States of such measures;
(iii) Assisting them in obtaining medical, psychological and other appropriate assistance;
(iv) Making available to the Court and the parties training in issues of trauma, sexual violence, security and confidentiality;
(v) Recommending, in consultation with the Office of the Prosecutor, the elaboration of a code of conduct, emphasizing the vital nature of security and confidentiality for investigators of the Court and of the defence and all intergovernmental and non-governmental organizations

acting at the request of the Court, as appropriate;

(vi) Cooperating with States, where necessary, in providing any of the measures stipulated in this rule;

(b) With respect to witnesses:

(i) Advising them where to obtain legal advice for the purpose of protecting their rights, in particular in relation to their testimony;

(ii) Assisting them when they are called to testify before the Court;

(iii) Taking gender-sensitive measures to facilitate the testimony of victims of sexual violence at all stages of the proceedings.

3. In performing its functions, the Unit shall give due regard to the particular needs of children, elderly persons and persons with disabilities. In order to facilitate the participation and protection of children as witnesses, the Unit may assign, as appropriate, and with the agreement of the parents or the legal guardian, a child-support person to assist a child through all stages of the proceedings.

Rule 18

Responsibilities of the Unit

For the efficient and effective performance of its work, the

Victims and Witnesses Unit shall:

(a) Ensure that the staff in the Unit maintain confidentiality at all times;

(b) While recognizing the specific interests of the Office of the Prosecutor, the defence and the witnesses, respect the interests of the witness, including, where necessary, by maintaining an appropriate separation of the services provided to the prosecution and defence witnesses, and act impartially when cooperating with all parties and in accordance with the rulings and decisions of the Chambers;

(c) Have administrative and technical assistance available for witnesses, victims who appear before the Court, and others who are at risk on account of testimony given by such witnesses, during all stages of the proceedings and thereafter, as reasonably appropriate;

(d) Ensure training of its staff with respect to victims' and witnesses' security, integrity and dignity, including matters related to gender and cultural sensitivity;

(e) Where appropriate, cooperate with intergovernmental and non-governmental organizations.

Rule 19

Expertise in the Unit

In addition to the staff mentioned in article 43, paragraph 6, and subject to article 44, the Victims and Witnesses Unit may include, as appropriate, persons with expertise, inter alia, in the following areas:

(a) Witness protection and security;

(b) Legal and administrative matters, including areas of humanitarian and criminal law;

(c) Logistics administration;

(d) Psychology in criminal proceedings;

(e) Gender and cultural diversity;

(f) Children, in particular traumatized children;

(g) Elderly persons, in particular in connection with armed conflict and exile trauma;

(h) Persons with disabilities;

(i) Social work and counselling;

(j) Health care;

(k) Interpretation and translation.

Subsection 3

Counsel for the defence

Rule 20

Responsibilities of the Registrar relating to the rights of the defence

1. In accordance with article 43, paragraph 1, the Registrar

shall organize the staff of the Registry in a manner that promotes the rights of the defence, consistent with the principle of fair trial as defined in the Statute. For that purpose, the Registrar shall, inter alia:

(a) Facilitate the protection of confidentiality, as defined in article 67, paragraph 1 (b);

(b) Provide support, assistance, and information to all defence counsel appearing before the Court and, as appropriate, support for professional investigators necessary for the efficient and effective conduct of the defence;

(c) Assist arrested persons, persons to whom article 55, paragraph 2, applies and the accused in obtaining legal advice and the assistance of legal counsel;

(d) Advise the Prosecutor and the Chambers, as necessary, on relevant defence-related issues;

(e) Provide the defence with such facilities as may be necessary for the direct performance of the duty of the defence;

(f) Facilitate the dissemination of information and case law of the Court to defence counsel and, as appropriate, cooperate with national defence and bar associations or any independent representative body of counsel and legal associations referred to in sub-rule 3 to promote the specialization and training of lawyers in the law of the Statute and the Rules.

2. The Registrar shall carry out the functions stipulated in sub-rule 1, including the financial administration of the Registry, in such a manner as to ensure the professional

independence of defence counsel.

3. For purposes such as the management of legal assistance in accordance with rule 21 and the development of a Code of Professional Conduct in accordance with rule 8, the Registrar shall consult, as appropriate, with any independent representative body of counsel or legal associations, including any such body the establishment of which may be facilitated by the Assembly of States Parties.

Rule 21

Assignment of legal assistance

1. Subject to article 55, paragraph 2 (c), and article 67, paragraph 1 (d), criteria and procedures for assignment of legal assistance shall be established in the Regulations, based on a proposal by the Registrar, following consultations with any independent representative body of counsel or legal associations, as referred to in rule 20, sub-rule 3.

2. The Registrar shall create and maintain a list of counsel who meet the criteria set forth in rule 22 and the Regulations. The person shall freely choose his or her counsel from this list or other counsel who meets the required criteria and is willing to be included in the list.

3. A person may seek from the Presidency a review of a decision to refuse a request for assignment of counsel. The decision of the Presidency shall be final. If a request is refused,

a further request may be made by a person to the Registrar, upon showing a change in circumstances.

4. A person choosing to represent himself or herself shall so notify the Registrar in writing at the first opportunity.

5. Where a person claims to have insufficient means to pay for legal assistance and this is subsequently found not to be so, the Chamber dealing with the case at that time may make an order of contribution to recover the cost of providing counsel.

Rule 22

Appointment and qualifications of Counsel for the defence

1. A counsel for the defence shall have established competence in international or criminal law and procedure, as well as the necessary relevant experience, whether as judge, prosecutor, advocate or in other similar capacity, in criminal proceedings. A counsel for the defence shall have an excellent knowledge of and be fluent in at least one of the working languages of the Court. Counsel for the defence may be assisted by other persons, including professors of law, with relevant expertise.

2. Counsel for the defence engaged by a person exercising his or her right under the Statute to retain legal counsel of his or her choosing shall file a power of attorney with the Registrar at the earliest opportunity.

3. In the performance of their duties, Counsel for the defence shall be subject to the Statute, the Rules, the Regulations,

the Code of Professional Conduct for Counsel adopted in accordance with rule 8 and any other document adopted by the Court that may be relevant to the performance of their duties.

Section IV

Situations that may affect the functioning of the Court

Subsection 1
Removal from office and disciplinary measures

Rule 23
General principle

A judge, the Prosecutor, a Deputy Prosecutor, the Registrar and a Deputy Registrar shall be removed from office or shall be subject to disciplinary measures in such cases and with such guarantees as are established in the Statute and the Rules.

Rule 24
Definition of serious misconduct and serious breach of duty

1. For the purposes of article 46, paragraph 1 (a), "serious misconduct" shall be constituted by conduct that:

(a) If it occurs in the course of official duties, is incompatible with official functions, and causes or is likely to cause serious harm to the proper administration of justice before the Court or the proper internal functioning of the Court, such as:

(i) Disclosing facts or information that he or she has acquired in the course of his or her duties or on a matter which is sub judice, where such disclosure is seriously prejudicial to the judicial proceedings or to any person;

(ii) Concealing information or circumstances of a nature sufficiently serious to have precluded him or her from holding office;

(iii) Abuse of judicial office in order to obtain unwarranted favourable treatment from any authorities, officials or professionals; or

(b) If it occurs outside the course of official duties, is of a grave nature that causes or is likely to cause serious harm to the standing of the Court.

2. For the purposes of article 46, paragraph 1 (a), a "serious breach of duty" occurs where a person has been grossly negligent in the performance of his or her duties or has knowingly acted in contravention of those duties. This may include, inter alia, situations where the person:

Interfering in the exercise of the functions of a person referred to in article 47;

(ii) Repeatedly failing to comply with or ignoring

requests made by the Presiding Judge or by the Presidency in the exercise of their lawful authority;

(iii) Failing to enforce the disciplinary measures to which the Registrar or a Deputy Registrar and other officers of the Court are subject when a judge knows or should know of a serious breach of duty on their part; or

(b) If it occurs outside the course of official duties, causes or is likely to cause harm to the standing of the Court.

2. Nothing in this rule precludes the possibility of the conduct set out in sub-rule 1 (a) constituting "serious misconduct" or "serious breach of duty" for the purposes of article 46, paragraph 1 (a).

Rule 26

Receipt of complaints

1. For the purposes of article 46, paragraph 1, and article 47, any complaint concerning any conduct defined under rules 24 and 25 shall include the grounds on which it is based, the identity of the complainant and, if available, any relevant evidence. The complaint shall remain confidential.

2. All complaints shall be transmitted to the Presidency, which may also initiate proceedings on its own motion, and which shall, pursuant to the Regulations, set aside anonymous or manifestly unfounded complaints and transmit the other

complaints to the competent organ. The Presidency shall be assisted in this task by one or more judges, appointed on the basis of automatic rotation, in accordance with the Regulations.

Rule 27

Common provisions on the rights of the defence

Rule 28

Suspension from duty

Where an allegation against a person who is the subject of a complaint is of a sufficiently serious nature, the person may be suspended from duty pending the final decision of the competent organ.

Rule 29

Procedure in the event of a request for removal from office

1. In the case of a judge, the Registrar or a Deputy Registrar, the question of removal from office shall be put to a vote at a plenary session.

2. The Presidency shall advise the President of the Bureau of the Assembly of States Parties in writing of any recommendation adopted in the case of a judge, and any decision adopted in the

case of the Registrar or a Deputy Registrar.

3.The Prosecutor shall advise the President of the Bureau of the Assembly of States Parties in writing of any recommendation he or she makes in the case of a Deputy Prosecutor.

4.Where the conduct is found not to amount to serious misconduct or a serious breach of duty, it may be decided in accordance with article 47 that the person concerned has engaged in misconduct of a less serious nature and a disciplinary measure imposed.

Rule 30

Procedure in the event of a request for disciplinary measures

1. In the case of a judge, the Registrar or a Deputy Registrar, any decision to impose a disciplinary measure shall be taken by the Presidency.

2. In the case of the Prosecutor, any decision to impose a disciplinary measure shall be taken by an absolute majority of the Bureau of the Assembly of States Parties.

3. In the case of a Deputy Prosecutor:

(a) Any decision to give a reprimand shall be taken by the Prosecutor;

(b) Any decision to impose a pecuniary sanction shall be taken by an absolute majority of the Bureau of the Assembly of

States Parties upon the recommendation of the Prosecutor.

4. Reprimands shall be recorded in writing and shall be transmitted to the President of the Bureau of the Assembly of States Parties.

Rule 31

Removal from office

Once removal from office has been pronounced, it shall take effect immediately. The person concerned shall cease to form part of the Court, including for unfinished cases in which he or she was taking part.

Rule 32

Disciplinary measures

The disciplinary measures that may be imposed are:

(a) A reprimand; or

(b) A pecuniary sanction that may not exceed six months of the salary paid by the Court to the person concerned.

Subsection 2

Excusing, disqualification, death and resignation

Rule 33
Excusing of a judge, the Prosecutor or a Deputy Prosecutor

1. A judge, the Prosecutor or a Deputy Prosecutor seeking to be excused from his or her functions shall make a request in writing to the Presidency, setting out the grounds upon which he or she should be excused.

Rule 34
Disqualification of a judge, the Prosecutor or a Deputy Prosecutor

1. In addition to the grounds set out in article 41, paragraph 2, and article 42, paragraph 7, the grounds for disqualification of a judge, the Prosecutor or a Deputy Prosecutor shall include, inter alia, the following:

(a) Personal interest in the case, including a spousal, parental or other close family, personal or professional relationship, or a subordinate relationship, with any of the parties;

(b) Involvement, in his or her private capacity, in any legal proceedings initiated prior to his or her involvement in the case, or initiated by him or her subsequently, in which the person being investigated or prosecuted was or is an opposing party;

(c) Performance of functions, prior to taking office, during which he or she could be expected to have formed an opinion on the case in question, on the parties or on their legal representatives that, objectively, could adversely affect the required impartiality of the person concerned;

(d) Expression of opinions, through the communications media, in writing or in public actions, that, objectively, could adversely affect the required impartiality of the person concerned.

2. Subject to the provisions set out in article 41, paragraph 2, and article 42, paragraph 8, a request for disqualification shall be made in writing as soon as there is knowledge of the grounds on which it is based. The request shall state the grounds and attach any relevant evidence, and shall be transmitted to the person concerned, who shall be entitled to present written submissions.

3. Any question relating to the disqualification of the Prosecutor or a Deputy Prosecutor shall be decided by a majority of the judges of the Appeals Chamber.

Rule 35

Duty of a judge, the Prosecutor or a Deputy Prosecutor to request to beexcused

Where a judge, the Prosecutor or a Deputy Prosecutor has reason to believe that a ground for disqualification exists in relation to him or her, he or she shall make a request to be excused and shall not wait for a request for disqualification to be made in accordance with article 41, paragraph 2, or article 42, paragraph 7, and rule 34. The request shall be made and the Presidency shall deal with it in accordance with rule 33.

Rule 36

Death of a judge, the Prosecutor, a Deputy Prosecutor, the Registrar or a Deputy Registrar

The Presidency shall inform, in writing, the President of the Bureau of the Assembly of States Parties of the death of a judge, the Prosecutor, a Deputy Prosecutor, the Registrar or a Deputy Registrar.

Rule 37

Resignation of a judge, the Prosecutor, a Deputy Prosecutor, the Registrar or a Deputy Registrar

Subsection 3

Replacements and alternate judges

Rule 38
Replacements

1. A judge may be replaced for objective and justified reasons, inter alia:

(a) Resignation;
(b) Accepted excuse;
(c) Disqualification;
(d) Removal from office;
(e) Death.

2. Replacement shall take place in accordance with the pre-established procedure in the Statute, the Rules and the Regulations.

Rule 39
Alternate judges

Where an alternate judge has been assigned by the Presidency to a Trial Chamber pursuant to article 74, paragraph 1, he or she shall sit through all proceedings and deliberations of the case, but may not take any part therein and shall not exercise any of the functions of the members of the Trial Chamber hearing the case, unless and until he or she is required to replace a member of the Trial Chamber if that member is unable to continue attending. Alternate judges shall be designated in accordance with a procedure pre-established by the Court.

Section V

Publication, languages and translation

Rule 40

Publication of decisions in official languages of the Court

2. Decisions on confirmation of charges under article 61, paragraph 7, and on offences against the administration of justice under article 70, paragraph 3, shall be published in all the official languages of the Court when the Presidency determines that they resolve fundamental issues.

3. The Presidency may decide to publish other decisions in all the official languages when such decisions concern major issues relating to the interpretation or the implementation of the Statute or concern a major issue of general interest.

Rule 41

Working languages of the Court

1. For the purposes of article 50, paragraph 2, the Presidency

shall authorize the use of an official language of the Court as a working language when:

(a) That language is understood and spoken by the majority of those involved in a case before the Court and any of the participants in the proceedings so requests; or

(b) The Prosecutor and the defence so request.

2. The Presidency may authorize the use of an official language of the Court as a working language if it considers that it would facilitate the efficiency of the proceedings.

Rule 42

Translation and interpretation services

Rule 43

Procedure applicable to the publication of documents of the Court

Chapter 3 Jurisdiction and admissibility

Section I

Declarations and referrals relating to articles 11, 12, 13 and 14

Rule 44

Declaration provided for in article 12, paragraph 3

1. The Registrar, at the request of the Prosecutor, may inquire of a State that is not a Party to the Statute or that has become a Party to the Statute after its entry into force, on a confidential basis, whether it intends to make the declaration provided for in article 12, paragraph 3.

2. When a State lodges, or declares to the Registrar its intent to lodge, a declaration with the Registrar pursuant to article 12, paragraph 3, or when the Registrar acts pursuant to sub-rule 1, the Registrar shall inform the State concerned that the declaration under article 12, paragraph 3, has as a consequence the acceptance of jurisdiction with respect to the crimes referred to in article 5 of relevance to the situation and the provisions of Part 9, and any rules thereunder concerning States Parties, shall apply.

Rule 45

Referral of a situation to the Prosecutor

Section II

Initiation of investigations under article 15

Rule 46

Information provided to the Prosecutor under article 15, paragraphs 1 and 2

Where information is submitted under article 15, paragraph 1, or where oral or written testimony is received pursuant to article 15, paragraph 2, at the seat of the Court, the Prosecutor shall protect the confidentiality of such information and testimony or take any other necessary measures, pursuant to his or her duties under the Statute.

Rule 47

Testimony under article 15, paragraph 2

1. The provisions of rules 111 and 112 shall apply, mutatis mutandis, to testimony received by the Prosecutor pursuant to article 15, paragraph 2.

2. When the Prosecutor considers that there is a serious risk that it might not be possible for the testimony to be taken subsequently, he or she may request the Pre-Trial Chamber to take such measures as may be necessary to ensure the efficiency and integrity of the proceedings and, in particular, to appoint a counsel or a judge from the Pre-Trial Chamber to be present during the taking of the testimony in order to protect the rights of the defence. If the testimony is subsequently presented in the proceedings, its admissibility shall be governed by article

69, paragraph 4, and given such weight as determined by the relevant Chamber.

Rule 48

Determination of reasonable basis to proceed with an investigation under article 15, paragraph 3

In determining whether there is a reasonable basis to proceed with an investigation under article 15, paragraph 3, the Prosecutor shall consider the factors set out in article 53, paragraph 1 (a) to (c).

Rule 49

Decision and notice under article 15, paragraph 6

Rule 50

Procedure for authorization by the Pre-Trial Chamber of the commencement of the investigation

Section III

Challenges and preliminary rulings under articles 17, 18 and 19

Rule 51

Information provided under article 17

In considering the matters referred to in article 17, paragraph 2, and in the context of the circumstances of the case, the Court may consider, inter alia, information that the State referred to in article 17, paragraph 1, may choose to bring to the attention of the Court showing that its courts meet internationally recognized norms and standards for the independent and impartial prosecution of similar conduct, or that the State has confirmed in writing to the Prosecutor that the case is being investigated or prosecuted.

Rule 52

Notification provided for in article 18, paragraph 1

Rule 53

Deferral provided for in article 18, paragraph 2

When a State requests a deferral pursuant to article 18, paragraph 2, that State shall make this request in writing and provide information concerning its investigation, taking into account article 18, paragraph 2. The Prosecutor may request additional information from that State.

Rule 54
Application by the Prosecutor under article 18, paragraph 2

1. An application submitted by the Prosecutor to the Pre-Trial Chamber in accordance with article 18, paragraph 2, shall be in writing and shall contain the basis for the application. The information provided by the State under rule 53 shall be communicated by the Prosecutor to the Pre-Trial Chamber.

2. The Prosecutor shall inform that State in writing when he or she makes an application to the Pre-Trial Chamber under article 18, paragraph 2, and shall include in the notice a summary of the basis of the application.

Rule 55
Proceedings concerning article 18, paragraph 2

1. The Pre-Trial Chamber shall decide on the procedure to be followed and may take appropriate measures for the proper conduct of the proceedings. It may hold a hearing.

2. The Pre-Trial Chamber shall examine the Prosecutor's application and any observations submitted by a State that requested a deferral in accordance with article 18, paragraph 2, and shall consider the factors in article 17 in deciding whether to authorize an investigation.

3. The decision and the basis for the decision of the Pre-

Trial Chamber shall be communicated as soon as possible to the Prosecutor and to the State that requested a deferral of an investigation.

Rule 56

Application by the Prosecutor following review under article 18, paragraph 3

Rule 57

Provisional measures under article 18, paragraph 6

Rule 58

Proceedings under article 19

1. A request or application made under article 19 shall be in writing and contain the basis for it.

2. When a Chamber receives a request or application raising a challenge or question concerning its jurisdiction or the admissibility of a case in accordance with article 19, paragraph 2 or 3, or is acting on its own motion as provided for in article 19, paragraph 1, it shall decide on the procedure to be followed and may take appropriate measures for the proper conduct of the proceedings. It may hold a hearing. It may join the challenge or question to a confirmation or a trial proceeding as long as this does not cause undue delay, and in this circumstance shall hear

and decide on the challenge or question first.

3. The Court shall transmit a request or application received under sub-rule 2 to the Prosecutor and to the person referred to in article 19, paragraph 2, who has been surrendered to the Court or who has appeared voluntarily or pursuant to a summons, and shall allow them to submit written observations to the request or application within a period of time determined by the Chamber.

4. The Court shall rule on any challenge or question of jurisdiction first and then on any challenge or question of admissibility.

Rule 59

Participation in proceedings under article 19, paragraph 3

1. For the purpose of article 19, paragraph 3, the Registrar shall inform the following of any question or challenge of jurisdiction or admissibility which has arisen pursuant to article 19, paragraphs 1, 2 and 3:

(a) Those who have referred a situation pursuant to article 13;

(b) The victims who have already communicated with the Court in relation to that case or their legal representatives.

2. The Registrar shall provide those referred to in sub-rule 1,

in a manner consistent with the duty of the Court regarding the confidentiality of information, the protection of any person and the preservation of evidence, with a summary of the grounds on which the jurisdiction of the Court or the admissibility of the case has been challenged.

3. Those receiving the information, as provided for in sub-rule 1, may make representation in writing to the competent Chamber within such time limit as it considers appropriate.

Rule 60

Competent organ to receive challenges

If a challenge to the jurisdiction of the Court or to the admissibility of a case is made after a confirmation of the charges but before the constitution or designation of the Trial Chamber, it shall be addressed to the Presidency, which shall refer it to the Trial Chamber as soon as the latter is constituted or designated in accordance with rule 130.

Rule 61

Provisional measures under article 19, paragraph 8

Rule 62

Proceedings under article 19, paragraph 10

1. If the Prosecutor makes a request under article 19, paragraph 10, he or she shall make the request to the Chamber that made the latest ruling on admissibility. The provisions of rules 58, 59 and 61 shall be applicable.

2. The State or States whose challenge to admissibility under article 19, paragraph 2, provoked the decision of inadmissibility provided for in article 19, paragraph 10, shall be notified of the request of the Prosecutor and shall be given a time limit within which to make representations.

Chapter 4 Provisions relating to various stages of the proceedings

Section I

Evidence

Rule 63

General provisions relating to evidence

1. The rules of evidence set forth in this chapter, together with article 69, shall apply in proceedings before all Chambers.

2. A Chamber shall have the authority, in accordance with the discretion described in article 64, paragraph 9, to assess freely all evidence submitted in order to determine its relevance or admissibility in accordance with article 69.

3. A Chamber shall rule on an application of a party or on

its own motion, made under article 64, subparagraph 9 (a), concerning admissibility when it is based on the grounds set out in article 69, paragraph 7.

4. Without prejudice to article 66, paragraph 3, a Chamber shall not impose a legal requirement that corroboration is required in order to prove any crime within the jurisdiction of the Court, in particular, crimes of sexual violence.

5. The Chambers shall not apply national laws governing evidence, other than in accordance with article 21.

Rule 64

Procedure relating to the relevance or admissibility of evidence

1. An issue relating to relevance or admissibility must be raised at the time when the evidence is submitted to a Chamber. Exceptionally, when those issues were not known at the time when the evidence was submitted, it may be raised immediately after the issue has become known. The Chamber may request that the issue be raised in writing. The written motion shall be communicated by the Court to all those who participate in the proceedings, unless otherwise decided by the Court.

2. A Chamber shall give reasons for any rulings it makes on evidentiary matters. These reasons shall be placed in the record of the proceedings if they have not already been incorporated into the record during the course of the proceedings in

accordance with article 64, paragraph 10, and rule 137, sub-rule 1.

3. Evidence ruled irrelevant or inadmissible shall not be considered by the Chamber.

Rule 65

Compellability of witnesses

Rule 66

Solemn undertaking

1. Except as described in sub-rule 2, every witness shall, in accordance with article 69, paragraph 1, make the following solemn undertaking before testifying:

"I solemnly declare that I will speak the truth, the whole truth and nothing but the truth."

2. A person under the age of 18 or a person whose judgement has been impaired and who, in the opinion of the Chamber, does not understand the nature of a solemn undertaking may be allowed to testify without this solemn undertaking if the Chamber considers that the person is able to describe matters of which he or she has knowledge and that the person understands the meaning of the duty to speak the truth.

3. Before testifying, the witness shall be informed of the offence defined in article 70, paragraph 1 (a).

Rule 67

Live testimony by means of audio or video-link technology

1. In accordance with article 69, paragraph 2, a Chamber may allow a witness to give viva voce (oral) testimony before the Chamber by means of audio or video technology, provided that such technology permits the witness to be examined by the Prosecutor, the defence, and by the Chamber itself, at the time that the witness so testifies.

2. The examination of a witness under this rule shall be conducted in accordance with the relevant rules of this chapter.

3. The Chamber, with the assistance of the Registry, shall ensure that the venue chosen for the conduct of the audio or video-link testimony is conducive to the giving of truthful and open testimony and to the safety, physical and psychological well-being, dignity and privacy of the witness.

Rule 68

Prior recorded testimony

When the Pre-Trial Chamber has not taken measures under article 56, the Trial Chamber may, in accordance with article 69, paragraph 2, allow the introduction of previously recorded audio or video testimony of a witness, or the transcript or other documented evidence of such testimony, provided that:

(a) If the witness who gave the previously recorded testimony is not present before the Trial Chamber, both the Prosecutor and the defence had the opportunity to examine the witness during the recording; or

(b) If the witness who gave the previously recorded testimony is present before the Trial Chamber, he or she does not object to the submission of the previously recorded testimony and the Prosecutor, the defence and the Chamber have the opportunity to examine the witness during the proceedings.

Rule 69

Agreements as to evidence

The Prosecutor and the defence may agree that an alleged fact, which is contained in the charges, the contents of a document, the expected testimony of a witness or other evidence is not contested and, accordingly, a Chamber may consider such alleged fact as being proven, unless the Chamber is of the opinion that a more complete presentation of the alleged facts is required in the interests of justice, in particular the interests of the victims.

Rule 70

Principles of evidence in cases of sexual violence

In cases of sexual violence, the Court shall be guided by and, where appropriate, apply the following principles:

(a) Consent cannot be inferred by reason of any words or conduct of a victim where force, threat of force, coercion or taking advantage of a coercive environment undermined the victim's ability to give voluntary and genuine consent;

(b) Consent cannot be inferred by reason of any words or conduct of a victim where the victim is incapable of giving genuine consent;

(c) Consent cannot be inferred by reason of the silence of, or lack of resistance by, a victim to the alleged sexual violence;

(d) Credibility, character or predisposition to sexual availability of a victim or witness cannot be inferred by reason of the sexual nature of the prior or subsequent conduct of a victim or witness.

Rule 71

Evidence of other sexual conduct

In the light of the definition and nature of the crimes within the jurisdiction of the Court, and subject to article 69, paragraph 4, a Chamber shall not admit evidence of the prior or subsequent sexual conduct of a victim or witness.

Rule 72

In camera procedure to consider relevance or admissibility of evidence

1. Where there is an intention to introduce or elicit, including by means of the questioning of a victim or witness, evidence that the victim consented to an alleged crime of sexual violence, or evidence of the words, conduct, silence or lack of resistance of a victim or witness as referred to in principles (a) through (d) of rule 70, notification shall be provided to the Court which shall describe the substance of the evidence intended to be introduced or elicited and the relevance of the evidence to the issues in the case.

2. In deciding whether the evidence referred to in sub-rule 1 is relevant or admissible, a Chamber shall hear in camera the views of the Prosecutor, the defence, the witness and the victim or his or her legal representative, if any, and shall take into account whether that evidence has a sufficient degree of probative value to an issue in the case and the prejudice that such evidence may cause, in accordance with article 69, paragraph 4. For this purpose, the Chamber shall have regard to article 21, paragraph 3, and articles 67 and 68, and shall be guided by principles (a) to (d) of rule 70, especially with respect to the proposed questioning of a victim.

3. Where the Chamber determines that the evidence referred to in sub-rule 2 is admissible in the proceedings, the Chamber shall state on the record the specific purpose for which the

evidence is admissible. In evaluating the evidence during the proceedings, the Chamber shall apply principles (a) to (d) of rule 70.

Rule 73

Privileged communications and information

1. Without prejudice to article 67, paragraph 1 (b), communications made in the context of the professional relationship between a person and his or her legal counsel shall be regarded as privileged, and consequently not subject to disclosure, unless:

(a) The person consents in writing to such disclosure; or

(b) The person voluntarily disclosed the content of the communication to a third party, and that third party then gives evidence of that disclosure.

2. Having regard to rule 63, sub-rule 5, communications made in the context of a class of professional or other confidential relationships shall be regarded as privileged, and consequently not subject to disclosure, under the same terms as in sub-rules 1 (a) and 1 (b) if a Chamber decides in respect of that class that:

(a) Communications occurring within that class of relationship are made in the course of a confidential relationship producing a reasonable expectation of privacy and non-disclosure;

(b) Confidentiality is essential to the nature and type of relationship between the person and the confidant; and

(c) Recognition of the privilege would further the objectives of the Statute and the Rules.

3. In making a decision under sub-rule 2, the Court shall give particular regard to recognizing as privileged those communications made in the context of the professional relationship between a person and his or her medical doctor, psychiatrist, psychologist or counsellor, in particular those related to or involving victims, or between a person and a member of a religious clergy; and in the latter case, the Court shall recognize as privileged those communications made in the context of a sacred confession where it is an integral part of the practice of that religion.

4. The Court shall regard as privileged, and consequently not subject to disclosure, including by way of testimony of any present or past official or employee of the International Committee of the Red Cross (ICRC), any information, documents or other evidence which it came into the possession of in the course, or as a consequence, of the performance by ICRC of its functions under the Statutes of the International Red Cross and Red Crescent Movement, unless:

(a) After consultations undertaken pursuant to sub-rule 6, ICRC does not object in writing to such disclosure, or otherwise has waived this privilege; or

(b) Such information, documents or other evidence is contained in public statements and documents of ICRC.

5. Nothing in sub-rule 4 shall affect the admissibility of the same evidence obtained from a source other than ICRC and its officials or employees when such evidence has also been acquired by this source independently of ICRC and its officials or employees.

6. If the Court determines that ICRC information, documents or other evidence are of great importance for a particular case, consultations shall be held between the Court and ICRC in order to seek to resolve the matter by cooperative means, bearing in mind the circumstances of the case, the relevance of the evidence sought, whether the evidence could be obtained from a source other than ICRC, the interests of justice and of victims, and the performance of the Court's and ICRC's functions.

Rule 74
Self-incrimination by a witness

1. Unless a witness has been notified pursuant to rule 190, the Chamber shall notify a witness of the provisions of this rule before his or her testimony.

2. Where the Court determines that an assurance with respect to self-incrimination should be provided to a particular witness,

it shall provide the assurances under sub-rule 3, paragraph (c), before the witness attends, directly or pursuant to a request under article 93, paragraph (1) (e).

3.(a) A witness may object to making any statement that might tend to incriminate him or her.

(b) Where the witness has attended after receiving an assurance under sub-rule 2, the Court may require the witness to answer the question or questions.

(c) In the case of other witnesses, the Chamber may require the witness to answer the question or questions, after assuring the witness that the evidence provided in response to the questions:

(i) Will be kept confidential and will not be disclosed to the public or any State; and

(ii) Will not be used either directly or indirectly against that person in any subsequent prosecution by the Court, except under articles 70 and 71.

4. Before giving such an assurance, the Chamber shall seek the views of the Prosecutor, ex parte, to determine if the assurance should be given to this particular witness.

5. In determining whether to require the witness to answer, the Chamber shall consider:

(a) The importance of the anticipated evidence;

(b) Whether the witness would be providing unique evidence;

(c) The nature of the possible incrimination, if known; and

(d) The sufficiency of the protections for the witness, in the particular circumstances.

6. If the Chamber determines that it would not be appropriate to provide an assurance to this witness, it shall not require the witness to answer the question. If the Chamber determines not to require the witness to answer, it may still continue the questioning of the witness on other matters.

7. In order to give effect to the assurance, the Chamber shall:

(a) Order that the evidence of the witness be given in camera;

(b) Order that the identity of the witness and the content of the evidence given shall not be disclosed, in any manner, and provide that the breach of any such order will be subject to sanction under article 71;

(c) Specifically advise the Prosecutor, the accused, the defence counsel, the legal representative of the victim and any Court staff present of the consequences of a breach of the order under subparagraph (b);

(d) Order the sealing of any record of the proceedings; and

(e) Use protective measures with respect to any decision of the Court to ensure that the identity of the witness and the content of the evidence given are not disclosed.

8. Where the Prosecutor is aware that the testimony of any witness may raise issues with respect to self-incrimination, he or she shall request an in camera hearing and advise the Chamber of this, in advance of the testimony of the witness. The Chamber may impose the measures outlined in sub-rule 7 for all or a part of the testimony of that witness.

9. The accused, the defence counsel or the witness may advise the Prosecutor or the Chamber that the testimony of a witness will raise issues of self-incrimination before the witness testifies and the Chamber may take the measures outlined in sub-rule 7.

10. If an issue of self-incrimination arises in the course of the proceedings, the Chamber shall suspend the taking of the testimony and provide the witness with an opportunity to obtain legal advice if he or she so requests for the purpose of the application of the rule.

Rule 75

Incrimination by family members

1. A witness appearing before the Court, who is a spouse, child or parent of an accused person, shall not be required by a Chamber to make any statement that might tend to incriminate that accused person. However, the witness may choose to make

such a statement.

2. In evaluating the testimony of a witness, a Chamber may take into account that the witness, referred to in sub-rule 1, objected to reply to a question which was intended to contradict a previous statement made by the witness, or the witness was selective in choosing which questions to answer.

Section II

Disclosure

Rule 76

Pre-trial disclosure relating to prosecution witnesses

1. The Prosecutor shall provide the defence with the names of witnesses whom the Prosecutor intends to call to testify and copies of any prior statements made by those witnesses. This shall be done sufficiently in advance to enable the adequate preparation of the defence.

2. The Prosecutor shall subsequently advise the defence of the names of any additional prosecution witnesses and provide copies of their statements when the decision is made to call those witnesses.

3. The statements of prosecution witnesses shall be made available in original and in a language which the accused fully understands and speaks.

4. This rule is subject to the protection and privacy of victims

and witnesses and the protection of confidential information as provided for in the Statute and rules 81 and 82.

Rule 77

Inspection of material in possession or control of the Prosecutor

Rule 78

Inspection of material in possession or control of the defence

The defence shall permit the Prosecutor to inspect any books, documents, photographs and other tangible objects in the possession or control of the defence, which are intended for use by the defence as evidence for the purposes of the confirmation hearing or at trial.

Rule 79

Disclosure by the defence

1. The defence shall notify the Prosecutor of its intent to:

(a) Raise the existence of an alibi, in which case the notification shall specify the place or places at which the accused claims to have been present at the time of the alleged crime and the names of witnesses and any other evidence upon which the accused intends to rely to establish the alibi; or

(b) Raise a ground for excluding criminal responsibility provided for in article 31, paragraph 1, in which case the notification shall specify the names of witnesses and any other evidence upon which the accused intends to rely to establish the ground.

2. With due regard to time limits set forth in other rules, notification under sub-rule 1 shall be given sufficiently in advance to enable the Prosecutor to prepare adequately and to respond. The Chamber dealing with the matter may grant the Prosecutor an adjournment to address the issue raised by the defence.

3. Failure of the defence to provide notice under this rule shall not limit its right to raise matters dealt with in sub-rule 1 and to present evidence.

4. This rule does not prevent a Chamber from ordering disclosure of any other evidence.

Rule 80

Procedures for raising a ground for excluding criminal responsibility under article 31, paragraph 3

1. The defence shall give notice to both the Trial Chamber and the Prosecutor if it intends to raise a ground for excluding

criminal responsibility under article 31, paragraph 3. This shall be done sufficiently in advance of the commencement of the trial to enable the Prosecutor to prepare adequately for trial.

2. Following notice given under sub-rule 1, the Trial Chamber shall hear both the Prosecutor and the defence before deciding whether the defence can raise a ground for excluding criminal responsibility.

3. If the defence is permitted to raise the ground, the Trial Chamber may grant the Prosecutor an adjournment to address that ground.

Rule 81

Restrictions on disclosure

1. Reports, memoranda or other internal documents prepared by a party, its assistants or representatives in connection with the investigation or preparation of the case are not subject to disclosure.

2. Where material or information is in the possession or control of the Prosecutor which must be disclosed in accordance with the Statute, but disclosure may prejudice further or ongoing investigations, the Prosecutor may apply to the Chamber dealing with the matter for a ruling as to whether the material or information must be disclosed to the defence. The matter shall be heard on an ex parte basis by the Chamber. However, the Prosecutor may not introduce such material or

information into evidence during the confirmation hearing or the trial without adequate prior disclosure to the accused.

3. Where steps have been taken to ensure the confidentiality of information, in accordance with articles 54, 57, 64, 72 and 93, and, in accordance with article 68, to protect the safety of witnesses and victims and members of their families, such information shall not be disclosed, except in accordance with those articles. When the disclosure of such information may create a risk to the safety of the witness, the Court shall take measures to inform the witness in advance.

4. The Chamber dealing with the matter shall, on its own motion or at the request of the Prosecutor, the accused or any State, take the necessary steps to ensure the confidentiality of information, in accordance with articles 54, 72 and 93, and, in accordance with article 68, to protect the safety of witnesses and victims and members of their families, including by authorizing the non-disclosure of their identity prior to the commencement of the trial.

5. Where material or information is in the possession or control of the Prosecutor which is withheld under article 68, paragraph 5, such material and information may not be subsequently introduced into evidence during the confirmation hearing or the trial without adequate prior disclosure to the accused.

6. Where material or information is in the possession or control of the defence which is subject to disclosure, it may be withheld in circumstances similar to those which would

allow the Prosecutor to rely on article 68, paragraph 5, and a summary thereof submitted instead. Such material and information may not be subsequently introduced into evidence during the confirmation hearing or the trial without adequate prior disclosure to the Prosecutor.

Rule 82

Restrictions on disclosure of material and information protected under article 54, paragraph 3 (e)

1. Where material or information is in the possession or control of the Prosecutor which is protected under article 54, paragraph 3 (e), the Prosecutor may not subsequently introduce such material or information into evidence without the prior consent of the provider of the material or information and adequate prior disclosure to the accused.

2. If the Prosecutor introduces material or information protected under article 54, paragraph 3 (e), into evidence, a Chamber may not order the production of additional evidence received from the provider of the initial material or information, nor may a Chamber for the purpose of obtaining such additional evidence itself summon the provider or a representative of the provider as a witness or order their attendance.

3. If the Prosecutor calls a witness to introduce in evidence any material or information which has been protected under article 54, paragraph 3 (e), a Chamber may not compel that

witness to answer any question relating to the material or information or its origin, if the witness declines to answer on grounds of confidentiality.

4. The right of the accused to challenge evidence which has been protected under article 54, paragraph 3 (e), shall remain unaffected subject only to the limitations contained in sub-rules 2 and 3.

5. A Chamber dealing with the matter may order, upon application by the defence, that, in the interests of justice, material or information in the possession of the accused, which has been provided to the accused under the same conditions as set forth in article 54, paragraph 3 (e), and which is to be introduced into evidence, shall be subject mutatis mutandis to sub-rules 1, 2 and 3.

Rule 83

Ruling on exculpatory evidence under article 67, paragraph 2

The Prosecutor may request as soon as practicable a hearing on an ex parte basis before the Chamber dealing with the matter for the purpose of obtaining a ruling under article 67, paragraph 2.

Rule 84

Disclosure and additional evidence for trial

In order to enable the parties to prepare for trial and to facilitate the fair and expeditious conduct of the proceedings, the Trial Chamber shall, in accordance with article 64, paragraphs 3 (c) and 6 (d), and article 67, paragraph (2), and subject to article 68, paragraph 5, make any necessary orders for the disclosure of documents or information not previously disclosed and for the production of additional evidence. To avoid delay and to ensure that the trial commences on the set date, any such orders shall include strict time limits which shall be kept under review by the Trial Chamber.

Section III

Victims and witnesses

Subsection 1

Definition and general principle relating to victims

Rule 85
Definition of victims

For the purposes of the Statute and the Rules of Procedure and Evidence:

(a) "Victims" means natural persons who have suffered harm as a result of the commission of any crime within the jurisdiction of the Court;

(b) Victims may include organizations or institutions that

have sustained direct harm to any of their property which is dedicated to religion, education, art or science or charitable purposes, and to their historic monuments, hospitals and other places and objects for humanitarian purposes.

Rule 86

General principle

A Chamber in making any direction or order, and other organs of the Court in performing their functions under the Statute or the Rules, shall take into account the needs of all victims and witnesses in accordance with article 68, in particular, children, elderly persons, persons with disabilities and victims of sexual or gender violence.

Subsection 2

Protection of victims and witnesses

Rule 87

Protective measures

1. Upon the motion of the Prosecutor or the defence or upon the request of a witness or a victim or his or her legal representative, if any, or on its own motion, and after having consulted with the Victims and Witnesses Unit, as appropriate, a Chamber may order measures to protect a victim, a witness

or another person at risk on account of testimony given by a witness pursuant to article 68, paragraphs 1 and 2. The Chamber shall seek to obtain, whenever possible, the consent of the person in respect of whom the protective measure is sought prior to ordering the protective measure.

2. A motion or request under sub-rule 1 shall be governed by rule 134, provided that:

(a) Such a motion or request shall not be submitted ex parte;

(b) A request by a witness or by a victim or his or her legal representative, if any, shall be served on both the Prosecutor and the defence, each of whom shall have the opportunity to respond;

(c) A motion or request affecting a particular witness or a particular victim shall be served on that witness or victim or his or her legal representative, if any, in addition to the other party, each of whom shall have the opportunity to respond;

(d) When the Chamber proceeds on its own motion, notice and opportunity to respond shall be given to the Prosecutor and the defence, and to any witness or any victim or his or her legal representative, if any, who would be affected by such protective measure; and

(e) A motion or request may be filed under seal, and, if so filed, shall remain sealed until otherwise ordered by a Chamber. Responses to motions or requests filed under seal shall also be filed under seal.

3. A Chamber may, on a motion or request under sub-rule

1, hold a hearing, which shall be conducted in camera, to determine whether to order measures to prevent the release to the public or press and information agencies, of the identity or the location of a victim, a witness or other person at risk on account of testimony given by a witness by ordering, inter alia:

(a) That the name of the victim, witness or other person at risk on account of testimony given by a witness or any information which could lead to his or her identification, be expunged from the public records of the Chamber;

(b) That the Prosecutor, the defence or any other participant in the proceedings be prohibited from disclosing such information to a third party;

(c) That testimony be presented by electronic or other special means, including the use of technical means enabling the alteration of pictures or voice, the use of audio-visual technology, in particular videoconferencing and closed-circuit television, and the exclusive use of the sound media;

(d) That a pseudonym be used for a victim, a witness or other person at risk on account of testimony given by a witness; or

(e) That a Chamber conduct part of its proceedings in camera.

Rule 88

Special measures

1. Upon the motion of the Prosecutor or the defence, or

upon the request of a witness or a victim or his or her legal representative, if any, or on its own motion, and after having consulted with the Victims and Witnesses Unit, as appropriate, a Chamber may, taking into account the views of the victim or witness, order special measures such as, but not limited to, measures to facilitate the testimony of a traumatized victim or witness, a child, an elderly person or a victim of sexual violence, pursuant to article 68, paragraphs 1 and 2. The Chamber shall seek to obtain, whenever possible, the consent of the person in respect of whom the special measure is sought prior to ordering that measure.

2. A Chamber may hold a hearing on a motion or a request under sub-rule 1, if necessary in camera or ex parte, to determine whether to order any such special measure, including but not limited to an order that a counsel, a legal representative, a psychologist or a family member be permitted to attend during the testimony of the victim or the witness.

3. For inter partes motions or requests filed under this rule, the provisions of rule 87, sub-rules 2 (b) to (d), shall apply mutatis mutandis.

4. A motion or request filed under this rule may be filed under seal, and if so filed shall remain sealed until otherwise ordered by a Chamber. Any responses to inter partes motions or requests filed under seal shall also be filed under seal.

5. Taking into consideration that violations of the privacy of a witness or victim may create risk to his or her security, a Chamber shall be vigilant in controlling the manner of

questioning a witness or victim so as to avoid any harassment or intimidation, paying particular attention to attacks on victims of crimes of sexual violence.

Subsection 3

Participation of victims in the proceedings

Rule 89
Application for participation of victims in the proceedings

1. In order to present their views and concerns, victims shall make written application to the Registrar, who shall transmit the application to the relevant Chamber. Subject to the provisions of the Statute, in particular article 68, paragraph 1, the Registrar shall provide a copy of the application to the Prosecutor and the defence, who shall be entitled to reply within a time limit to be set by the Chamber. Subject to the provisions of sub-rule 2, the Chamber shall then specify the proceedings and manner in which participation is considered appropriate, which may include making opening and closing statements.

2. The Chamber, on its own initiative or on the application of the Prosecutor or the defence, may reject the application if it considers that the person is not a victim or that the criteria set forth in article 68, paragraph 3, are not otherwise fulfilled. A victim whose application has been rejected may file a new

application later in the proceedings.

3. An application referred to in this rule may also be made by a person acting with the consent of the victim, or a person acting on behalf of a victim, in the case of a victim who is a child or, when necessary, a victim who is disabled.

4. Where there are a number of applications, the Chamber may consider the applications in such a manner as to ensure the effectiveness of the proceedings and may issue one decision.

Rule 90

Legal representatives of victims

1. A victim shall be free to choose a legal representative.

2. Where there are a number of victims, the Chamber may, for the purposes of ensuring the effectiveness of the proceedings, request the victims or particular groups of victims, if necessary with the assistance of the Registry, to choose a common legal representative or representatives. In facilitating the coordination of victim representation, the Registry may provide assistance, inter alia, by referring the victims to a list of counsel, maintained by the Registry, or suggesting one or more common legal representatives.

3. If the victims are unable to choose a common legal representative or representatives within a time limit that the Chamber may decide, the Chamber may request the Registrar to choose one or more common legal representatives.

4. The Chamber and the Registry shall take all reasonable steps to ensure that in the selection of common legal representatives, the distinct interests of the victims, particularly as provided in article 68, paragraph 1, are represented and that any conflict of interest is avoided.

5. A victim or group of victims who lack the necessary means to pay for a common legal representative chosen by the Court may receive assistance from the Registry, including, as appropriate, financial assistance.

6. A legal representative of a victim or victims shall have the qualifications set forth in rule 22, sub-rule 1.

Rule 91

Participation of legal representatives in the proceedings

1. A Chamber may modify a previous ruling under rule 89.

2. A legal representative of a victim shall be entitled to attend and participate in the proceedings in accordance with the terms of the ruling of the Chamber and any modification thereof given under rules 89 and 90. This shall include participation in hearings unless, in the circumstances of the case, the Chamber concerned is of the view that the representative's intervention should be confined to written observations or submissions. The Prosecutor and the defence shall be allowed to reply to any oral or written observation by the legal representative for victims.

3. (a) When a legal representative attends and participates

in accordance with this rule, and wishes to question a witness, including questioning under rules 67 and 68, an expert or the accused, the legal representative must make application to the Chamber. The Chamber may require the legal representative to provide a written note of the questions and in that case the questions shall be communicated to the Prosecutor and, if appropriate, the defence, who shall be allowed to make observations within a time limit set by the Chamber.

(b) The Chamber shall then issue a ruling on the request, taking into account the stage of the proceedings, the rights of the accused, the interests of witnesses, the need for a fair, impartial and expeditious trial and in order to give effect to article 68, paragraph 3. The ruling may include directions on the manner and order of the questions and the production of documents in accordance with the powers of the Chamber under article 64. The Chamber may, if it considers it appropriate, put the question to the witness, expert or accused on behalf of the victim's legal representative.

4. For a hearing limited to reparations under article 75, the restrictions on questioning by the legal representative set forth in sub-rule 2 shall not apply. In that case, the legal representative may, with the permission of the Chamber concerned, question witnesses, experts and the person concerned.

Rule 92
Notification to victims and their legal representatives

1. This rule on notification to victims and their legal representatives shall apply to all proceedings before the Court, except in proceedings provided for in Part 2.

2. In order to allow victims to apply for participation in the proceedings in accordance with rule 89, the Court shall notify victims concerning the decision of the Prosecutor not to initiate an investigation or not to prosecute pursuant to article 53. Such a notification shall be given to victims or their legal representatives who have already participated in the proceedings or, as far as possible, to those who have communicated with the Court in respect of the situation or case in question. The Chamber may order the measures outlined in sub-rule 8 if it considers it appropriate in the particular circumstances.

3. In order to allow victims to apply for participation in the proceedings in accordance with rule 89, the Court shall notify victims regarding its decision to hold a hearing to confirm charges pursuant to article 61. Such a notification shall be given to victims or their legal representatives who have already participated in the proceedings or, as far as possible, to those who have communicated with the Court in respect of the case in question.

4. When a notification for participation as provided for in sub-rules 2 and 3 has been given, any subsequent notification as referred to in sub-rules 5 and 6 shall only be provided to

victims or their legal representatives who may participate in the proceedings in accordance with a ruling of the Chamber pursuant to rule 89 and any modification thereof.

5. In a manner consistent with the ruling made under rules 89 to 91, victims or their legal representatives participating in proceedings shall, in respect of those proceedings, be notified by the Registrar in a timely manner of:

(a) Proceedings before the Court, including the date of hearings and any postponements thereof, and the date of delivery of the decision;

(b) Requests, submissions, motions and other documents relating to such requests, submissions or motions.

6. Where victims or their legal representatives have participated in a certain stage of the proceedings, the Registrar shall notify them as soon as possible of the decisions of the Court in those proceedings.

7. Notifications as referred to in sub-rules 5 and 6 shall be in writing or, where written notification is not possible, in any other form as appropriate. The Registry shall keep a record of all notifications. Where necessary, the Registrar may seek the cooperation of States Parties in accordance with article 93, paragraph 1 (d) and (l).

8. For notification as referred to in sub-rule 3 and otherwise at the request of a Chamber, the Registrar shall take necessary measures to give adequate publicity to the proceedings. In

doing so, the Registrar may seek, in accordance with Part 9, the cooperation of relevant States Parties, and seek the assistance of intergovernmental organizations.

Rule 93

Views of victims or their legal representatives

A Chamber may seek the views of victims or their legal representatives participating pursuant to rules 89 to 91 on any issue, inter alia, in relation to issues referred to in rules 107, 109, 125, 128, 136, 139 and 191. In addition, a Chamber may seek the views of other victims, as appropriate.

Subsection 4

Reparations to victims

Rule 94

Procedure upon request

1. A victim's request for reparations under article 75 shall be made in writing and filed with the Registrar. It shall contain the following particulars:

(a) The identity and address of the claimant;
(b) A description of the injury, loss or harm;
(c) The location and date of the incident and, to the extent

possible, the identity of the person or persons the victim believes to be responsible for the injury, loss or harm;

(d) Where restitution of assets, property or other tangible items is sought, a description of them;

(e) Claims for compensation;

(f) Claims for rehabilitation and other forms of remedy;

(g) To the extent possible, any relevant supporting documentation, including names and addresses of witnesses.

2. At commencement of the trial and subject to any protective measures, the Court shall ask the Registrar to provide notification of the request to the person or persons named in the request or identified in the charges and, to the extent possible, to any interested persons or any interested States. Those notified shall file with the Registry any representation made under article 75, paragraph 3.

Rule 95

Procedure on the motion of the Court

1. In cases where the Court intends to proceed on its own motion pursuant to article 75, paragraph 1, it shall ask the Registrar to provide notification of its intention to the person or persons against whom the Court is considering making a determination, and, to the extent possible, to victims, interested persons and interested States. Those notified shall file with the Registry any representation made under article 75,

paragraph 3.

2. If, as a result of notification under sub-rule 1:

(a) A victim makes a request for reparations, that request will be determined as if it had been brought under rule 94;

(b) A victim requests that the Court does not make an order for reparations, the Court shall not proceed to make an individual order in respect of that victim.

Rule 96

Publication of reparation proceedings

1. Without prejudice to any other rules on notification of proceedings, the Registrar shall, insofar as practicable, notify the victims or their legal representatives and the person or persons concerned. The Registrar shall also, having regard to any information provided by the Prosecutor, take all the necessary measures to give adequate publicity of the reparation proceedings before the Court, to the extent possible, to other victims, interested persons and interested States.

2. In taking the measures described in sub-rule 1, the Court may seek, in accordance with Part 9, the cooperation of relevant States Parties, and seek the assistance of intergovernmental organizations in order to give publicity, as widely as possible and by all possible means, to the reparation proceedings before

the Court.

Rule 97

Assessment of reparations

1. Taking into account the scope and extent of any damage, loss or injury, the Court may award reparations on an individualized basis or, where it deems it appropriate, on a collective basis or both.

2. At the request of victims or their legal representatives, or at the request of the convicted person, or on its own motion, the Court may appoint appropriate experts to assist it in determining the scope, extent of any damage, loss and injury to, or in respect of victims and to suggest various options concerning the appropriate types and modalities of reparations. The Court shall invite, as appropriate, victims or their legal representatives, the convicted person as well as interested persons and interested States to make observations on the reports of the experts.

3. In all cases, the Court shall respect the rights of victims and the convicted person.

Rule 98

Trust Fund

1. Individual awards for reparations shall be made directly

against a convicted person.

2. The Court may order that an award for reparations against a convicted person be deposited with the Trust Fund where at the time of making the order it is impossible or impracticable to make individual awards directly to each victim. The award for reparations thus deposited in the Trust Fund shall be separated from other resources of the Trust Fund and shall be forwarded to each victim as soon as possible.

3. The Court may order that an award for reparations against a convicted person be made through the Trust Fund where the number of the victims and the scope, forms and modalities of reparations makes a collective award more appropriate.

4. Following consultations with interested States and the Trust Fund, the Court may order that an award for reparations be made through the Trust Fund to an intergovernmental, international or national organization approved by the Trust Fund.

5. Other resources of the Trust Fund may be used for the benefit of victims subject to the provisions of article 79.

Rule 99

Cooperation and protective measures for the purpose of forfeiture under articles 57, paragraph 3 (e), and 75, paragraph 4

1. The Pre-Trial Chamber, pursuant to article 57, paragraph 3 (e), or the Trial Chamber, pursuant to article 75, paragraph 4,

may, on its own motion or on the application of the Prosecutor or at the request of the victims or their legal representatives who have made a request for reparations or who have given a written undertaking to do so, determine whether measures should be requested.

2. Notice is not required unless the Court determines, in the particular circumstances of the case, that notification could not jeopardize the effectiveness of the measures requested. In the latter case, the Registrar shall provide notification of the proceedings to the person against whom a request is made and so far as is possible to any interested persons or interested States.

3. If an order is made without prior notification, the relevant Chamber shall request the Registrar, as soon as is consistent with the effectiveness of the measures requested, to notify those against whom a request is made and, to the extent possible, to any interested persons or any interested States and invite them to make observations as to whether the order should be revoked or otherwise modified.

4. The Court may make orders as to the timing and conduct of any proceedings necessary to determine these issues.

Section IV

Miscellaneous provisions

Rule 100

Place of the proceedings

1. In a particular case, where the Court considers that it would be in the interests of justice, it may decide to sit in a State other than the host State.

2. An application or recommendation changing the place where the Court sits may be filed at any time after the initiation of an investigation, either by the Prosecutor, the defence or by a majority of the judges of the Court. Such an application or recommendation shall be addressed to the Presidency. It shall be made in writing and specify in which State the Court would sit. The Presidency shall satisfy itself of the views of the relevant Chamber.

3. The Presidency shall consult the State where the Court intends to sit. If that State agrees that the Court can sit in that State, then the decision to sit in a State other than the host State shall be taken by the judges, in plenary session, by a two-thirds majority.

Rule 101

Time limits

1. In making any order setting time limits regarding the conduct of any proceedings, the Court shall have regard to the need to facilitate fair and expeditious proceedings, bearing in mind in particular the rights of the defence and the victims.

2. Taking into account the rights of the accused, in particular under article 67, paragraph (1) (c), all those participating in the proceedings to whom any order is directed shall endeavour to act as expeditiously as possible, within the time limit ordered by the Court.

Rule 102

Communications other than in writing

Rule 103

Amicus curiae and other forms of submission

1. At any stage of the proceedings, a Chamber may, if it considers it desirable for the proper determination of the case, invite or grant leave to a State, organization or person to submit, in writing or orally, any observation on any issue that the Chamber deems appropriate.

2. The Prosecutor and the defence shall have the opportunity to respond to the observations submitted under sub-rule 1.

3. A written observation submitted under sub-rule 1 shall be filed with the Registrar, who shall provide copies to the Prosecutor and the defence. The Chamber shall determine

what time limits shall apply to the filing of such observations.

Chapter 5

Investigation and prosecution

Section I

Decision of the Prosecutor regarding the initiation of an investigation under article 53, paragraphs 1 and 2

Rule 104

Evaluation of information by the Prosecutor

1. In acting pursuant to article 53, paragraph 1, the Prosecutor shall, in evaluating the information made available to him or her, analyse the seriousness of the information received.
2. For the purposes of sub-rule 1, the Prosecutor may seek additional information from States, organs of the United Nations, intergovernmental and non-governmental organizations, or other reliable sources that he or she deems appropriate, and may receive written or oral testimony at the seat of the Court. The procedure set out in rule 47 shall apply to the receiving of such testimony.

Rule 105

Notification of a decision by the Prosecutor not to initiate an investigation

1. When the Prosecutor decides not to initiate an investigation under article 53, paragraph 1, he or she shall promptly inform in writing the State or States that referred a situation under article 14, or the Security Council in respect of a situation covered by article 13, paragraph (b).

2. When the Prosecutor decides not to submit to the Pre-Trial Chamber a request for authorization of an investigation, rule 49 shall apply.

3. The notification referred to in sub-rule 1 shall contain the conclusion of the Prosecutor and, having regard to article 68, paragraph 1, the reasons for the conclusion of a person in accordance with article 60, paragraph 3, at least every 120 days and may do so at any time on the request of the person or the Prosecutor.

3. After the first appearance, a request for interim release must be made in writing. The Prosecutor shall be given notice of such a request. The Pre-Trial Chamber shall decide after having received observations in writing of the Prosecutor and the detained person. The Pre-Trial Chamber may decide to hold a hearing, at the request of the Prosecutor or the detained person or on its own initiative. A hearing must be held at least once every year.

Rule 119

Conditional release

1. The Pre-Trial Chamber may set one or more conditions restricting liberty, including the following:

(a) The person must not travel beyond territorial limits set by the Pre-Trial Chamber without the explicit agreement of the Chamber;

(b) The person must not go to certain places or associate with certain persons as specified by the Pre-Trial Chamber;

(c) The person must not contact directly or indirectly victims or witnesses;

(d) The person must not engage in certain professional activities;

(e) The person must reside at a particular address as specified by the Pre-Trial Chamber;

(f) The person must respond when summoned by an authority or qualified person designated by the Pre-Trial Chamber;

(g) The person must post bond or provide real or personal security or surety, for which the amount and the schedule and mode of payment shall be determined by the Pre-Trial Chamber;

(h) The person must supply the Registrar with all identity documents, particularly his or her passport.

2. At the request of the person concerned or the Prosecutor or on its own initiative, the Pre-Trial Chamber may at any time decide to amend the conditions set pursuant to sub-rule 1.

3. Before imposing or amending any conditions restricting

liberty, the Pre-Trial Chamber shall seek the views of the Prosecutor, the person concerned, any relevant State and victims that have communicated with the Court in that case and whom the Chamber considers could be at risk as a result of a release or conditions imposed.

4. If the Pre-Trial Chamber is convinced that the person concerned has failed to comply with one or more of the obligations imposed, it may, on such basis, at the request of the Prosecutor or on its own initiative, issue a warrant of arrest in respect of the person.

5. When the Pre-Trial Chamber issues a summons to appear pursuant to article 58, paragraph 7, and intends to set conditions restricting liberty, it shall ascertain the relevant provisions of the national law of the State receiving the summons. In a manner that is in keeping with the national law of the State receiving the summons, the Pre-Trial Chamber shall proceed in accordance with sub-rules 1, 2 and 3. If the Pre-Trial Chamber receives information that the person concerned has failed to comply with conditions imposed, it shall proceed in accordance with sub-rule 4.

Rule 120

Instruments of restraint

Section V

Proceedings with regard to the confirmation of charges under article 61

Rule 121

Proceedings before the confirmation hearing

(b) The Pre-Trial Chamber shall hold status conferences to ensure that disclosure takes place under satisfactory conditions. For each case, a judge of the Pre-Trial Chamber shall be appointed to organize such status conferences, on his or her own motion, or at the request of the Prosecutor or the person;

(c) All evidence disclosed between the Prosecutor and the person for the purposes of the confirmation hearing shall be communicated to the Pre-Trial Chamber.

3. The Prosecutor shall provide to the Pre-Trial Chamber and the person, no later than 30 days before the date of the confirmation hearing, a detailed description of the charges together with a list of the evidence which he or she intends to present at the hearing.

4. Where the Prosecutor intends to amend the charges pursuant to article 61, paragraph 4, he or she shall notify the Pre-Trial Chamber and the person no later than 15 days before the date of the hearing of the amended charges together with a

list of evidence that the Prosecutor intends to bring in support of those charges at the hearing.

5. Where the Prosecutor intends to present new evidence at the hearing, he or she shall provide the Pre-Trial Chamber and the person with a list of that evidence no later than 15 days before the date of the hearing.

6. If the person intends to present evidence under article 61, paragraph 6, he or she shall provide a list of that evidence to the Pre-Trial Chamber no later than 15 days before the date of the hearing. The Pre-Trial Chamber shall transmit the list to the Prosecutor without delay. The person shall provide a list of evidence that he or she intends to present in response to any amended charges or a new list of evidence provided by the Prosecutor.

7. The Prosecutor or the person may ask the Pre-Trial Chamber to postpone the date of the confirmation hearing. The Pre-Trial Chamber may also, on its own motion, decide to postpone the hearing.

8. The Pre-Trial Chamber shall not take into consideration charges and evidence presented after the time limit, or any extension thereof, has expired.

9. The Prosecutor and the person may lodge written submissions with the Pre-Trial Chamber, on points of fact and on law, including grounds for excluding criminal responsibility set forth in article 31, paragraph 1, no later than three days before the date of the hearing. A copy of these submissions shall be transmitted immediately to the Prosecutor or the person, as

the case may be.

10. The Registry shall create and maintain a full and accurate record of all proceedings before the Pre-Trial Chamber, including all documents transmitted to the Chamber pursuant to this rule. Subject to any restrictions concerning confidentiality and the protection of national security information, the record may be consulted by the Prosecutor, the person and victims or their legal representatives participating in the proceedings pursuant to rules 89 to 91.

Rule 122

Proceedings at the confirmation hearing in the presence of the person charged

1. The Presiding Judge of the Pre-Trial Chamber shall ask the officer of the Registry assisting the Chamber to read out the charges as presented by the Prosecutor. The Presiding Judge shall determine how the hearing is to be conducted and, in particular, may establish the order and the conditions under which he or she intends the evidence contained in the record of the proceedings to be presented.

2. If a question or challenge concerning jurisdiction or admissibility arises, rule 58 applies.

3. Before hearing the matter on the merits, the Presiding Judge of the Pre-Trial Chamber shall ask the Prosecutor and the person whether they intend to raise objections or make

observations concerning an issue related to the proper conduct of the proceedings prior to the confirmation hearing.

4. At no subsequent point may the objections and observations made under sub-rule 3 be raised or made again in the confirmation or trial proceedings.

5. If objections or observations referred to in sub-rule 3 are presented, the Presiding Judge of the Pre-Trial Chamber shall invite those referred to in sub-rule 3 to present their arguments, in the order which he or she shall establish. The person shall have the right to reply.

6. If the objections raised or observations made are those referred to in sub-rule 3, the Pre-Trial Chamber shall decide whether to join the issue raised with the examination of the charges and the evidence, or to separate them, in which case it shall adjourn the confirmation hearing and render a decision on the issues raised.

7. During the hearing on the merits, the Prosecutor and the person shall present their arguments in accordance with article 61, paragraphs 5 and 6.

8. The Pre-Trial Chamber shall permit the Prosecutor and the person, in that order, to make final observations.

9. Subject to the provisions of article 61, article 69 shall apply mutatis mutandis at the confirmation hearing.

Rule 123

Measures to ensure the presence of the person concerned at the confirmation hearing

1. When a warrant of arrest or summons to appear in accordance with article 58, paragraph 7, has been issued for a person by the Pre-Trial Chamber and the person is arrested or served with the summons, the Pre-Trial Chamber shall ensure that the person is notified of the provisions of article 61, paragraph 2.

2. The Pre-Trial Chamber may hold consultations with the Prosecutor, at the request of the latter or on its own initiative, in order to determine whether there is cause to hold a hearing on confirmation of charges under the conditions set forth in article 61, paragraph 2 (b). When the person concerned has a counsel known to the Court, the consultations shall be held in the presence of the counsel unless the Pre-Trial Chamber decides otherwise.

3. The Pre-Trial Chamber shall ensure that a warrant of arrest for the person concerned has been issued and, if the warrant of arrest has not been executed within a reasonable period of time after the issuance of the warrant, that all reasonable measures have been taken to locate and arrest the person.

Rule 124

Waiver of the right to be present at the confirmation hearing

1. If the person concerned is available to the Court but wishes

to waive the right to be present at the hearing on confirmation of charges, he or she shall submit a written request to the Pre-Trial Chamber, which may then hold consultations with the Prosecutor and the person concerned, assisted or represented by his or her counsel.

2. A confirmation hearing pursuant to article 61, paragraph 2 (a), shall only be held when the Pre-Trial Chamber is satisfied that the person concerned understands the right to be present at the hearing and the consequences of waiving this right.

3. The Pre-Trial Chamber may authorize and make provision for the person to observe the hearing from outside the courtroom through the use of communications technology, if required.

4. The waiving of the right to be present at the hearing does not prevent the Pre-Trial Chamber from receiving written observations on issues before the Chamber from the person concerned.

Rule 125

Decision to hold the confirmation hearing in the absence of the person concerned

1. After holding consultations under rules 123 and 124, the Pre-Trial Chamber shall decide whether there is cause to hold a hearing on confirmation of charges in the absence of the person concerned, and in that case, whether the person

may be represented by counsel. The Pre-Trial Chamber shall, when appropriate, set a date for the hearing and make the date public.

2. The decision of the Pre-Trial Chamber shall be notified to the Prosecutor and, if possible, to the person concerned or his or her counsel.

3. If the Pre-Trial Chamber decides not to hold a hearing on confirmation of charges in the absence of the person concerned, and the person is not available to the Court, the confirmation of charges may not take place until the person is available to the Court. The Pre-Trial Chamber may review its decision at any time, at the request of the Prosecutor or on its own initiative.

4. If the Pre-Trial Chamber decides not to hold a hearing on confirmation of charges in the absence of the person concerned, and the person is available to the Court, it shall order the person to appear.

Rule 126

Confirmation hearing in the absence of the person concerned

1. The provisions of rules 121 and 122 shall apply mutatis mutandis to the preparation for and holding of a hearing on confirmation of charges in the absence of the person concerned.

2. If the Pre-Trial Chamber has determined that the person

concerned shall be represented by counsel, the counsel shall have the opportunity to exercise the rights of that person.

3. When the person who has fled is subsequently arrested and the Court has confirmed the charges upon which the Prosecutor intends to pursue the trial, the person charged shall be committed to the Trial Chamber established under article 61, paragraph 11. The person charged may request in writing that the Trial Chamber refer issues to the Pre-Trial Chamber that are necessary for the Chamber's effective and fair functioning in accordance with article 64, paragraph 4.

Section VI

Closure of the pre-trial phase

Rule 127

Procedure in the event of different decisions on multiple charges

Rule 128

Amendment of the charges

1. If the Prosecutor seeks to amend charges already confirmed before the trial has begun, in accordance with article 61, the Prosecutor shall make a written request to the Pre-Trial

Chamber, and that Chamber shall so notify the accused.

2. Before deciding whether to authorize the amendment, the Pre-Trial Chamber may request the accused and the Prosecutor to submit written observations on certain issues of fact or law.

3. If the Pre-Trial Chamber determines that the amendments proposed by the Prosecutor constitute additional or more serious charges, it shall proceed, as appropriate, in accordance with rules 121 and 122 or rules 123 to 126.

Rule 129

Notification of the decision on the confirmation of charges

Rule 130

Constitution of the Trial Chamber

When the Presidency constitutes a Trial Chamber and refers the case to it, the Presidency shall transmit the decision of the Pre-Trial Chamber and the record of the proceedings to the Trial Chamber. The Presidency may also refer the case to a previously constituted Trial Chamber.

Chapter 6

Trial procedure

Rule 131

Record of the proceedings transmitted by the Pre-Trial Chamber

1. The Registrar shall maintain the record of the proceedings transmitted by the Pre-Trial Chamber, pursuant to rule 121, sub-rule 10.

2. Subject to any restrictions concerning confidentiality and the protection of national security information, the record may be consulted by the Prosecutor, the defence, the representatives of States when they participate in the proceedings, and the victims or their legal representatives participating in the proceedings pursuant to rules 89 to 91.

Rule 132

Status conferences

1. Promptly after it is constituted, the Trial Chamber shall hold a status conference in order to set the date of the trial. The Trial Chamber, on its own motion, or at the request of the Prosecutor or the defence, may postpone the date of the trial. The Trial Chamber shall notify the trial date to all those participating in the proceedings. The Trial Chamber shall

ensure that this date and any postponements are made public.

2. In order to facilitate the fair and expeditious conduct of the proceedings, the Trial Chamber may confer with the parties by holding status conferences as necessary.

Rule 133

Motions challenging admissibility or jurisdiction

Rule 134

Motions relating to the trial proceedings

1. Prior to the commencement of the trial, the Trial Chamber on its own motion, or at the request of the Prosecutor or the defence, may rule on any issue concerning the conduct of the proceedings. Any request from the Prosecutor or the defence shall be in writing and, unless the request is for an ex parte procedure, served on the other party. For all requests other than those submitted for an ex parte procedure, the other party shall have the opportunity to file a response.

2. At the commencement of the trial, the Trial Chamber shall ask the Prosecutor and the defence whether they have any objections or observations concerning the conduct of the proceedings which have arisen since the confirmation hearings. Such objections or observations may not be raised or made again on a subsequent occasion in the trial proceedings, without leave of the Trial Chamber in this proceeding.

3. After the commencement of the trial, the Trial Chamber, on its own motion, or at the request of the Prosecutor or the defence, may rule on issues that arise during the course of the trial.

Rule 135

Medical examination of the accused

1. The Trial Chamber may, for the purpose of discharging its obligations under article 64, paragraph 8 (a), or for any other reasons, or at the request of a party, order a medical, psychiatric or psychological examination of the accused, under the conditions set forth in rule 113.

2. The Trial Chamber shall place its reasons for any such order on the record.

3. The Trial Chamber shall appoint one or more experts from the list of experts approved by the Registrar, or an expert approved by the Trial Chamber at the request of a party.

4. Where the Trial Chamber is satisfied that the accused is unfit to stand trial, it shall order that the trial be adjourned. The Trial Chamber may, on its own motion or at the request of the prosecution or the defence, review the case of the accused. In any event, the case shall be reviewed every 120 days unless there are reasons to do otherwise. If necessary, the Trial Chamber may order further examinations of the accused. When the Trial Chamber is satisfied that the accused has become fit to stand

trial, it shall proceed in accordance with rule 132.

Rule 136

Joint and separate trials

Rule 137

Record of the trial proceedings

1. In accordance with article 64, paragraph 10, the Registrar shall take measures to make, and preserve, a full and accurate record of all proceedings, including transcripts, audio- and video-recordings and other means of capturing sound or image.

2. A Trial Chamber may order the disclosure of all or part of the record of closed proceedings when the reasons for ordering its non-disclosure no longer exist.

3. The Trial Chamber may authorize persons other than the Registrar to take photographs, audio- and video-recordings and other means of capturing the sound or image of the trial.

Rule 138

Custody of evidence

The Registrar shall retain and preserve, as necessary, all the evidence and other materials offered during the hearing, subject to any order of the Trial Chamber.

Rule 139

Decision on admission of guilt

1. After having proceeded in accordance with article 65, paragraph 1, the Trial Chamber, in order to decide whether to proceed in accordance with article 65, paragraph 4, may invite the views of the Prosecutor and the defence.

2. The Trial Chamber shall then make its decision on the admission of guilt and shall give reasons for this decision, which shall be placed on the record.

Rule 140

Directions for the conduct of the proceedings and testimony

1. If the Presiding Judge does not give directions under article 64, paragraph 8, the Prosecutor and the defence shall agree on the order and manner in which the evidence shall be submitted to the Trial Chamber. If no agreement can be reached, the Presiding Judge shall issue directions.

2. In all cases, subject to article 64, paragraphs 8 (b) and 9, article 69, paragraph 4, and rule 88, sub-rule 5, a witness may be questioned as follows:

(a) A party that submits evidence in accordance with article 69, paragraph 3, by way of a witness, has the right to question that witness;

(b) The prosecution and the defence have the right to question that witness about relevant matters related to the witness's testimony and its reliability, the credibility of the witness and other relevant matters;

(c) The Trial Chamber has the right to question a witness before or after a witness is questioned by a participant referred to in sub-rules 2 (a) or (b);

(d) The defence shall have the right to be the last to examine a witness.

3. Unless otherwise ordered by the Trial Chamber, a witness other than an expert, or an investigator if he or she has not yet testified, shall not be present when the testimony of another witness is given. However, a witness who has heard the testimony of another witness shall not for that reason alone be disqualified from testifying. When a witness testifies after hearing the testimony of others, this fact shall be noted in the record and considered by the Trial Chamber when evaluating the evidence.

Rule 141

Closure of evidence and closing statements

1. The Presiding Judge shall declare when the submission of evidence is closed.

2. The Presiding Judge shall invite the Prosecutor and the

defence to make their closing statements. The defence shall always have the opportunity to speak last.

Rule 142

Deliberations

1. After the closing statements, the Trial Chamber shall retire to deliberate, in camera. The Trial Chamber shall inform all those who participated in the proceedings of the date on which the Trial Chamber will pronounce its decision. The pronouncement shall be made within a reasonable period of time after the Trial Chamber has retired to deliberate.

2. When there is more than one charge, the Trial Chamber shall decide separately on each charge. When there is more than one accused, the Trial Chamber shall decide separately on the charges against each accused.

Rule 143

Additional hearings on matters related to sentence or reparations

Pursuant to article 76, paragraphs 2 and 3, for the purpose of holding a further hearing on matters related to sentence and, if applicable, reparations, the Presiding Judge shall set the date of the further hearing. This hearing can be postponed, in exceptional circumstances, by the Trial Chamber, on its own motion or at the request of the Prosecutor, the defence or the legal representatives of the victims participating in the proceedings pursuant to rules 89 to 91 and, in respect of reparations hearings, those victims who have made a request under rule 94.

Rule 144
Delivery of the decisions of the Trial Chamber

1. Decisions of the Trial Chamber concerning admissibility of a case, the jurisdiction of the Court, criminal responsibility of the accused, sentence and reparations shall be pronounced in public and, wherever possible, in the presence of the accused, the Prosecutor, the victims or the legal representatives of the victims participating in the proceedings pursuant to rules 89 to 91, and the representatives of the States which have participated in the proceedings.

2. Copies of all the above-mentioned decisions shall be provided as soon as possible to:

(a) All those who participated in the proceedings, in a working language of the Court;

(b) The accused, in a language he or she fully understands or speaks, if necessary to meet the requirements of fairness under article 67, paragraph 1 (f).

Chapter 7

Penalties

Rule 145

Determination of sentence

Before making an order pursuant to article 79, paragraph 2, a Chamber may request the representatives of the Fund to submit written or oral observations to it.

Chapter 8

Appeal and revision

Section I

General provisions

Rule 149

Rules governing proceedings in the Appeals Chamber

Parts 5 and 6 and rules governing proceedings and the submission of evidence in the Pre-Trial and Trial Chambers shall apply mutatis mutandis to proceedings in the Appeals Chamber.

Section II

Appeals against convictions, acquittals, sentences and reparation orders

Rule 150

Appeal

1. Subject to sub-rule 2, an appeal against a decision of conviction or acquittal under article 74, a sentence under article 76 or a reparation order under article 75 may be filed not later than 30 days from the date on which the party filing the appeal is notified of the decision, the sentence or the reparation order.

2. The Appeals Chamber may extend the time limit set out in sub-rule 1, for good cause, upon the application of the party seeking to file the appeal.

3. The appeal shall be filed with the Registrar.

4. If an appeal is not filed as set out in sub-rules 1 to 3, the decision, the sentence or the reparation order of the Trial Chamber shall become final.

Rule 151

Procedure for the appeal

1. Upon the filing of an appeal under rule 150, the Registrar shall transmit the trial record to the Appeals Chamber.

2. The Registrar shall notify all parties who participated in the proceedings before the Trial Chamber that an appeal has been filed.

Rule 152

Discontinuance of the appeal

Rule 153

Judgement on appeals against reparation orders

1. The Appeals Chamber may confirm, reverse or amend a reparation order made under article 75.
2. The judgement of the Appeals Chamber shall be delivered in accordance with article 83, paragraphs 4 and 5.

Section III

Appeals against other decisions

Rule 154

Appeals that do not require the leave of the Court

1. An appeal may be filed under article 81, paragraph 3 (c) (ii), or article 82, paragraph 1 (a) or (b), not later than five days from the date upon which the party filing the appeal is notified of the decision.

2. An appeal may be filed under article 82, paragraph 1 (c), not later than two days from the date upon which the party filing the appeal is notified of the decision.

3. Rule 150, sub-rules 3 and 4, shall apply to appeals filed under sub-rules 1 and 2 of this rule.

Rule 155

Appeals that require leave of the Court

1. When a party wishes to appeal a decision under article 82, paragraph 1 (d), or article 82, paragraph 2, that party shall, within five days of being notified of that decision, make a written application to the Chamber that gave the decision, setting out the reasons for the request for leave to appeal.

2. The Chamber shall render a decision and shall notify all parties who participated in the proceedings that gave rise to the decision referred to in sub-rule 1.

Rule 156

Procedure for the appeal

Discontinuance of the appeal

Any party who has filed an appeal under rule 154 or who has obtained the leave of a Chamber to appeal a decision under rule 155 may discontinue the appeal at any time before judgement has been delivered. In such case, the party shall file with the

Registrar a written notice of discontinuance of appeal. The Registrar shall inform the other parties that such a notice has been filed.

Rule 158

Judgement on the appeal

Section IV

Revision of conviction or sentence

Rule 159

Application for revision

1. An application for revision provided for in article 84, paragraph 1, shall be in writing and shall set out the grounds on which the revision is sought. It shall as far as possible be accompanied by supporting material.

2. The determination on whether the application is meritorious shall be taken by a majority of the judges of the Appeals Chamber and shall be supported by reasons in writing.

3. Notification of the decision shall be sent to the applicant and, as far as possible, to all the parties who participated in the proceedings related to the initial decision.

Rule 160

Transfer for the purpose of revision

1. For the conduct of the hearing provided for in rule 161, the relevant Chamber shall issue its order sufficiently in advance to enable the transfer of the sentenced person to the seat of the Court, as appropriate.

2. The determination of the Court shall be communicated without delay to the State of enforcement.

3. The provisions of rule 206, sub-rule 3, shall be applicable.

Rule 161

Determination on revision

1. On a date which it shall determine and shall communicate to the applicant and to all those having received notification under rule 159, sub-rule 3, the relevant Chamber shall hold a hearing to determine whether the conviction or sentence should be revised.

2. For the conduct of the hearing, the relevant Chamber shall exercise, mutatis mutandis, all the powers of the Trial Chamber pursuant to Part 6 and the rules governing proceedings and the submission of evidence in the Pre-Trial and Trial Chambers.

3. The determination on revision shall be governed by the applicable provisions of article 83, paragraph 4.

Chapter 9

Offences and misconduct against the Court

Section I

Offences against the administration of justice under article 70.

Rule 162

Exercise of jurisdiction

1. Before deciding whether to exercise jurisdiction, the Court may consult with States Parties that may have jurisdiction over the offence.

2. In making a decision whether or not to exercise jurisdiction, the Court may consider, in particular:

(a) The availability and effectiveness of prosecution in a State Party;

(b) The seriousness of an offence;

(c) The possible joinder of charges under article 70 with charges under articles 5 to 8;

(d) The need to expedite proceedings;

(e) Links with an ongoing investigation or a trial before the Court; and

(f) Evidentiary considerations.

3. The Court shall give favourable consideration to a request from the host State for a waiver of the power of the Court to exercise jurisdiction in cases where the host State considers such a waiver to be of particular importance.

4. If the Court decides not to exercise its jurisdiction, it may request a State Party to exercise jurisdiction pursuant to article 70, paragraph 4.

Rule 163

Application of the Statute and the Rules

1. Unless otherwise provided in sub-rules 2 and 3, rule 162 and rules 164 to 169, the Statute and the Rules shall apply mutatis mutandis to the Court's investigation, prosecution and punishment of offences defined in article 70.

2. The provisions of Part 2, and any rules thereunder, shall not apply, with the exception of article 21.

3. The provisions of Part 10, and any rules thereunder, shall not apply, with the exception of articles 103, 107, 109 and 111.

Rule 164

Periods of limitation

1. If the Court exercises jurisdiction in accordance with rule 162, it shall apply the periods of limitation set forth in this

rule.

2. Offences defined in article 70 shall be subject to a period of limitation of five years from the date on which the offence was committed, provided that during this period no investigation or prosecution has been initiated. The period of limitation shall be interrupted if an investigation or prosecution has been initiated during this period, either before the Court or by a State Party with jurisdiction over the case pursuant to article 70, paragraph 4 (a).

3. Enforcement of sanctions imposed with respect to offences defined in article 70 shall be subject to a period of limitation of 10 years from the date on which the sanction has become final. The period of limitation shall be interrupted with the detention of the convicted person or while the person concerned is outside the territory of the States Parties.

Rule 165

Investigation, prosecution and trial

1. The Prosecutor may initiate and conduct investigations with respect to the offences defined in article 70 on his or her own initiative, on the basis of information communicated by a Chamber or any reliable source.

2. Articles 53 and 59, and any rules thereunder, shall not apply.

3. For purposes of article 61, the Pre-Trial Chamber may

make any of the determinations set forth in that article on the basis of written submissions, without a hearing, unless the interests of justice otherwise require.

4. A Trial Chamber may, as appropriate and taking into account the rights of the defence, direct that there be joinder of charges under article 70 with charges under articles 5 to 8.

Rule 166

Sanctions under article 70

1. If the Court imposes sanctions with respect to article 70, this rule shall apply.

2. Article 77, and any rules thereunder, shall not apply, with the exception of an order of forfeiture under article 77, paragraph 2 (b), which may be ordered in addition to imprisonment or a fine or both.

3. Each offence may be separately fined and those fines may be cumulative. Under no circumstances may the total amount exceed 50 per cent of the value of the convicted person's identifiable assets, liquid or realizable, and property, after deduction of an appropriate amount that would satisfy the financial needs of the convicted person and his or her dependants.

4. In imposing a fine the Court shall allow the convicted person a reasonable period in which to pay the fine. The Court may provide for payment of a lump sum or by way of

instalments during that period.

5. If the convicted person does not pay a fine imposed in accordance with the conditions set forth in sub-rule 4, appropriate measures may be taken by the Court pursuant to rules 217 to 222 and in accordance with article 109. Where, in cases of continued wilful non-payment, the Court, on its own motion or at the request of the Prosecutor, is satisfied that all available enforcement measures have been exhausted, it may as a last resort impose a term of imprisonment in accordance with article 70, paragraph 3. In the determination of such term of imprisonment, the Court shall take into account the amount of fine paid.

Rule 167

International cooperation and judicial assistance

1. With regard to offences under article 70, the Court may request a State to provide any form of international cooperation or judicial assistance corresponding to those forms set forth in Part 9. In any such request, the Court shall indicate that the basis for the request is an investigation or prosecution of offences under article 70.

2. The conditions for providing international cooperation or judicial assistance to the Court with respect to offences under article 70 shall be those set forth in article 70, paragraph 2.

Rule 168

Ne bis in idem

In respect of offences under article 70, no person shall be tried before the Court with respect to conduct which formed the basis of an offence for which the person has already been convicted or acquitted by the Court or another court.

Rule 169

Immediate arrest

In the case of an alleged offence under article 70 committed in the presence of a Chamber, the Prosecutor may orally request that Chamber to order the immediate arrest of the person concerned.

Section II

Misconduct before the Court under article 71

Rule 170

Disruption of proceedings

Having regard to article 63, paragraph 2, the Presiding Judge of the Chamber dealing with the matter may, after giving a warning:

(a) Order a person disrupting the proceedings of the Court to leave or be removed from the courtroom; or,

(b) In case of repeated misconduct, order the interdiction of that person from attending the proceedings.

Rule 171

Refusal to comply with a direction by the Court

Rule 172

Conduct covered by both articles 70 and 71

If conduct covered by article 71 also constitutes one of the offences defined in article 70, the Court shall proceed in accordance with article 70 and rules 162 to 169.

Chapter 10

Compensation to an arrested or convicted person

Rule 173

Request for compensation

1. Anyone seeking compensation on any of the grounds indicated in article 85 shall submit a request, in writing, to the Presidency, which shall designate a Chamber composed of

three judges to consider the request. These judges shall not have participated in any earlier judgement of the Court regarding the person making the request.

2. The request for compensation shall be submitted not later than six months from the date the person making the request was notified of the decision of the Court concerning:

(a) The unlawfulness of the arrest or detention under article 85, paragraph 1;

(b) The reversal of the conviction under article 85, paragraph 2;

(c) The existence of a grave and manifest miscarriage of justice under article 85, paragraph 3.

3. The request shall contain the grounds and the amount of compensation requested.

4. The person requesting compensation shall be entitled to legal assistance.

Rule 174

Procedure for seeking compensation

1. A request for compensation and any other written observation by the person filing the request shall be transmitted to the Prosecutor, who shall have an opportunity to respond in writing. Any observations by the Prosecutor shall be notified to

the person filing the request.

2. The Chamber designated under rule 173, sub-rule 1, may either hold a hearing or determine the matter on the basis of the request and any written observations by the Prosecutor and the person filing the request. A hearing shall be held if the Prosecutor or the person seeking compensation so requests.

3. The decision shall be taken by the majority of the judges. The decision shall be notified to the Prosecutor and to the person filing the request.

Rule 175
Amount of compensation

In establishing the amount of any compensation in conformity with article 85, paragraph 3, the Chamber designated under rule 173, sub-rule 1, shall take into consideration the consequences of the grave and manifest miscarriage of justice on the personal, family, social and professional situation of the person filing the request.

Chapter 11

International cooperation and judicial assistance

Section I

Requests for cooperation under article 87

Rule 176

Organs of the Court responsible for the transmission and receipt of any communications relating to international cooperation and judicial assistance

1. Upon and subsequent to the establishment of the Court, the Registrar shall obtain from the Secretary-General of the United Nations any communication made by States pursuant to article 87, paragraphs 1 (a) and 2.

2. The Registrar shall transmit the requests for cooperation made by the Chambers and shall receive the responses, information and documents from requested States. The Office of the Prosecutor shall transmit the requests for cooperation made by the Prosecutor and shall receive the responses, information and documents from requested States.

3. The Registrar shall be the recipient of any communication from States concerning subsequent changes in the designation of the national channels charged with receiving requests for cooperation, as well as of any change in the language in which requests for cooperation should be made, and shall, upon

request, make such information available to States Parties as may be appropriate.

4. The provisions of sub-rule 2 are applicable mutatis mutandis where the Court requests information, documents or other forms of cooperation and assistance from an intergovernmental organization.

5. The Registrar shall transmit any communications referred to in sub-rules 1 and 3 and rule 177, sub-rule 2, as appropriate, to the Presidency or the Office of the Prosecutor, or both.

Rule 177

Channels of communication

1. Communications concerning the national authority charged with receiving requests for cooperation made upon ratification, acceptance, approval or accession shall provide all relevant information about such authorities.

2. When an intergovernmental organization is asked to assist the Court under article 87, paragraph 6, the Registrar shall, when necessary, ascertain its designated channel of communication and obtain all relevant information relating thereto.

Rule 178

Language chosen by States Parties under article 87, paragraph 2

Rule 179

Language of requests directed to States not party to the Statute

When a State not party to the Statute has agreed to provide assistance to the Court under article 87, paragraph 5, and has not made a choice of language for such requests, the requests for cooperation shall either be in or be accompanied by a translation into one of the working languages of the Court.

Rule 180

Changes in the channels of communication or the languages of requests for cooperation

1. Changes concerning the channel of communication or the language a State has chosen under article 87, paragraph 2, shall be communicated in writing to the Registrar at the earliest opportunity.

2. Such changes shall take effect in respect of requests for cooperation made by the Court at a time agreed between the Court and the State or, in the absence of such an agreement, 45 days after the Court has received the communication and, in all cases, without prejudice to current requests or requests in progress.

Section II

Surrender, transit and competing requests under articles 89 and 90

Rule 181

Challenge to admissibility of a case before a national court

When a situation described in article 89, paragraph 2, arises, and without prejudice to the provisions of article 19 and of rules 58 to 62 on procedures applicable to challenges to the jurisdiction of the Court or the admissibility of a case, the Chamber dealing with the case, if the admissibility ruling is still pending, shall take steps to obtain from the requested State all the relevant information about the ne bis in idem challenge brought by the person.

Rule 182

Request for transit under article 89, paragraph 3 (e)

1. In situations described in article 89, paragraph 3 (e), the Court may transmit the request for transit by any medium capable of delivering a written record.

2. When the time limit provided for in article 89, paragraph 3 (e), has expired and the person concerned has been released, such a release is without prejudice to a subsequent arrest of the person in accordance with the provisions of article 89 or article

92.

Rule 183

Possible temporary surrender

Following the consultations referred to in article 89, paragraph 4, the requested State may temporarily surrender the person sought in accordance with conditions determined between the requested State and the Court. In such case the person shall be kept in custody during his or her presence before the Court and shall be transferred to the requested State once his or her presence before the Court is no longer required, at the latest when the proceedings have been completed.

Rule 184

Arrangements for surrender

1. The requested State shall immediately inform the Registrar when the person sought by the Court is available for surrender.
2. The person shall be surrendered to the Court by the date and in the manner agreed upon between the authorities of the requested State and the Registrar.
3. If circumstances prevent the surrender of the person by the date agreed, the authorities of the requested State and the Registrar shall agree upon a new date and manner by which the

person shall be surrendered.

4. The Registrar shall maintain contact with the authorities of the host State in relation to the arrangements for the surrender of the person to the Court.

Rule 185

Release of a person from the custody of the Court other than upon completion of sentence

1. Subject to sub-rule 2, where a person surrendered to the Court is released from the custody of the Court because the Court does not have jurisdiction, the case is inadmissible under article 17, paragraph 1 (b), (c) or (d), the charges have not been confirmed under article 61, the person has been acquitted at trial or on appeal, or for any other reason, the Court shall, as soon as possible, make such arrangements as it considers appropriate for the transfer of the person, taking into account the views of the person, to a State which is obliged to receive him or her, to another State which agrees to receive him or her, or to a State which has requested his or her extradition with the consent of the original surrendering State. In this case, the host State shall facilitate the transfer in accordance with the agreement referred to in article 3, paragraph 2, and the related arrangements.

2. Where the Court has determined that the case is inadmissible under article 17, paragraph 1 (a), the Court

shall make arrangements, as appropriate, for the transfer of the person to a State whose investigation or prosecution has formed the basis of the successful challenge to admissibility, unless the State that originally surrendered the person requests his or her return.

Rule 186

Competing requests in the context of a challenge to the admissibility of the case

In situations described in article 90, paragraph 8, the requested State shall provide the notification of its decision to the Prosecutor in order to enable him or her to act in accordance with article 19, paragraph 10.

Section III

Documents for arrest and surrender under articles 91 and 92

Rule 187

Translation of documents accompanying request for surrender

For the purposes of article 67, paragraph 1 (a), and in accordance with rule 117, sub-rule 1, the request under article 91 shall be accompanied, as appropriate, by a translation of the warrant of arrest or of the judgement of conviction and by a translation of the text of any relevant provisions of the Statute, in a language that the person fully understands and speaks.

Rule 188

Time limit for submission of documents after provisional arrest

For the purposes of article 92, paragraph 3, the time limit for receipt by the requested State of the request for surrender and the documents supporting the request shall be 60 days from the date of the provisional arrest.

Rule 189

Transmission of documents supporting the request

When a person has consented to surrender in accordance with the provisions of article 92, paragraph 3, and the requested State proceeds to surrender the person to the Court, the Court shall not be required to provide the documents described in article 91 unless the requested State indicates otherwise.

Section IV

Cooperation under article 93

Rule 190

Instruction on self-incrimination accompanying request

for witness

Rule 191

Assurance provided by the Court under article 93, paragraph 2

The Chamber dealing with the case, on its own motion or at the request of the Prosecutor, defence or witness or expert concerned, may decide, after taking into account the views of the Prosecutor and the witness or expert concerned, to provide the assurance described in article 93, paragraph 2.

Rule 192

Transfer of a person in custody

1. Transfer of a person in custody to the Court in accordance with article 93, paragraph 7, shall be arranged by the national authorities concerned in liaison with the Registrar and the authorities of the host State.

2. The Registrar shall ensure the proper conduct of the transfer, including the supervision of the person while in the custody of the Court.

3. The person in custody before the Court shall have the right to raise matters concerning the conditions of his or her detention with the relevant Chamber.

4. In accordance with article 93, paragraph 7 (b), when the

purposes of the transfer have been fulfilled, the Registrar shall arrange for the return of the person in custody to the requested State.

Rule 193

Temporary transfer of the person from the State of enforcement

Rule 194

Cooperation requested from the Court

1. In accordance with article 93, paragraph 10, and consistent with article 96, mutatis mutandis, a State may transmit to the Court a request for cooperation or assistance to the Court, either in or accompanied by a translation into one of the working languages of the Court.

2. Requests described in sub-rule 1 are to be sent to the Registrar, which shall transmit them, as appropriate, either to the Prosecutor or to the Chamber concerned.

3. If protective measures within the meaning of article 68 have been adopted, the Prosecutor or Chamber, as appropriate, shall consider the views of the Chamber which ordered the measures as well as those of the relevant victim or witness, before deciding on the request.

4. If the request relates to documents or evidence as described

in article 93, paragraph 10 (b) (ii), the Prosecutor or Chamber, as appropriate, shall obtain the written consent of the relevant State before proceeding with the request.

5. When the Court decides to grant the request for cooperation or assistance from a State, the request shall be executed, insofar as possible, following any procedure outlined therein by the requesting State and permitting persons specified in the request to be present.

Section V

Cooperation under article 98

Rule 195

Provision of information

1. When a requested State notifies the Court that a request for surrender or assistance raises a problem of execution in respect of article 98, the requested State shall provide any information relevant to assist the Court in the application of article 98. Any concerned third State or sending State may provide additional information to assist the Court.

2. The Court may not proceed with a request for the surrender of a person without the consent of a sending State if, under article 98, paragraph 2, such a request would be inconsistent with obligations under an international agreement pursuant to which the consent of a sending State is required prior to the

surrender of a person of that State to the Court.

Section VI

Rule of speciality under article 101

Rule 196

Provision of views on article 101, paragraph 1

Rule 197

Extension of the surrender

When the Court has requested a waiver of the requirements of article 101, paragraph 1, the requested State may ask the Court to obtain and provide the views of the person surrendered to the Court.

Chapter 12

Enforcement

Section I

Role of States in enforcement of sentences of imprisonment and change in designation of State of enforcement under articles 103 and 104

Rule 198

Communications between the Court and States

Unless the context otherwise requires, article 87 and rules 176 to 180 shall apply, as appropriate, to communications between the Court and a State on matters relating to enforcement of sentences.

Rule 199

Organ responsible under Part 10

Unless provided otherwise in the Rules, the functions of the Court under Part 10 shall be exercised by the Presidency.

Rule 200

List of States of enforcement

Rule 201

Principles of equitable distribution

(b) The prospect of the resocialization and successful resettlement of the sentenced person;

(c) Whether the early release of the sentenced person would give rise to significant social instability;

(d) Any significant action taken by the sentenced person for the benefit of the victims as well as any impact on the victims and their families as a result of the early release;

(e) Individual circumstances of the sentenced person, including a worsening state of physical or mental health or advanced age.

Rule 224

Procedure for review concerning reduction of sentence

1. For the application of article 110, paragraph 3, three judges of the Appeals Chamber appointed by that Chamber shall conduct a hearing, unless they decide otherwise in a particular case, for exceptional reasons. The hearing shall be conducted with the sentenced person, who may be assisted by his or her counsel, with interpretation, as may be required. Those three judges shall invite the Prosecutor, the State of enforcement of any penalty under article 77 or any reparation order pursuant to article 75 and, to the extent possible, the victims or their legal representatives who participated in the proceedings, to participate in the hearing or to submit written observations. Under exceptional circumstances, this hearing may be conducted by way of a videoconference or in the State of enforcement by a judge delegated by the Appeals Chamber.

2. The same three judges shall communicate the decision and the reasons for it to all those who participated in the review proceedings as soon as possible.

3. For the application of article 110, paragraph 5, three

judges of the Appeals Chamber appointed by that Chamber shall review the question of reduction of sentence every three years, unless it establishes a shorter interval in its decision taken pursuant to article 110, paragraph 3. In case of a significant change in circumstances, those three judges may permit the sentenced person to apply for a review within the three-year period or such shorter period as may have been set by the three judges.

4. For any review under article 110, paragraph 5, three judges of the Appeals Chamber appointed by that Chamber shall invite written representations from the sentenced person or his or her counsel, the Prosecutor, the State of enforcement of any penalty under article 77 and any reparation order pursuant to article 75 and, to the extent possible, the victims or their legal representatives who participated in the proceedings. The three judges may also decide to hold a hearing.

5. The decision and the reasons for it shall be communicated to all those who participated in the review proceedings as soon as possible.

Section VI

Escape

Rule 225

Measures under article 111 in the event of escape

1. If the sentenced person has escaped, the State of enforcement shall, as soon as possible, advise the Registrar by any medium capable of delivering a written record. The Presidency shall then proceed in accordance with Part 9.

2. However, if the State in which the sentenced person is located agrees to surrender him or her to the State of enforcement, pursuant to either international agreements or its national legislation, the State of enforcement shall so advise the Registrar in writing. The person shall be surrendered to the State of enforcement as soon as possible, if necessary in consultation with the Registrar, who shall provide all necessary assistance, including, if necessary, the presentation of requests for transit to the States concerned, in accordance with rule 207. The costs associated with the surrender of the sentenced person shall be borne by the Court if no State assumes responsibility for them.

3. If the sentenced person is surrendered to the Court pursuant to Part 9, the Court shall transfer him or her to the State of enforcement. Nevertheless, the Presidency may, acting on its own motion or at the request of the Prosecutor or of the initial State of enforcement and in accordance with article 103 and rules 203 to 206, designate another State, including the State to the territory of which the sentenced person has fled.

4. In all cases, the entire period of detention in the territory of the State in which the sentenced person was in custody after his or her escape and, where sub-rule 3 is applicable, the period of detention at the seat of the Court following the surrender of the

sentenced person from the State in which he or she was located shall be deducted from the sentence remaining to be served.

ROME STATUTE OF THE INTERNATIONAL CRIMINAL COURT

PREAMBLE

The States Parties to this Statute,

Conscious that all peoples are united by common bonds, their cultures pieced together in a shared heritage, and concerned that this delicate mosaic may be shattered at any time,

Mindful that during this century millions of children, women and men have been victims of unimaginable atrocities that deeply shock the conscience of humanity,

Recognizing that such grave crimes threaten the peace, security and well-being of the world,

Affirming that the most serious crimes of concern to the international community as a whole must not go unpunished and that their effective prosecution must be ensured by taking measures at the national level and by enhancing international cooperation,

Determined to put an end to impunity for the perpetrators of these crimes and thus to contribute to the prevention of such crimes,

Recalling that it is the duty of every State to exercise its criminal jurisdiction over those responsible for international crimes,

Reaffirming the Purposes and Principles of the Charter of the United Nations, and in particular that all States shall refrain from the threat or use of force against the territorial integrity or political independence of any State, or in any other manner inconsistent with the Purposes of the United Nations,

Emphasizing in this connection that nothing in this Statute shall be taken as authorizing any State Party to intervene in an armed conflict or in the internal affairs of any State,

Determined to these ends and for the sake of present and future generations, to establish an independent permanent International Criminal Court in relationship with the United Nations system, with jurisdiction over the most serious crimes of concern to the international community as a whole,

Emphasizing that the International Criminal Court established under this Statute shall be complementary to national criminal jurisdictions,

Resolved to guarantee lasting respect for and the enforcement of international justice,

Have agreed as follows

PART 1. ESTABLISHMENT OF THE COURT

Article 1
The Court

An International Criminal Court ("the Court") is hereby established. It shall be a permanent institution and shall have the power to exercise its jurisdiction over persons for the most serious crimes of international concern, as referred to in this Statute, and shall be complementary to national criminal jurisdictions. The jurisdiction and functioning of the Court shall be governed by the provisions of this Statute.

Article 2
Relationship of the Court with the United Nations

The Court shall be brought into relationship with the United Nations through an agreement to be approved by the Assembly of States Parties to this Statute and thereafter concluded by the President of the Court on its behalf.

Article 3
Seat of the Court

1. The seat of the Court shall be established at The Hague in the Netherlands ("the host State").

2. The Court shall enter into a headquarters agreement with

the host State, to be approved by the Assembly of States Parties and thereafter concluded by the President of the Court on its behalf.

3. The Court may sit elsewhere, whenever it considers it desirable, as provided in this Statute.

Article 4
Legal status and powers of the Court

1. The Court shall have international legal personality. It shall also have such legal capacity as may be necessary for the exercise of its functions and the fulfilment of its purposes.

2. The Court may exercise its functions and powers, as provided in this Statute, on the territory of any State Party and, by special agreement, on the territory of any other State.

PART 2. JURISDICTION, ADMISSIBILITY AND APPLICABLE LAW

Article 5
Crimes within the jurisdiction of the Court

1. The jurisdiction of the Court shall be limited to the most serious crimes of concern to the international community as a whole. The Court has jurisdiction in accordance with this

Statute with respect to the following crimes:

(a) The crime of genocide;

(b) Crimes against humanity;

(c) War crimes;

(d) The crime of aggression.

2. The Court shall exercise jurisdiction over the crime of aggression once a provision is adopted in accordance with articles 121 and 123 defining the crime and setting out the conditions under which the Court shall exercise jurisdiction with respect to this crime. Such a provision shall be consistent with the relevant provisions of the Charter of the United Nations.

Article 6
Genocide

For the purpose of this Statute, "genocide" means any of the following acts committed with intent to destroy, in whole or in part, a national, ethnical, racial or religious group, as such:

(a) Killing members of the group;

(b) Causing serious bodily or mental harm to members of the group;

(c) Deliberately inflicting on the group conditions of life calculated to bring about its physical destruction in whole or in part;

(d) Imposing measures intended to prevent births within the group;
(e) Forcibly transferring children of the group to another group.

Article 7
Crimes against humanity

1. For the purpose of this Statute, "crime against humanity" means any of the following acts when committed as part of a widespread or systematic attack directed against any civilian population, with knowledge of the attack:

(a) Murder;
(b) Extermination;
(c) Enslavement;
(d) Deportation or forcible transfer of population;
(e) Imprisonment or other severe deprivation of physical liberty in violation of fundamental rules of international law;
(f) Torture;
(g) Rape, sexual slavery, enforced prostitution, forced pregnancy, enforced sterilization, or any other form of sexual violence of comparable gravity;
(h) Persecution against any identifiable group or collectivity on political, racial, national, ethnic, cultural, religious, gender as defined in paragraph 3, or other grounds that are universally recognized as impermissible under international law, in connection with any act referred to in this paragraph or any

crime within the jurisdiction of the Court;

(i) Enforced disappearance of persons;

(j) The crime of apartheid;

(k) Other inhumane acts of a similar character intentionally causing great suffering, or serious injury to body or to mental or physical health.

2. For the purpose of paragraph 1:

(a) "Attack directed against any civilian population" means a course of conduct involving the multiple commission of acts referred to in paragraph 1 against any civilian population, pursuant to or in furtherance of a State or organizational policy to commit such attack;

(b) "Extermination" includes the intentional infliction of conditions of life, inter alia the deprivation of access to food and medicine, calculated to bring about the destruction of part of a population;

(c) "Enslavement" means the exercise of any or all of the powers attaching to the right of ownership over a person and includes the exercise of such power in the course of trafficking in persons, in particular women and children;

(d) "Deportation or forcible transfer of population" means forced displacement of the persons concerned by expulsion or other coercive acts from the area in which they are lawfully present, without grounds permitted under international law;

(e) "Torture" means the intentional infliction of severe pain or suffering, whether physical or mental, upon a person in the custody or under the control of the accused; except that torture shall not include pain or suffering arising only from, inherent in or incidental to, lawful sanctions;

(f) "Forced pregnancy" means the unlawful confinement of a woman forcibly made pregnant, with the intent of affecting the ethnic composition of any population or carrying out other grave violations of international law. This definition shall not in any way be interpreted as affecting national laws relating to pregnancy;

(g) "Persecution" means the intentional and severe deprivation of fundamental rights contrary to international law by reason of the identity of the group or collectivity;

(h) "The crime of apartheid" means inhumane acts of a character similar to those referred to in paragraph 1, committed in the context of an institutionalized regime of systematic oppression and domination by one racial group over any other racial group or groups and committed with the intention of maintaining that regime;

(i) "Enforced disappearance of persons" means the arrest, detention or abduction of persons by, or with the authorization, support or acquiescence of, a State or a political organization, followed by a refusal to acknowledge that deprivation of freedom or to give information on the fate or whereabouts of those persons, with the intention of removing them from the protection of the law for a prolonged period of time.

3. For the purpose of this Statute, it is understood that the

term "gender" refers to the two sexes, male and female, within the context of society. The term "gender" does not indicate any meaning different from the above.

Article 8
War crimes

1. The Court shall have jurisdiction in respect of war crimes in particular when committed as part of a plan or policy or as part of a large-scale commission of such crimes.

2. For the purpose of this Statute, "war crimes" means:

(a) Grave breaches of the Geneva Conventions of 12 August 1949, namely, any of the following acts against persons or property protected under the provisions of the relevant Geneva Convention:

(i) Wilful killing;

(ii) Torture or inhuman treatment, including biological experiments;

(iii) Wilfully causing great suffering, or serious injury to body or health;

(iv) Extensive destruction and appropriation of property, not justified by military necessity and carried out unlawfully and wantonly;

(v)Compelling a prisoner of war or other protected person to serve in the forces of a hostile Power;

(vi)Wilfully depriving a prisoner of war or other

protected person of the rights of fair and regular trial;

(vii) Unlawful deportation or transfer or unlawful confinement;

(viii) Taking of hostages.

(b) Other serious violations of the laws and customs applicable in international armed conflict, within the established framework of international law, namely, any of the following acts:

(i) Intentionally directing attacks against the civilian population as such or against individual civilians not taking direct part in hostilities;

(ii) Intentionally directing attacks against civilian objects, that is, objects which are not military objectives;

(iii) Intentionally directing attacks against personnel, installations, material, units or vehicles involved in a humanitarian assistance or peacekeeping mission in accordance with the Charter of the United Nations, as long as they are entitled to the protection given to civilians or civilian objects under the international law of armed conflict;

(iv) Intentionally launching an attack in the knowledge that such attack will cause incidental loss of life or injury to civilians or damage to civilian objects or widespread, long-term and severe damage to the natural environment which would be clearly excessive in relation to the concrete and direct overall military advantage anticipated;

(v) Attacking or bombarding, by whatever means, towns, villages, dwellings or buildings which are undefended and which are not military objectives;

(vi) Killing or wounding a combatant who, having laid down his arms or having no longer means of defence, has surrendered at discretion;

(vii) Making improper use of a flag of truce, of the flag or of the military insignia and uniform of the enemy or of the United Nations, as well as of the distinctive emblems of the Geneva Conventions, resulting in death or serious personal injury;

(viii) The transfer, directly or indirectly, by the Occupying Power of parts of its own civilian population into the territory it occupies, or the deportation or transfer of all or parts of the population of the occupied territory within or outside this territory;

(ix) Intentionally directing attacks against buildings dedicated to religion, education, art, science or charitable purposes, historic monuments, hospitals and places where the sick and wounded are collected, provided they are not military objectives;

(x) Subjecting persons who are in the power of an adverse party to physical mutilation or to medical or scientific experiments of any kind which are neither justified by the medical, dental or hospital treatment of the person concerned nor carried out in his or her interest, and which cause death to or seriously endanger the health of such person or persons;

(xi) Killing or wounding treacherously individuals belonging to the hostile nation or army;

(xii) Declaring that no quarter will be given;

(xiii) Destroying or seizing the enemy's property unless such destruction or seizure be imperatively demanded by the necessities of war;

(xiv) Declaring abolished, suspended or inadmissible in a court of law the rights and actions of the nationals of the hostile party;

(xv) Compelling the nationals of the hostile party to take part in the operations of war directed against their own country, even if they were in the belligerent's service before the commencement of the war;

(xvi) Pillaging a town or place, even when taken by assault;

(xvii)Employing poison or poisoned weapons;

(xviii) Employing asphyxiating, poisonous or other gases, and all analogous liquids, materials or devices;

(xix) Employing bullets which expand or flatten easily in the human body, such as bullets with a hard envelope which does not entirely cover the core or is pierced with incisions;

(xx) Employing weapons, projectiles and material and methods of warfare which are of a nature to cause superfluous injury or unnecessary suffering or which are inherently indiscriminate in violation of the international law of armed conflict, provided that such weapons, projectiles and material and methods of warfare are the subject of a comprehensive prohibition and are included in an annex to this Statute, by an amendment in accordance with the relevant provisions set forth in articles 121 and 123;

(xxi) Committing outrages upon personal dignity, in particular humiliating and degrading treatment;

(xxii) Committing rape, sexual slavery, enforced prostitution, forced pregnancy, as defined in article 7, paragraph 2 (f), enforced sterilization, or any other form of sexual violence also constituting a grave breach of the Geneva Conventions;

(xxiii) Utilizing the presence of a civilian or other protected person to render certain points, areas or military forces immune from military operations;

(xxiv) Intentionally directing attacks against buildings, material, medical units and transport, and personnel using the distinctive emblems of the Geneva Conventions in conformity with international law;

(xxv) Intentionally using starvation of civilians as a method of warfare by depriving them of objects indispensable to their survival, including wilfully impeding relief supplies as provided for under the Geneva Conventions;

(xxvi) Conscripting or enlisting children under the age

of fifteen years into the national armed forces or using them to participate actively in hostilities.

(c) In the case of an armed conflict not of an international character, serious violations of article 3 common to the four Geneva Conventions of 12 August 1949, namely, any of the following acts committed against persons taking no active part in the hostilities, including members of armed forces who have laid down their arms and those placed hors de combat by sickness, wounds, detention or any other cause:

(i) Violence to life and person, in particular murder of all kinds, mutilation, cruel treatment and torture;

(ii) Committing outrages upon personal dignity, in particular humiliating and degrading treatment;

(iii) Taking of hostages;

(iv) The passing of sentences and the carrying out of executions without previous judgement pronounced by a regularly constituted court, affording all judicial guarantees which are generally recognized as indispensable.

(d) Paragraph 2 (c) applies to armed conflicts not of an international character and thus does not apply to situations of internal disturbances and tensions, such as riots, isolated and sporadic acts of violence or other acts of a similar nature.

(e) Other serious violations of the laws and customs applicable in armed conflicts not of an international character, within the established framework of international law, namely, any of the following acts:

(i) Intentionally directing attacks against the civilian population as such or against individual civilians not taking direct part in hostilities;

(ii) Intentionally directing attacks against buildings, material, medical units and transport, and personnel using the distinctive emblems of the Geneva Conventions in conformity with international law;

(iii) Intentionally directing attacks against personnel, installations, material, units or vehicles involved in a humanitarian assistance or peacekeeping mission in accordance with the Charter of the United Nations, as long as they are entitled to the protection given to civilians or civilian objects under the international law of armed conflict;

(iv) Intentionally directing attacks against buildings dedicated to religion, education, art, science or charitable purposes, historic monuments, hospitals and places where the sick and wounded are collected, provided they are not military objectives;

(v) Pillaging a town or place, even when taken by assault;

(vi) Committing rape, sexual slavery, enforced prostitution, forced pregnancy, as defined in article 7, paragraph 2 (f), enforced sterilization, and any other form of sexual violence also constituting a serious violation of article 3 common to the four Geneva Conventions;

(vii) Conscripting or enlisting children under the age of fifteen years into armed forces or groups or using them to participate actively in hostilities;

(viii) Ordering the displacement of the civilian population for reasons related to the conflict, unless the security of the civilians involved or imperative military reasons so demand;

(ix) Killing or wounding treacherously a combatant adversary;

(x) Declaring that no quarter will be given;

(xi) Subjecting persons who are in the power of another party to the conflict to physical mutilation or to medical or scientific experiments of any kind which are neither justified by the medical, dental or hospital treatment of the person concerned nor carried out in his or her interest, and which cause death to or seriously endanger the health of such person or persons;

(xii) Destroying or seizing the property of an adversary unless such destruction or seizure be imperatively demanded by the necessities of the conflict;

(f) Paragraph 2 (e) applies to armed conflicts not of an international character and thus does not apply to situations of internal disturbances and tensions, such as riots, isolated and sporadic acts of violence or other acts of a similar nature. It applies to armed conflicts that take place in the territory of a State when there is protracted armed conflict between governmental authorities and organized armed groups or between such groups.

3. Nothing in paragraph 2 (c) and (e) shall affect the responsibility of a Government to maintain or re-establish law and order in the State or to defend the unity and territorial integrity of the State, by all legitimate means.

Article 9
Elements of Crimes

1. Elements of Crimes shall assist the Court in the interpretation and application of articles 6, 7 and 8. They shall be adopted by a two-thirds majority of the members of the Assembly of States Parties.

2. Amendments to the Elements of Crimes may be proposed by:

(a) Any State Party;
(b) The judges acting by an absolute majority;
(c) The Prosecutor.

Such amendments shall be adopted by a two-thirds majority of the members of the Assembly of States Parties.

3. The Elements of Crimes and amendments thereto shall be consistent with this Statute.

Article 10

Nothing in this Part shall be interpreted as limiting or prejudicing in any way existing or developing rules of international law for purposes other than this Statute.

Article 11
Jurisdiction ratione temporis

1. The Court has jurisdiction only with respect to crimes committed after the entry into force of this Statute.

2. If a State becomes a Party to this Statute after its entry into force, the Court may exercise its jurisdiction only with respect to crimes committed after the entry into force of this Statute for that State, unless that State has made a declaration under article 12, paragraph 3.

Article 12
Preconditions to the exercise of jurisdiction

1. A State which becomes a Party to this Statute thereby accepts the jurisdiction of the Court with respect to the crimes referred to in article 5.

2. In the case of article 13, paragraph (a) or (c), the Court may exercise its jurisdiction if one or more of the following States are Parties to this Statute or have accepted the jurisdiction of the Court in accordance with paragraph 3:

(a) The State on the territory of which the conduct in question occurred or, if the crime was committed on board a vessel or aircraft, the State of registration of that vessel or aircraft;

(b) The State of which the person accused of the crime is a national.

3. If the acceptance of a State which is not a Party to this Statute is required under paragraph 2, that State may, by declaration lodged with the Registrar, accept the exercise of jurisdiction by the Court with respect to the crime in question. The accepting State shall cooperate with the Court without any delay or exception in accordance with Part 9.

Article 13
Exercise of jurisdiction

The Court may exercise its jurisdiction with respect to a crime referred to in article 5 in accordance with the provisions of this Statute if:

(a) A situation in which one or more of such crimes appears to have been committed is referred to the Prosecutor by a State Party in accordance with article 14;

(b) A situation in which one or more of such crimes appears to have been committed is referred to the Prosecutor by the Security Council acting under Chapter VII of the Charter of the United Nations; or

(c) The Prosecutor has initiated an investigation in respect of such a crime in accordance with article 15.

Article 14
Referral of a situation by a State Party

1. A State Party may refer to the Prosecutor a situation in which one or more crimes within the jurisdiction of the Court appear to have been committed requesting the Prosecutor to investigate the situation for the purpose of determining whether one or more specific persons should be charged with the commission of such crimes.

2. As far as possible, a referral shall specify the relevant circumstances and be accompanied by such supporting documentation as is available to the State referring the situation.

Article 15
Prosecutor

1. The Prosecutor may initiate investigations proprio motu on the basis of information on crimes within the jurisdiction of the Court.

2. The Prosecutor shall analyse the seriousness of the information received. For this purpose, he or she may seek additional information from States, organs of the United Nations, intergovernmental or non-governmental organizations, or other reliable sources that he or she deems

appropriate, and may receive written or oral testimony at the seat of the Court.

3. If the Prosecutor concludes that there is a reasonable basis to proceed with an investigation, he or she shall submit to the Pre-Trial Chamber a request for authorization of an investigation, together with any supporting material collected. Victims may make representations to the Pre-Trial Chamber, in accordance with the Rules of Procedure and Evidence.

4. If the Pre-Trial Chamber, upon examination of the request and the supporting material, considers that there is a reasonable basis to proceed with an investigation, and that the case appears to fall within the jurisdiction of the Court, it shall authorize the commencement of the investigation, without prejudice to subsequent determinations by the Court with regard to the jurisdiction and admissibility of a case.

5. The refusal of the Pre-Trial Chamber to authorize the investigation shall not preclude the presentation of a subsequent request by the Prosecutor based on new facts or evidence regarding the same situation.

6. If, after the preliminary examination referred to in paragraphs 1 and 2, the Prosecutor concludes that the information provided does not constitute a reasonable basis for an investigation, he or she shall inform those who provided the information. This shall not preclude the Prosecutor from considering further information submitted to him or her regarding the same situation in the light of new facts or evidence.

Article 16
Deferral of investigation or prosecution

No investigation or prosecution may be commenced or proceeded with under this Statute for a period of 12 months after the Security Council, in a resolution adopted under Chapter VII of the Charter of the United Nations, has requested the Court to that effect; that request may be renewed by the Council under the same conditions.

Article 17
Issues of admissibility

1. Having regard to paragraph 10 of the Preamble and article 1, the Court shall determine that a case is inadmissible where:

(a) The case is being investigated or prosecuted by a State which has jurisdiction over it, unless the State is unwilling or unable genuinely to carry out the investigation or prosecution;

(b) The case has been investigated by a State which has jurisdiction over it and the State has decided not to prosecute the person concerned, unless the decision resulted from the unwillingness or inability of the State genuinely to prosecute;

(c) The person concerned has already been tried for conduct which is the subject of the complaint, and a trial by the Court is not permitted under article 20, paragraph 3;

(d) The case is not of sufficient gravity to justify further action by the Court.

2. In order to determine unwillingness in a particular case, the Court shall consider, having regard to the principles of due process recognized by international law, whether one or more of the following exist, as applicable:

(a) The proceedings were or are being undertaken or the national decision was made for the purpose of shielding the person concerned from criminal responsibility for crimes within the jurisdiction of the Court referred to in article 5;

(b) There has been an unjustified delay in the proceedings which in the circumstances is inconsistent with an intent to bring the person concerned to justice;

(c) The proceedings were not or are not being conducted independently or impartially, and they were or are being conducted in a manner which, in the circumstances, is inconsistent with an intent to bring the person concerned to justice.

3. In order to determine inability in a particular case, the Court shall consider whether, due to a total or substantial collapse or unavailability of its national judicial system, the State is unable to obtain the accused or the necessary evidence and testimony or otherwise unable to carry out its proceedings.

Article 18
Preliminary rulings regarding admissibility

1. When a situation has been referred to the Court pursuant to article 13 (a) and the Prosecutor has determined that there would be a reasonable basis to commence an investigation, or the Prosecutor initiates an investigation pursuant to articles 13 (c) and 15, the Prosecutor shall notify all States Parties and those States which, taking into account the information available, would normally exercise jurisdiction over the crimes concerned. The Prosecutor may notify such States on a confidential basis and, where the Prosecutor believes it necessary to protect persons, prevent destruction of evidence or prevent the absconding of persons, may limit the scope of the information provided to States.

2. Within one month of receipt of that notification, a State may inform the Court that it is investigating or has investigated its nationals or others within its jurisdiction with respect to criminal acts which may constitute crimes referred to in article 5 and which relate to the information provided in the notification to States. At the request of that State, the Prosecutor shall defer to the State's investigation of those persons unless the Pre-Trial Chamber, on the application of the Prosecutor, decides to authorize the investigation.

3. The Prosecutor's deferral to a State's investigation shall be open to review by the Prosecutor six months after the date of deferral or at any time when there has been a significant change

of circumstances based on the State's unwillingness or inability genuinely to carry out the investigation.

4. The State concerned or the Prosecutor may appeal to the Appeals Chamber against a ruling of the Pre-Trial Chamber, in accordance with article 82. The appeal may be heard on an expedited basis.

5. When the Prosecutor has deferred an investigation in accordance with paragraph 2, the Prosecutor may request that the State concerned periodically inform the Prosecutor of the progress of its investigations and any subsequent prosecutions. States Parties shall respond to such requests without undue delay.

6. Pending a ruling by the Pre-Trial Chamber, or at any time when the Prosecutor has deferred an investigation under this article, the Prosecutor may, on an exceptional basis, seek authority from the Pre-Trial Chamber to pursue necessary investigative steps for the purpose of preserving evidence where there is a unique opportunity to obtain important evidence or there is a significant risk that such evidence may not be subsequently available.

7. A State which has challenged a ruling of the Pre-Trial Chamber under this article may challenge the admissibility of a case under article 19 on the grounds of additional significant facts or significant change of circumstances.

Article 19
Challenges to the jurisdiction of the Court or the admissibility of a case

1. The Court shall satisfy itself that it has jurisdiction in any case brought before it. The Court may, on its own motion, determine the admissibility of a case in accordance with article 17.

2. Challenges to the admissibility of a case on the grounds referred to in article 17 or challenges to the jurisdiction of the Court may be made by:

(a) An accused or a person for whom a warrant of arrest or a summons to appear has been issued under article 58;

(b) A State which has jurisdiction over a case, on the ground that it is investigating or prosecuting the case or has investigated or prosecuted; or

(c) A State from which acceptance of jurisdiction is required under article 12.

3. The Prosecutor may seek a ruling from the Court regarding a question of jurisdiction or admissibility. In proceedings with respect to jurisdiction or admissibility, those who have referred the situation under article 13, as well as victims, may also submit observations to the Court.

4. The admissibility of a case or the jurisdiction of the Court may be challenged only once by any person or State referred to in paragraph 2. The challenge shall take place prior to or at the

commencement of the trial. In exceptional circumstances, the Court may grant leave for a challenge to be brought more than once or at a time later than the commencement of the trial. Challenges to the admissibility of a case, at the commencement of a trial, or subsequently with the leave of the Court, may be based only on article 17, paragraph 1 (c).

5. A State referred to in paragraph 2 (b) and (c) shall make a challenge at the earliest opportunity.

6. Prior to the confirmation of the charges, challenges to the admissibility of a case or challenges to the jurisdiction of the Court shall be referred to the Pre-Trial Chamber. After confirmation of the charges, they shall be referred to the Trial Chamber. Decisions with respect to jurisdiction or admissibility may be appealed to the Appeals Chamber in accordance with article 82.

7. If a challenge is made by a State referred to in paragraph 2 (b) or (c), the Prosecutor shall suspend the investigation until such time as the Court makes a determination in accordance with article 17.

8. Pending a ruling by the Court, the Prosecutor may seek authority from the Court:

(a) To pursue necessary investigative steps of the kind referred to in article 18, paragraph 6;

(b) To take a statement or testimony from a witness or complete the collection and examination of evidence which had begun prior to the making of the challenge; and

(c) In cooperation with the relevant States, to prevent the absconding of persons in respect of whom the Prosecutor has already requested a warrant of arrest under article 58.

9. The making of a challenge shall not affect the validity of any act performed by the Prosecutor or any order or warrant issued by the Court prior to the making of the challenge.

10. If the Court has decided that a case is inadmissible under article 17, the Prosecutor may submit a request for a review of the decision when he or she is fully satisfied that new facts have arisen which negate the basis on which the case had previously been found inadmissible under article 17.

11. If the Prosecutor, having regard to the matters referred to in article 17, defers an investigation, the Prosecutor may request that the relevant State make available to the Prosecutor information on the proceedings. That information shall, at the request of the State concerned, be confidential. If the Prosecutor thereafter decides to proceed with an investigation, he or she shall notify the State to which deferral of the proceedings has taken place.

Article 20
Ne bis in idem

1. Except as provided in this Statute, no person shall be tried before the Court with respect to conduct which formed the basis of crimes for which the person has been convicted or acquitted by the Court.

2. No person shall be tried by another court for a crime referred to in article 5 for which that person has already been convicted or acquitted by the Court.

3. No person who has been tried by another court for conduct also proscribed under article 6, 7 or 8 shall be tried by the Court with respect to the same conduct unless the proceedings in the other court:

(a) Were for the purpose of shielding the person concerned from criminal responsibility for crimes within the jurisdiction of the Court; or

(b) Otherwise were not conducted independently or impartially in accordance with the norms of due process recognized by international law and were conducted in a manner which, in the circumstances, was inconsistent with an intent to bring the person concerned to justice.

Article 21
Applicable law

1. The Court shall apply:

(a) In the first place, this Statute, Elements of Crimes and its Rules of Procedure and Evidence;

(b) In the second place, where appropriate, applicable treaties and the principles and rules of international law, including the established principles of the international law of armed conflict;

(c) Failing that, general principles of law derived by the Court from national laws of legal systems of the world including, as appropriate, the national laws of States that would normally exercise jurisdiction over the crime, provided that those principles are not inconsistent with this Statute and with international law and internationally recognized norms and standards.

2. The Court may apply principles and rules of law as interpreted in its previous decisions.

3. The application and interpretation of law pursuant to this article must be consistent with internationally recognized human rights, and be without any adverse distinction founded on grounds such as gender as defined in article 7, paragraph 3, age, race, colour, language, religion or belief, political or other opinion, national, ethnic or social origin, wealth, birth or other status.

PART 3. GENERAL PRINCIPLES OF CRIMINAL LAW

Article 22
Nullum crimen sine lege

1. A person shall not be criminally responsible under this Statute unless the conduct in question constitutes, at the time it takes place, a crime within the jurisdiction of the Court.

2. The definition of a crime shall be strictly construed and shall not be extended by analogy. In case of ambiguity, the definition shall be interpreted in favour of the person being investigated, prosecuted or convicted.

3. This article shall not affect the characterization of any conduct as criminal under international law independently of this Statute.

Article 23
Nulla poena sine lege

A person convicted by the Court may be punished only in accordance with this Statute.

Article 24
Non-retroactivity ratione personae

1. No person shall be criminally responsible under this Statute for conduct prior to the entry into force of the Statute.

2. In the event of a change in the law applicable to a given case prior to a final judgement, the law more favourable to the person being investigated, prosecuted or convicted shall apply.

Article 25
Individual criminal responsibility

1. The Court shall have jurisdiction over natural persons

pursuant to this Statute.

2. A person who commits a crime within the jurisdiction of the Court shall be individually responsible and liable for punishment in accordance with this Statute.

3. In accordance with this Statute, a person shall be criminally responsible and liable for punishment for a crime within the jurisdiction of the Court if that person:

(a) Commits such a crime, whether as an individual, jointly with another or through another person, regardless of whether that other person is criminally responsible;

(b) Orders, solicits or induces the commission of such a crime which in fact occurs or is attempted;

(c) For the purpose of facilitating the commission of such a crime, aids, abets or otherwise assists in its commission or its attempted commission, including providing the means for its commission;

(d) In any other way contributes to the commission or attempted commission of such a crime by a group of persons acting with a common purpose. Such contribution shall be intentional and shall either:

(i) Be made with the aim of furthering the criminal activity or criminal purpose of the group, where such activity or purpose involves the commission of a crime within the jurisdiction of the Court; or

(ii)Be made in the knowledge of the intention of the

group to commit the crime;

(e) In respect of the crime of genocide, directly and publicly incites others to commit genocide;

(f) Attempts to commit such a crime by taking action that commences its execution by means of a substantial step, but the crime does not occur because of circumstances independent of the person's intentions. However, a person who abandons the effort to commit the crime or otherwise prevents the completion of the crime shall not be liable for punishment under this Statute for the attempt to commit that crime if that person completely and voluntarily gave up the criminal purpose.

4. No provision in this Statute relating to individual criminal responsibility shall affect the responsibility of States under international law.

Article 26
Exclusion of jurisdiction over persons under eighteen

The Court shall have no jurisdiction over any person who was under the age of 18 at the time of the alleged commission of a crime.

Article 27
Irrelevance of official capacity

1. This Statute shall apply equally to all persons without any distinction based on official capacity. In particular, official capacity as a Head of State or Government, a member of a Government or parliament, an elected representative or a government official shall in no case exempt a person from criminal responsibility under this Statute, nor shall it, in and of itself, constitute a ground for reduction of sentence.

2. Immunities or special procedural rules which may attach to the official capacity of a person, whether under national or international law, shall not bar the Court from exercising its jurisdiction over such a person.

Article 28
Responsibility of commanders and other superiors

In addition to other grounds of criminal responsibility under this Statute for crimes within the jurisdiction of the Court:

(a) A military commander or person effectively acting as a military commander shall be criminally responsible for crimes within the jurisdiction of the Court committed by forces under his or her effective command and control, or effective authority and control as the case may be, as a result of his or her failure to exercise control properly over such forces, where:

(i) That military commander or person either knew or, owing to the circumstances at the time, should have known that the forces were committing or about to commit such crimes; and

(ii) That military commander or person failed to take all necessary and reasonable measures within his or her power to prevent or repress their commission or to submit the matter to the competent authorities for investigation and prosecution.

(b)With respect to superior and subordinate relationships not described in paragraph (a), a superior shall be criminally responsible for crimes within the jurisdiction of the Court committed by subordinates under his or her effective authority and control, as a result of his or her failure to exercise control properly over such subordinates, where:

(i)The superior either knew, or consciously disregarded information which clearly indicated, that the subordinates were committing or about to commit such crimes;

(ii)The crimes concerned activities that were within the effective responsibility and control of the superior; and

(iii)The superior failed to take all necessary and reasonable measures within his or her power to prevent or repress their commission or to submit the matter to the competent authorities for investigation and prosecution.

Article 29
Non-applicability of statute of limitations

The crimes within the jurisdiction of the Court shall not be subject to any statute of limitations.

Article 30
Mental element

1. Unless otherwise provided, a person shall be criminally responsible and liable for punishment for a crime within the jurisdiction of the Court only if the material elements are committed with intent and knowledge.

2. For the purposes of this article, a person has intent where:

(a) In relation to conduct, that person means to engage in the conduct;

(b) In relation to a consequence, that person means to cause that consequence or is aware that it will occur in the ordinary course of events.

3. For the purposes of this article, "knowledge" means awareness that a circumstance exists or a consequence will occur in the ordinary course of events. "Know" and "knowingly" shall be construed accordingly.

Article 31
Grounds for excluding criminal responsibility

1. In addition to other grounds for excluding criminal responsibility provided for in this Statute, a person shall not be criminally responsible if, at the time of that person's conduct:

(a) The person suffers from a mental disease or defect that destroys that person's capacity to appreciate the unlawfulness or nature of his or her conduct, or capacity to control his or her conduct to conform to the requirements of law;

(b) The person is in a state of intoxication that destroys that person's capacity to appreciate the unlawfulness or nature of his or her conduct, or capacity to control his or her conduct to conform to the requirements of law, unless the person has become voluntarily intoxicated under such circumstances that the person knew, or disregarded the risk, that, as a result of the intoxication, he or she was likely to engage in conduct constituting a crime within the jurisdiction of the Court;

(c) The person acts reasonably to defend himself or herself or another person or, in the case of war crimes, property which is essential for the survival of the person or another person or property which is essential for accomplishing a military mission, against an imminent and unlawful use of force in a manner proportionate to the degree of danger to the person or the other person or property protected. The fact that the person was involved in a defensive operation conducted by forces shall not in itself constitute a ground for excluding criminal responsibility under this subparagraph;

(d) The conduct which is alleged to constitute a crime within the jurisdiction of the Court has been caused by duress resulting from a threat of imminent death or of continuing or imminent serious bodily harm against that person or another person, and the person acts necessarily and reasonably to avoid this threat, provided that the person does not intend to cause a greater harm than the one sought to be avoided. Such a threat may either be:

(i) Made by other persons; or

(ii) Constituted by other circumstances beyond that person's control.

2. The Court shall determine the applicability of the grounds for excluding criminal responsibility provided for in this Statute to the case before it.

3. At trial, the Court may consider a ground for excluding criminal responsibility other than those referred to in paragraph 1 where such a ground is derived from applicable law as set forth in article 21. The procedures relating to the consideration of such a ground shall be provided for in the Rules of Procedure and Evidence.

Article 32
Mistake of fact or mistake of law

1. A mistake of fact shall be a ground for excluding criminal responsibility only if it negates the mental element required by the crime.

2. A mistake of law as to whether a particular type of conduct is a crime within the jurisdiction of the Court shall not be a ground for excluding criminal responsibility. A mistake of law may, however, be a ground for excluding criminal responsibility if it negates the mental element required by such a crime, or as provided for in article 33.

Article 33
Superior orders and prescription of law

1. The fact that a crime within the jurisdiction of the Court has been committed by a person pursuant to an order of a Government or of a superior, whether military or civilian, shall not relieve that person of criminal responsibility unless:

(a) The person was under a legal obligation to obey orders of the Government or the superior in question;

(b) The person did not know that the order was unlawful; and

(c) The order was not manifestly unlawful.

2. For the purposes of this article, orders to commit genocide or crimes against humanity are manifestly unlawful.

PART 4. COMPOSITION AND ADMINISTRATION OF THE COURT

Article 34
Organs of the Court

The Court shall be composed of the following organs:

(a) The Presidency;

(b) An Appeals Division, a Trial Division and a Pre-Trial Division;

(c) The Office of the Prosecutor;

(d) The Registry.

Article 35
Service of judges

1. All judges shall be elected as full-time members of the Court and shall be available to serve on that basis from the commencement of their terms of office.

2. The judges composing the Presidency shall serve on a full-time basis as soon as they are elected.

3. The Presidency may, on the basis of the workload of the

Court and in consultation with its members, decide from time to time to what extent the remaining judges shall be required to serve on a full-time basis. Any such arrangement shall be without prejudice to the provisions of article 40.

4. The financial arrangements for judges not required to serve on a full-time basis shall be made in accordance with article 49.

Article 36
Qualifications, nomination and election of judges

1. Subject to the provisions of paragraph 2, there shall be 18 judges of the Court.

2. (a) The Presidency, acting on behalf of the Court, may propose an increase in the number of judges specified in paragraph 1, indicating the reasons why this is considered necessary and appropriate. The Registrar shall promptly circulate any such proposal to all States Parties.

(b) Any such proposal shall then be considered at a meeting of the Assembly of States Parties to be convened in accordance with article 112. The proposal shall be considered adopted if approved at the meeting by a vote of two thirds of the members of the Assembly of States Parties and shall enter into force at such time as decided by the Assembly of States Parties.

(c) (i)Once a proposal for an increase in the number of judges has been adopted under subparagraph (b), the election of the additional judges shall take place at the next session of the

Assembly of States Parties in accordance with paragraphs 3 to 8, and article 37, paragraph 2;

(ii) Once a proposal for an increase in the number of judges has been adopted and brought into effect under subparagraphs (b) and (c) (i), it shall be open to the Presidency at any time thereafter, if the workload of the Court justifies it, to propose a reduction in the number of judges, provided that the number of judges shall not be reduced below that specified in paragraph 1. The proposal shall be dealt with in accordance with the procedure laid down in subparagraphs (a) and (b). In the event that the proposal is adopted, the number of judges shall be progressively decreased as the terms of office of serving judges expire, until the necessary number has been reached.

3. (a) The judges shall be chosen from among persons of high moral character, impartiality and integrity who possess the qualifications required in their respective States for appointment to the highest judicial offices.

(b) Every candidate for election to the Court shall:

(i) Have established competence in criminal law and procedure, and the necessary relevant experience, whether as judge, prosecutor, advocate or in other similar capacity, in criminal proceedings; or

(ii) Have established competence in relevant areas of international law such as international humanitarian law and the law of human rights, and extensive experience in a professional legal capacity which is of relevance to the judicial work of the Court;

(c) Every candidate for election to the Court shall have an excellent knowledge of and be fluent in at least one of the working languages of the Court.

4. (a) Nominations of candidates for election to the Court may be made by any State Party to this Statute, and shall be made either:

(i) By the procedure for the nomination of candidates for appointment to the highest judicial offices in the State in question; or

(ii) By the procedure provided for the nomination of candidates for the International Court of Justice in the Statute of that Court.

Nominations shall be accompanied by a statement in the necessary detail specifying how the candidate fulfils the requirements of paragraph 3.

(b) Each State Party may put forward one candidate for any given election who need not necessarily be a national of that

State Party but shall in any case be a national of a State Party.

(c) The Assembly of States Parties may decide to establish, if appropriate, an Advisory Committee on nominations. In that event, the Committee's composition and mandate shall be established by the Assembly of States Parties.

5. For the purposes of the election, there shall be two lists of candidates:

List A containing the names of candidates with the qualifications specified in paragraph 3 (b) (i); and

List B containing the names of candidates with the qualifications specified in paragraph 3 (b) (ii).

A candidate with sufficient qualifications for both lists may choose on which list to appear. At the first election to the Court, at least nine judges shall be elected from list A and at least five judges from list B. Subsequent elections shall be so organized as to maintain the equivalent proportion on the Court of judges qualified on the two lists.

6. (a) The judges shall be elected by secret ballot at a meeting of the Assembly of States Parties convened for that purpose under article 112. Subject to paragraph 7, the persons elected to the Court shall be the 18 candidates who obtain the highest number of votes and a two-thirds majority of the States Parties present and voting.

(b) In the event that a sufficient number of judges is not

elected on the first ballot, successive ballots shall be held in accordance with the procedures laid down in subparagraph (a) until the remaining places have been filled.

7. No two judges may be nationals of the same State. A person who, for the purposes of membership of the Court, could be regarded as a national of more than one State shall be deemed to be a national of the State in which that person ordinarily exercises civil and political rights.

8. (a) The States Parties shall, in the selection of judges, take into account the need, within the membership of the Court, for:

(i) The representation of the principal legal systems of the world;

(ii) Equitable geographical representation; and

(iii) A fair representation of female and male judges.

(b) States Parties shall also take into account the need to include judges with legal expertise on specific issues, including, but not limited to, violence against women or children.

9. (a) Subject to subparagraph (b), judges shall hold office for a term of nine years and, subject to subparagraph (c) and to article 37, paragraph 2, shall not be eligible for re-election.

(b) At the first election, one third of the judges elected shall be selected by lot to serve for a term of three years; one third of the judges elected shall be selected by lot to serve for a term of six years; and the remainder shall serve for a term of nine years.

(c) A judge who is selected to serve for a term of three years under subparagraph (b) shall be eligible for re-election for a full term.

10. Notwithstanding paragraph 9, a judge assigned to a Trial or Appeals Chamber in accordance with article 39 shall continue in office to complete any trial or appeal the hearing of which has already commenced before that Chamber.

Article 37
Judicial vacancies

1. In the event of a vacancy, an election shall be held in accordance with article 36 to fill the vacancy.

2. A judge elected to fill a vacancy shall serve for the remainder of the predecessor's term and, if that period is three years or less, shall be eligible for re-election for a full term under article 36.

Article 38
The Presidency

1. The President and the First and Second Vice-Presidents

shall be elected by an absolute majority of the judges. They shall each serve for a term of three years or until the end of their respective terms of office as judges, whichever expires earlier. They shall be eligible for re-election once.

2. The First Vice-President shall act in place of the President in the event that the President is unavailable or disqualified. The Second Vice-President shall act in place of the President in the event that both the President and the First Vice-President are unavailable or disqualified.

3. The President, together with the First and Second Vice-Presidents, shall constitute the Presidency, which shall be responsible for:

(a) The proper administration of the Court, with the exception of the Office of the Prosecutor; and

(b)The other functions conferred upon it in accordance with this Statute.

4. In discharging its responsibility under paragraph 3 (a), the Presidency shall coordinate with and seek the concurrence of the Prosecutor on all matters of mutual concern.

Article 39
Chambers

1. As soon as possible after the election of the judges, the Court shall organize itself into the divisions specified in article

34, paragraph (b). The Appeals Division shall be composed of the President and four other judges, the Trial Division of not less than six judges and the Pre-Trial Division of not less than six judges. The assignment of judges to divisions shall be based on the nature of the functions to be performed by each division and the qualifications and experience of the judges elected to the Court, in such a way that each division shall contain an appropriate combination of expertise in criminal law and procedure and in international law. The Trial and Pre-Trial Divisions shall be composed predominantly of judges with criminal trial experience.

2. (a) The judicial functions of the Court shall be carried out in each division by Chambers.

(b) (i) The Appeals Chamber shall be composed of all the judges of the Appeals Division;

(ii) The functions of the Trial Chamber shall be carried out by three judges of the Trial Division;

(iii) The functions of the Pre-Trial Chamber shall be carried out either by three judges of the Pre-Trial Division or by a single judge of that division in accordance with this Statute and the Rules of Procedure and Evidence;

(c) Nothing in this paragraph shall preclude the simultaneous constitution of more than one Trial Chamber or Pre-Trial Chamber when the efficient management of the Court's workload so requires.

3. (a) Judges assigned to the Trial and Pre-Trial Divisions shall serve in those divisions for a period of three years, and thereafter until the completion of any case the hearing of which has already commenced in the division concerned.

(b)Judges assigned to the Appeals Division shall serve in that division for their entire term of office.

4. Judges assigned to the Appeals Division shall serve only in that division. Nothing in this article shall, however, preclude the temporary attachment of judges from the Trial Division to the Pre-Trial Division or vice versa, if the Presidency considers that the efficient management of the Court's workload so requires, provided that under no circumstances shall a judge who has participated in the pre-trial phase of a case be eligible to sit on the Trial Chamber hearing that case.

Article 40
Independence of the judges

1. The judges shall be independent in the performance of their functions.

2. Judges shall not engage in any activity which is likely to interfere with their judicial functions or to affect confidence in their independence.

3. Judges required to serve on a full-time basis at the seat

of the Court shall not engage in any other occupation of a professional nature.

4. Any question regarding the application of paragraphs 2 and 3 shall be decided by an absolute majority of the judges. Where any such question concerns an individual judge, that judge shall not take part in the decision.

Article 41
Excusing and disqualification of judges

1. The Presidency may, at the request of a judge, excuse that judge from the exercise of a function under this Statute, in accordance with the Rules of Procedure and Evidence.

2. (a) A judge shall not participate in any case in which his or her impartiality might reasonably be doubted on any ground. A judge shall be disqualified from a case in accordance with this paragraph if, inter alia, that judge has previously been involved in any capacity in that case before the Court or in a related criminal case at the national level involving the person being investigated or prosecuted. A judge shall also be disqualified on such other grounds as may be provided for in the Rules of Procedure and Evidence.

(b) The Prosecutor or the person being investigated or prosecuted may request the disqualification of a judge under this paragraph.

(c) Any question as to the disqualification of a judge shall be decided by an absolute majority of the judges. The challenged judge shall be entitled to present his or her comments on the matter, but shall not take part in the decision.

Article 42
The Office of the Prosecutor

1. The Office of the Prosecutor shall act independently as a separate organ of the Court. It shall be responsible for receiving referrals and any substantiated information on crimes within the jurisdiction of the Court, for examining them and for conducting investigations and prosecutions before the Court. A member of the Office shall not seek or act on instructions from any external source.

2. The Office shall be headed by the Prosecutor. The Prosecutor shall have full authority over the management and administration of the Office, including the staff, facilities and other resources thereof. The Prosecutor shall be assisted by one or more Deputy Prosecutors, who shall be entitled to carry out any of the acts required of the Prosecutor under this Statute. The Prosecutor and the Deputy Prosecutors shall be of different nationalities. They shall serve on a full-time basis.

3. The Prosecutor and the Deputy Prosecutors shall be persons of high moral character, be highly competent in and have extensive practical experience in the prosecution or trial of criminal cases. They shall have an excellent knowledge of and be fluent in at least one of the working languages of the Court.

4. The Prosecutor shall be elected by secret ballot by an absolute majority of the members of the Assembly of States Parties. The Deputy Prosecutors shall be elected in the same way from a list of candidates provided by the Prosecutor. The Prosecutor shall nominate three candidates for each position of Deputy Prosecutor to be filled. Unless a shorter term is decided upon at the time of their election, the Prosecutor and the Deputy Prosecutors shall hold office for a term of nine years and shall not be eligible for re-election.

5. Neither the Prosecutor nor a Deputy Prosecutor shall engage in any activity which is likely to interfere with his or her prosecutorial functions or to affect confidence in his or her independence. They shall not engage in any other occupation of a professional nature.

6. The Presidency may excuse the Prosecutor or a Deputy Prosecutor, at his or her request, from acting in a particular case.

7. Neither the Prosecutor nor a Deputy Prosecutor shall participate in any matter in which their impartiality might reasonably be doubted on any ground. They shall be disqualified from a case in accordance with this paragraph if, inter alia, they have previously been involved in any capacity in that case before the Court or in a related criminal case at the national level involving the person being investigated or prosecuted.

8. Any question as to the disqualification of the Prosecutor or a Deputy Prosecutor shall be decided by the Appeals

Chamber.

(a) The person being investigated or prosecuted may at any time request the disqualification of the Prosecutor or a Deputy Prosecutor on the grounds set out in this article;

(b) The Prosecutor or the Deputy Prosecutor, as appropriate, shall be entitled to present his or her comments on the matter;

9. The Prosecutor shall appoint advisers with legal expertise on specific issues, including, but not limited to, sexual and gender violence and violence against children.

Article 43
The Registry

1. The Registry shall be responsible for the non-judicial aspects of the administration and servicing of the Court, without prejudice to the functions and powers of the Prosecutor in accordance with article 42.

2. The Registry shall be headed by the Registrar, who shall be the principal administrative officer of the Court. The Registrar shall exercise his or her functions under the authority of the President of the Court.

3. The Registrar and the Deputy Registrar shall be persons of high moral character, be highly competent and have an excellent knowledge of and be fluent in at least one of the working languages of the Court.

4. The judges shall elect the Registrar by an absolute majority by secret ballot, taking into account any recommendation by the Assembly of States Parties. If the need arises and upon the recommendation of the Registrar, the judges shall elect, in the same manner, a Deputy Registrar.

5. The Registrar shall hold office for a term of five years, shall be eligible for re-election once and shall serve on a full-time basis. The Deputy Registrar shall hold office for a term of five years or such shorter term as may be decided upon by an absolute majority of the judges, and may be elected on the basis that the Deputy Registrar shall be called upon to serve as required.

6. The Registrar shall set up a Victims and Witnesses Unit within the Registry. This Unit shall provide, in consultation with the Office of the Prosecutor, protective measures and security arrangements, counselling and other appropriate assistance for witnesses, victims who appear before the Court, and others who are at risk on account of testimony given by such witnesses. The Unit shall include staff with expertise in trauma, including trauma related to crimes of sexual violence.

Article 44
Staff

1. The Prosecutor and the Registrar shall appoint such qualified staff as may be required to their respective offices. In the case of the Prosecutor, this shall include the appointment

of investigators.

2. In the employment of staff, the Prosecutor and the Registrar shall ensure the highest standards of efficiency, competency and integrity, and shall have regard, mutatis mutandis, to the criteria set forth in article 36, paragraph 8.

3. The Registrar, with the agreement of the Presidency and the Prosecutor, shall propose Staff Regulations which include the terms and conditions upon which the staff of the Court shall be appointed, remunerated and dismissed. The Staff Regulations shall be approved by the Assembly of States Parties.

4. The Court may, in exceptional circumstances, employ the expertise of gratis personnel offered by States Parties, intergovernmental organizations or non-governmental organizations to assist with the work of any of the organs of the Court. The Prosecutor may accept any such offer on behalf of the Office of the Prosecutor. Such gratis personnel shall be employed in accordance with guidelines to be established by the Assembly of States Parties.

Article 45
Solemn undertaking

Before taking up their respective duties under this Statute, the judges, the Prosecutor, the Deputy Prosecutors, the Registrar and the Deputy Registrar shall each make a solemn undertaking in open court to exercise his or her respective functions impartially and conscientiously.

Article 46
Removal from office

1. A judge, the Prosecutor, a Deputy Prosecutor, the Registrar or the Deputy Registrar shall be removed from office if a decision to this effect is made in accordance with paragraph 2, in cases where that person:

(a) Is found to have committed serious misconduct or a serious breach of his or her duties under this Statute, as provided for in the Rules of Procedure and Evidence; or

(b) Is unable to exercise the functions required by this Statute.

2. A decision as to the removal from office of a judge, the Prosecutor or a Deputy Prosecutor under paragraph 1 shall be made by the Assembly of States Parties, by secret ballot:

(a) In the case of a judge, by a two-thirds majority of the States Parties upon a recommendation adopted by a two-thirds majority of the other judges;

(b) In the case of the Prosecutor, by an absolute majority of the States Parties;

(c) In the case of a Deputy Prosecutor, by an absolute majority of the States Parties upon the recommendation of the Prosecutor.

3. A decision as to the removal from office of the Registrar or Deputy Registrar shall be made by an absolute majority of the judges.

4. A judge, Prosecutor, Deputy Prosecutor, Registrar or Deputy Registrar whose conduct or ability to exercise the functions of the office as required by this Statute is challenged under this article shall have full opportunity to present and receive evidence and to make submissions in accordance with the Rules of Procedure and Evidence. The person in question shall not otherwise participate in the consideration of the matter.

Article 47
Disciplinary measures

A judge, Prosecutor, Deputy Prosecutor, Registrar or Deputy Registrar who has committed misconduct of a less serious nature than that set out in article 46, paragraph 1, shall be subject to disciplinary measures, in accordance with the Rules of Procedure and Evidence.

Article 48
Privileges and immunities

1. The Court shall enjoy in the territory of each State Party such privileges and immunities as are necessary for the

fulfilment of its purposes.

2. The judges, the Prosecutor, the Deputy Prosecutors and the Registrar shall, when engaged on or with respect to the business of the Court, enjoy the same privileges and immunities as are accorded to heads of diplomatic missions and shall, after the expiry of their terms of office, continue to be accorded immunity from legal process of every kind in respect of words spoken or written and acts performed by them in their official capacity.

3. The Deputy Registrar, the staff of the Office of the Prosecutor and the staff of the Registry shall enjoy the privileges and immunities and facilities necessary for the performance of their functions, in accordance with the agreement on the privileges and immunities of the Court.

4. Counsel, experts, witnesses or any other person required to be present at the seat of the Court shall be accorded such treatment as is necessary for the proper functioning of the Court, in accordance with the agreement on the privileges and immunities of the Court.

5. The privileges and immunities of:

(a) A judge or the Prosecutor may be waived by an absolute majority of the judges;

(b) The Registrar may be waived by the Presidency;

(c) The Deputy Prosecutors and staff of the Office of the Prosecutor may be waived by the Prosecutor;

(d) The Deputy Registrar and staff of the Registry may be

waived by the Registrar.

Article 49
Salaries, allowances and expenses

The judges, the Prosecutor, the Deputy Prosecutors, the Registrar and the Deputy Registrar shall receive such salaries, allowances and expenses as may be decided upon by the Assembly of States Parties. These salaries and allowances shall not be reduced during their terms of office.

Article 50
Official and working languages

1. The official languages of the Court shall be Arabic, Chinese, English, French, Russian and Spanish. The judgements of the Court, as well as other decisions resolving fundamental issues before the Court, shall be published in the official languages. The Presidency shall, in accordance with the criteria established by the Rules of Procedure and Evidence, determine which decisions may be considered as resolving fundamental issues for the purposes of this paragraph.

2. The working languages of the Court shall be English and French. The Rules of Procedure and Evidence shall determine the cases in which other official languages may be used as working languages.

3. At the request of any party to a proceeding or a State allowed to intervene in a proceeding, the Court shall authorize a language other than English or French to be used by such a party or State, provided that the Court considers such authorization to be adequately justified.

Article 51
Rules of Procedure and Evidence

1. The Rules of Procedure and Evidence shall enter into force upon adoption by a two-thirds majority of the members of the Assembly of States Parties.

2. Amendments to the Rules of Procedure and Evidence may be proposed by:

(a) Any State Party;

(b) The judges acting by an absolute majority; or

(c) The Prosecutor.

Such amendments shall enter into force upon adoption by a two-thirds majority of the members of the Assembly of States Parties.

3. After the adoption of the Rules of Procedure and Evidence, in urgent cases where the Rules do not provide for a specific situation before the Court, the judges may, by a two-thirds majority, draw up provisional Rules to be applied until

adopted, amended or rejected at the next ordinary or special session of the Assembly of States Parties.

4. The Rules of Procedure and Evidence, amendments thereto and any provisional Rule shall be consistent with this Statute. Amendments to the Rules of Procedure and Evidence as well as provisional Rules shall not be applied retroactively to the detriment of the person who is being investigated or prosecuted or who has been convicted.

5. In the event of conflict between the Statute and the Rules of Procedure and Evidence, the Statute shall prevail.

Article 52
Regulations of the Court

1. The judges shall, in accordance with this Statute and the Rules of Procedure and Evidence, adopt, by an absolute majority, the Regulations of the Court necessary for its routine functioning.

2. The Prosecutor and the Registrar shall be consulted in the elaboration of the Regulations and any amendments thereto.

3. The Regulations and any amendments thereto shall take effect upon adoption unless otherwise decided by the judges. Immediately upon adoption, they shall be circulated to States Parties for comments. If within six months there are no objections from a majority of States Parties, they shall remain in force.

PART 5. INVESTIGATION AND PROSECUTION

Article 53
Initiation of an investigation

1. The Prosecutor shall, having evaluated the information made available to him or her, initiate an investigation unless he or she determines that there is no reasonable basis to proceed under this Statute. In deciding whether to initiate an investigation, the Prosecutor shall consider whether:

(a) The information available to the Prosecutor provides a reasonable basis to believe that a crime within the jurisdiction of the Court has been or is being committed;

(b) The case is or would be admissible under article 17; and

(c) Taking into account the gravity of the crime and the interests of victims, there are nonetheless substantial reasons to believe that an investigation would not serve the interests of justice.

If the Prosecutor determines that there is no reasonable basis to proceed and his or her determination is based solely on subparagraph (c) above, he or she shall inform the Pre-Trial Chamber.

2. If, upon investigation, the Prosecutor concludes that there is not a sufficient basis for a prosecution because:

(a) There is not a sufficient legal or factual basis to seek a warrant or summons under article 58;

(b) The case is inadmissible under article 17; or

(c) A prosecution is not in the interests of justice, taking into account all the circumstances, including the gravity of the crime, the interests of victims and the age or infirmity of the alleged perpetrator, and his or her role in the alleged crime;

the Prosecutor shall inform the Pre-Trial Chamber and the State making a referral under article 14 or the Security Council in a case under article 13, paragraph (b), of his or her conclusion and the reasons for the conclusion.

3. (a) At the request of the State making a referral under article 14 or the Security Council under article 13, paragraph (b), the Pre-Trial Chamber may review a decision of the Prosecutor under paragraph 1 or 2 not to proceed and may request the Prosecutor to reconsider that decision.

(b) In addition, the Pre-Trial Chamber may, on its own initiative, review a decision of the Prosecutor not to proceed if it is based solely on paragraph 1 (c) or 2 (c). In such a case, the decision of the Prosecutor shall be effective only if confirmed by the Pre-Trial Chamber.

4. The Prosecutor may, at any time, reconsider a decision whether to initiate an investigation or prosecution based on new facts or information.

Article 54
Duties and powers of the Prosecutor with respect to investigations

1. The Prosecutor shall:

(a) In order to establish the truth, extend the investigation to cover all facts and evidence relevant to an assessment of whether there is criminal responsibility under this Statute, and, in doing so, investigate incriminating and exonerating circumstances equally;

(b) Take appropriate measures to ensure the effective investigation and prosecution of crimes within the jurisdiction of the Court, and in doing so, respect the interests and personal circumstances of victims and witnesses, including age, gender as defined in article 7, paragraph 3, and health, and take into account the nature of the crime, in particular where it involves sexual violence, gender violence or violence against children; and

(c) Fully respect the rights of persons arising under this Statute.

2. The Prosecutor may conduct investigations on the territory of a State:

(a) In accordance with the provisions of Part 9; or

(b) As authorized by the Pre-Trial Chamber under article 57, paragraph 3 (d).

3. The Prosecutor may:

(a) Collect and examine evidence;

(b) Request the presence of and question persons being investigated, victims and witnesses;

(c) Seek the cooperation of any State or intergovernmental organization or arrangement in accordance with its respective competence and/or mandate;

(d) Enter into such arrangements or agreements, not inconsistent with this Statute, as may be necessary to facilitate the cooperation of a State, intergovernmental organization or person;

(e) Agree not to disclose, at any stage of the proceedings, documents or information that the Prosecutor obtains on the condition of confidentiality and solely for the purpose of generating new evidence, unless the provider of the information consents; and

(f) Take necessary measures, or request that necessary measures be taken, to ensure the confidentiality of information, the protection of any person or the preservation of evidence.

Article 55
Rights of persons during an investigation

1. In respect of an investigation under this Statute, a person:

(a) Shall not be compelled to incriminate himself or herself or to confess guilt;

(b) Shall not be subjected to any form of coercion, duress or threat, to torture or to any other form of cruel, inhuman or degrading treatment or punishment;

(c) Shall, if questioned in a language other than a language the person fully understands and speaks, have, free of any cost, the assistance of a competent interpreter and such translations as are necessary to meet the requirements of fairness; and

(d) Shall not be subjected to arbitrary arrest or detention, and shall not be deprived of his or her liberty except on such grounds and in accordance with such procedures as are established in this Statute.

2. Where there are grounds to believe that a person has committed a crime within the jurisdiction of the Court and that person is about to be questioned either by the Prosecutor, or by national authorities pursuant to a request made under Part 9, that person shall also have the following rights of which he or she shall be informed prior to being questioned:

(a) To be informed, prior to being questioned, that there are grounds to believe that he or she has committed a crime within the jurisdiction of the Court;

(b) To remain silent, without such silence being a consideration in the determination of guilt or innocence;

(c) To have legal assistance of the person's choosing, or, if the person does not have legal assistance, to have legal assistance assigned to him or her, in any case where the interests of justice so require, and without payment by the person in any such case if the person does not have sufficient means to pay for it; and

(d) To be questioned in the presence of counsel unless the person has voluntarily waived his or her right to counsel.

Article 56
Role of the Pre-Trial Chamber in relation to a unique investigative opportunity

1.(a)Where the Prosecutor considers an investigation to present a unique opportunity to take testimony or a statement from a witness or to examine, collect or test evidence, which may not be available subsequently for the purposes of a trial, the Prosecutor shall so inform the Pre-Trial Chamber.

(b) In that case, the Pre-Trial Chamber may, upon request of the Prosecutor, take such measures as may be necessary to ensure the efficiency and integrity of the proceedings and, in particular, to protect the rights of the defence.

(c) Unless the Pre-Trial Chamber orders otherwise, the Prosecutor shall provide the relevant information to the person who has been arrested or appeared in response to a summons in connection with the investigation referred to in subparagraph (a), in order that he or she may be heard on the matter.

2. The measures referred to in paragraph 1 (b) may include:

(a) Making recommendations or orders regarding procedures to be followed;

(b) Directing that a record be made of the proceedings;

(c) Appointing an expert to assist;

(d) Authorizing counsel for a person who has been arrested, or appeared before the Court in response to a summons, to participate, or where there has not yet been such an arrest or appearance or counsel has not been designated, appointing another counsel to attend and represent the interests of the defence;

(e) Naming one of its members or, if necessary, another available judge of the Pre-Trial or Trial Division to observe and make recommendations or orders regarding the collection and preservation of evidence and the questioning of persons;

(f) Taking such other action as may be necessary to collect or preserve evidence.

3. (a) Where the Prosecutor has not sought measures pursuant to this article but the Pre-Trial Chamber considers that such measures are required to preserve evidence that it deems would be essential for the defence at trial, it shall consult with the Prosecutor as to whether there is good reason for the Prosecutor's failure to request the measures. If upon consultation, the Pre-Trial Chamber concludes that the Prosecutor's failure to request such measures is unjustified, the Pre-Trial Chamber may take such measures on its own initiative.

(b) A decision of the Pre-Trial Chamber to act on its own initiative under this paragraph may be appealed by the Prosecutor. The appeal shall be heard on an expedited basis.

4. The admissibility of evidence preserved or collected for trial pursuant to this article, or the record thereof, shall be governed at trial by article 69, and given such weight as determined by the Trial Chamber.

Article 57
Functions and powers of the Pre-Trial Chamber

1. Unless otherwise provided in this Statute, the Pre-Trial Chamber shall exercise its functions in accordance with the provisions of this article.

2. (a) Orders or rulings of the Pre-Trial Chamber issued under articles 15, 18, 19, 54, paragraph 2, 61, paragraph 7, and 72 must be concurred in by a majority of its judges.

(b) In all other cases, a single judge of the Pre-Trial Chamber may exercise the functions provided for in this Statute, unless otherwise provided for in the Rules of Procedure and Evidence or by a majority of the Pre-Trial Chamber.

3. In addition to its other functions under this Statute, the Pre-Trial Chamber may:

(a) At the request of the Prosecutor, issue such orders

and warrants as may be required for the purposes of an investigation;

(b) Upon the request of a person who has been arrested or has appeared pursuant to a summons under article 58, issue such orders, including measures such as those described in article 56, or seek such cooperation pursuant to Part 9 as may be necessary to assist the person in the preparation of his or her defence;

(c) Where necessary, provide for the protection and privacy of victims and witnesses, the preservation of evidence, the protection of persons who have been arrested or appeared in response to a summons, and the protection of national security information;

(d) Authorize the Prosecutor to take specific investigative steps within the territory of a State Party without having secured the cooperation of that State under Part 9 if, whenever possible having regard to the views of the State concerned, the Pre-Trial Chamber has determined in that case that the State is clearly unable to execute a request for cooperation due to the unavailability of any authority or any component of its judicial system competent to execute the request for cooperation under Part 9.

(e) Where a warrant of arrest or a summons has been issued under article 58, and having due regard to the strength of the evidence and the rights of the parties concerned, as provided for in this Statute and the Rules of Procedure and Evidence, seek the cooperation of States pursuant to article 93, paragraph 1, (k) to take protective measures for the purpose of forfeiture, in particular for the ultimate benefit of victims.

Article 58
Issuance by the Pre-Trial Chamber of a warrant of arrest or a summons to appear

1. At any time after the initiation of an investigation, the Pre-Trial Chamber shall, on the application of the Prosecutor, issue a warrant of arrest of a person if, having examined the application and the evidence or other information submitted by the Prosecutor, it is satisfied that:

(a) There are reasonable grounds to believe that the person has committed a crime within the jurisdiction of the Court; and

(b) The arrest of the person appears necessary:

(i) To ensure the person's appearance at trial,

(ii) To ensure that the person does not obstruct or endanger the investigation or the court proceedings, or

(iii) Where applicable, to prevent the person from continuing with the commission of that crime or a related crime which is within the jurisdiction of the Court and which arises out of the same circumstances.

2. The application of the Prosecutor shall contain:

(a) The name of the person and any other relevant identifying information;

(b) A specific reference to the crimes within the jurisdiction of the Court which the person is alleged to have committed;

(c) A concise statement of the facts which are alleged to constitute those crimes;

(d) A summary of the evidence and any other information which establish reasonable grounds to believe that the person committed those crimes; and

(e) The reason why the Prosecutor believes that the arrest of the person is necessary.

3. The warrant of arrest shall contain:

(a) The name of the person and any other relevant identifying information;

(b) A specific reference to the crimes within the jurisdiction of the Court for which the person's arrest is sought; and

(c) A concise statement of the facts which are alleged to constitute those crimes.

4. The warrant of arrest shall remain in effect until otherwise ordered by the Court.

5. On the basis of the warrant of arrest, the Court may request the provisional arrest or the arrest and surrender of the person under Part 9.

6. The Prosecutor may request the Pre-Trial Chamber to

amend the warrant of arrest by modifying or adding to the crimes specified therein. The Pre-Trial Chamber shall so amend the warrant if it is satisfied that there are reasonable grounds to believe that the person committed the modified or additional crimes.

7. As an alternative to seeking a warrant of arrest, the Prosecutor may submit an application requesting that the Pre-Trial Chamber issue a summons for the person to appear. If the Pre-Trial Chamber is satisfied that there are reasonable grounds to believe that the person committed the crime alleged and that a summons is sufficient to ensure the person's appearance, it shall issue the summons, with or without conditions restricting liberty (other than detention) if provided for by national law, for the person to appear. The summons shall contain:

(a) The name of the person and any other relevant identifying information;

(b) The specified date on which the person is to appear;

(c) A specific reference to the crimes within the jurisdiction of the Court which the person is alleged to have committed; and

(d) A concise statement of the facts which are alleged to constitute the crime.

The summons shall be served on the person.

Article 59
Arrest proceedings in the custodial State

1. A State Party which has received a request for provisional arrest or for arrest and surrender shall immediately take steps to arrest the person in question in accordance with its laws and the provisions of Part 9.

2. A person arrested shall be brought promptly before the competent judicial authority in the custodial State which shall determine, in accordance with the law of that State, that:

(a) The warrant applies to that person;

(b) The person has been arrested in accordance with the proper process; and

(c) The person's rights have been respected.

3. The person arrested shall have the right to apply to the competent authority in the custodial State for interim release pending surrender.

4. In reaching a decision on any such application, the competent authority in the custodial State shall consider whether, given the gravity of the alleged crimes, there are urgent and exceptional circumstances to justify interim release and whether necessary safeguards exist to ensure that the custodial State can fulfil its duty to surrender the person to the Court. It shall not be open to the competent authority of the custodial State to consider whether the warrant of arrest was properly

issued in accordance with article 58, paragraph 1 (a) and (b).

5. The Pre-Trial Chamber shall be notified of any request for interim release and shall make recommendations to the competent authority in the custodial State. The competent authority in the custodial State shall give full consideration to such recommendations, including any recommendations on measures to prevent the escape of the person, before rendering its decision.

6. If the person is granted interim release, the Pre-Trial Chamber may request periodic reports on the status of the interim release.

7. Once ordered to be surrendered by the custodial State, the person shall be delivered to the Court as soon as possible.

Article 60
Initial proceedings before the Court

1. Upon the surrender of the person to the Court, or the person's appearance before the Court voluntarily or pursuant to a summons, the Pre-Trial Chamber shall satisfy itself that the person has been informed of the crimes which he or she is alleged to have committed, and of his or her rights under this Statute, including the right to apply for interim release pending trial.

2. A person subject to a warrant of arrest may apply for interim release pending trial. If the Pre-Trial Chamber is

satisfied that the conditions set forth in article 58, paragraph 1, are met, the person shall continue to be detained. If it is not so satisfied, the Pre-Trial Chamber shall release the person, with or without conditions.

3. The Pre-Trial Chamber shall periodically review its ruling on the release or detention of the person, and may do so at any time on the request of the Prosecutor or the person. Upon such review, it may modify its ruling as to detention, release or conditions of release, if it is satisfied that changed circumstances so require.

4. The Pre-Trial Chamber shall ensure that a person is not detained for an unreasonable period prior to trial due to inexcusable delay by the Prosecutor. If such delay occurs, the Court shall consider releasing the person, with or without conditions.

5. If necessary, the Pre-Trial Chamber may issue a warrant of arrest to secure the presence of a person who has been released.

Article 61
Confirmation of the charges before trial

1. Subject to the provisions of paragraph 2, within a reasonable time after the person's surrender or voluntary appearance before the Court, the Pre-Trial Chamber shall hold a hearing to confirm the charges on which the Prosecutor intends to seek trial. The hearing shall be held in the presence of the Prosecutor and the person charged, as well as his or her counsel.

2. The Pre-Trial Chamber may, upon request of the Prosecutor or on its own motion, hold a hearing in the absence of the person charged to confirm the charges on which the Prosecutor intends to seek trial when the person has:

(a) Waived his or her right to be present; or

(b) Fled or cannot be found and all reasonable steps have been taken to secure his or her appearance before the Court and to inform the person of the charges and that a hearing to confirm those charges will be held.

In that case, the person shall be represented by counsel where the Pre-Trial Chamber determines that it is in the interests of justice.

3. Within a reasonable time before the hearing, the person shall:

(a) Be provided with a copy of the document containing the charges on which the Prosecutor intends to bring the person to trial; and

(b) Be informed of the evidence on which the Prosecutor intends to rely at the hearing.

The Pre-Trial Chamber may issue orders regarding the disclosure of information for the purposes of the hearing.

4. Before the hearing, the Prosecutor may continue the

investigation and may amend or withdraw any charges. The person shall be given reasonable notice before the hearing of any amendment to or withdrawal of charges. In case of a withdrawal of charges, the Prosecutor shall notify the Pre-Trial Chamber of the reasons for the withdrawal.

5. At the hearing, the Prosecutor shall support each charge with sufficient evidence to establish substantial grounds to believe that the person committed the crime charged. The Prosecutor may rely on documentary or summary evidence and need not call the witnesses expected to testify at the trial.

6. At the hearing, the person may:

(a) Object to the charges;
(b) Challenge the evidence presented by the Prosecutor; and
(c) Present evidence.

7. The Pre-Trial Chamber shall, on the basis of the hearing, determine whether there is sufficient evidence to establish substantial grounds to believe that the person committed each of the crimes charged. Based on its determination, the Pre-Trial Chamber shall:

(a) Confirm those charges in relation to which it has determined that there is sufficient evidence, and commit the person to a Trial Chamber for trial on the charges as confirmed;

(b) Decline to confirm those charges in relation to which it has determined that there is insufficient evidence;

(c) Adjourn the hearing and request the Prosecutor to consider:

(i) Providing further evidence or conducting further investigation with respect to a particular charge; or

(ii) Amending a charge because the evidence submitted appears to establish a different crime within the jurisdiction of the Court.

8. Where the Pre-Trial Chamber declines to confirm a charge, the Prosecutor shall not be precluded from subsequently requesting its confirmation if the request is supported by additional evidence.

9. After the charges are confirmed and before the trial has begun, the Prosecutor may, with the permission of the Pre-Trial Chamber and after notice to the accused, amend the charges. If the Prosecutor seeks to add additional charges or to substitute more serious charges, a hearing under this article to confirm those charges must be held. After commencement of the trial, the Prosecutor may, with the permission of the Trial Chamber, withdraw the charges.

10. Any warrant previously issued shall cease to have effect with respect to any charges which have not been confirmed by the Pre-Trial Chamber or which have been withdrawn by the Prosecutor.

11. Once the charges have been confirmed in accordance with this article, the Presidency shall constitute a Trial Chamber which, subject to paragraph 9 and to article 64, paragraph 4, shall be responsible for the conduct of subsequent proceedings and may exercise any function of the Pre-Trial Chamber that is relevant and capable of application in those proceedings.

PART 6. THE TRIAL

Article 62
Place of trial

Unless otherwise decided, the place of the trial shall be the seat of the Court.

Article 63
Trial in the presence of the accused

1. The accused shall be present during the trial.

2. If the accused, being present before the Court, continues to disrupt the trial, the Trial Chamber may remove the accused and shall make provision for him or her to observe the trial and instruct counsel from outside the courtroom, through the use of communications technology, if required. Such measures shall be taken only in exceptional circumstances after other

reasonable alternatives have proved inadequate, and only for such duration as is strictly required.

Article 64
Functions and powers of the Trial Chamber

1. The functions and powers of the Trial Chamber set out in this article shall be exercised in accordance with this Statute and the Rules of Procedure and Evidence.

2. The Trial Chamber shall ensure that a trial is fair and expeditious and is conducted with full respect for the rights of the accused and due regard for the protection of victims and witnesses.

3. Upon assignment of a case for trial in accordance with this Statute, the Trial Chamber assigned to deal with the case shall:

(a) Confer with the parties and adopt such procedures as are necessary to facilitate the fair and expeditious conduct of the proceedings;

(b) Determine the language or languages to be used at trial; and

(c) Subject to any other relevant provisions of this Statute, provide for disclosure of documents or information not previously disclosed, sufficiently in advance of the commencement of the trial to enable adequate preparation for trial.

4. The Trial Chamber may, if necessary for its effective and fair functioning, refer preliminary issues to the Pre-Trial Chamber or, if necessary, to another available judge of the Pre-Trial Division.

5. Upon notice to the parties, the Trial Chamber may, as appropriate, direct that there be joinder or severance in respect of charges against more than one accused.

6. In performing its functions prior to trial or during the course of a trial, the Trial Chamber may, as necessary:

(a) Exercise any functions of the Pre-Trial Chamber referred to in article 61, paragraph 11;

(b) Require the attendance and testimony of witnesses and production of documents and other evidence by obtaining, if necessary, the assistance of States as provided in this Statute;

(c) Provide for the protection of confidential information;

(d) Order the production of evidence in addition to that already collected prior to the trial or presented during the trial by the parties;

(e) Provide for the protection of the accused, witnesses and victims; and

(f) Rule on any other relevant matters.

7. The trial shall be held in public. The Trial Chamber may, however, determine that special circumstances require that certain proceedings be in closed session for the purposes set forth in article 68, or to protect confidential or sensitive

information to be given in evidence.

8. (a)At the commencement of the trial, the Trial Chamber shall have read to the accused the charges previously confirmed by the Pre-Trial Chamber. The Trial Chamber shall satisfy itself that the accused understands the nature of the charges. It shall afford him or her the opportunity to make an admission of guilt in accordance with article 65 or to plead not guilty.

(b) At the trial, the presiding judge may give directions for the conduct of proceedings, including to ensure that they are conducted in a fair and impartial manner. Subject to any directions of the presiding judge, the parties may submit evidence in accordance with the provisions of this Statute.

9. The Trial Chamber shall have, inter alia, the power on application of a party or on its own motion to:

(a) Rule on the admissibility or relevance of evidence; and

(b) Take all necessary steps to maintain order in the course of a hearing.

10. The Trial Chamber shall ensure that a complete record of the trial, which accurately reflects the proceedings, is made and that it is maintained and preserved by the Registrar.

Article 65
Proceedings on an admission of guilt

1. Where the accused makes an admission of guilt pursuant to article 64, paragraph 8 (a), the Trial Chamber shall determine whether:

(a) The accused understands the nature and consequences of the admission of guilt;

(b) The admission is voluntarily made by the accused after sufficient consultation with defence counsel; and

(c) The admission of guilt is supported by the facts of the case that are contained in:

(i) The charges brought by the Prosecutor and admitted by the accused;

(ii) Any materials presented by the Prosecutor which supplement the charges and which the accused accepts; and

(iii) Any other evidence, such as the testimony of witnesses, presented by the Prosecutor or the accused.

2. Where the Trial Chamber is satisfied that the matters referred to in paragraph 1 are established, it shall consider the admission of guilt, together with any additional evidence presented, as establishing all the essential facts that are required to prove the crime to which the admission of guilt relates, and

may convict the accused of that crime.

3. Where the Trial Chamber is not satisfied that the matters referred to in paragraph 1 are established, it shall consider the admission of guilt as not having been made, in which case it shall order that the trial be continued under the ordinary trial procedures provided by this Statute and may remit the case to another Trial Chamber.

4. Where the Trial Chamber is of the opinion that a more complete presentation of the facts of the case is required in the interests of justice, in particular the interests of the victims, the Trial Chamber may:

(a) Request the Prosecutor to present additional evidence, including the testimony of witnesses; or

(b) Order that the trial be continued under the ordinary trial procedures provided by this Statute, in which case it shall consider the admission of guilt as not having been made and may remit the case to another Trial Chamber.

5. Any discussions between the Prosecutor and the defence regarding modification of the charges, the admission of guilt or the penalty to be imposed shall not be binding on the Court.

Article 66
Presumption of innocence

1. Everyone shall be presumed innocent until proved guilty

before the Court in accordance with the applicable law.

2. The onus is on the Prosecutor to prove the guilt of the accused.

3. In order to convict the accused, the Court must be convinced of the guilt of the accused beyond reasonable doubt.

Article 67
Rights of the accused

1. In the determination of any charge, the accused shall be entitled to a public hearing, having regard to the provisions of this Statute, to a fair hearing conducted impartially, and to the following minimum guarantees, in full equality:

(a) To be informed promptly and in detail of the nature, cause and content of the charge, in a language which the accused fully understands and speaks;

(b) To have adequate time and facilities for the preparation of the defence and to communicate freely with counsel of the accused's choosing in confidence;

(c) To be tried without undue delay;

(d) Subject to article 63, paragraph 2, to be present at the trial, to conduct the defence in person or through legal assistance of the accused's choosing, to be informed, if the accused does not have legal assistance, of this right and to have legal assistance assigned by the Court in any case where the interests of justice so require, and without payment if the accused lacks sufficient means to pay for it;

(e) To examine, or have examined, the witnesses against him or her and to obtain the attendance and examination of witnesses on his or her behalf under the same conditions as witnesses against him or her. The accused shall also be entitled to raise defences and to present other evidence admissible under this Statute;

(f) To have, free of any cost, the assistance of a competent interpreter and such translations as are necessary to meet the requirements of fairness, if any of the proceedings of or documents presented to the Court are not in a language which the accused fully understands and speaks;

(g) Not to be compelled to testify or to confess guilt and to remain silent, without such silence being a consideration in the determination of guilt or innocence;

(h) To make an unsworn oral or written statement in his or her defence; and

(i) Not to have imposed on him or her any reversal of the burden of proof or any onus of rebuttal.

2. In addition to any other disclosure provided for in this Statute, the Prosecutor shall, as soon as practicable, disclose to the defence evidence in the Prosecutor's possession or control which he or she believes shows or tends to show the innocence of the accused, or to mitigate the guilt of the accused, or which may affect the credibility of prosecution evidence. In case of

doubt as to the application of this paragraph, the Court shall decide.

Article 68
Protection of the victims and witnesses and their participation in the proceedings

1. The Court shall take appropriate measures to protect the safety, physical and psychological well-being, dignity and privacy of victims and witnesses. In so doing, the Court shall have regard to all relevant factors, including age, gender as defined in article 7, paragraph 3, and health, and the nature of the crime, in particular, but not limited to, where the crime involves sexual or gender violence or violence against children. The Prosecutor shall take such measures particularly during the investigation and prosecution of such crimes. These measures shall not be prejudicial to or inconsistent with the rights of the accused and a fair and impartial trial.

2. As an exception to the principle of public hearings provided for in article 67, the Chambers of the Court may, to protect victims and witnesses or an accused, conduct any part of the proceedings in camera or allow the presentation of evidence by electronic or other special means. In particular, such measures shall be implemented in the case of a victim of sexual violence or a child who is a victim or a witness, unless otherwise ordered by the Court, having regard to all the circumstances, particularly the views of the victim or witness.

3. Where the personal interests of the victims are affected, the Court shall permit their views and concerns to be presented and considered at stages of the proceedings determined to be appropriate by the Court and in a manner which is not prejudicial to or inconsistent with the rights of the accused and a fair and impartial trial. Such views and concerns may be presented by the legal representatives of the victims where the Court considers it appropriate, in accordance with the Rules of Procedure and Evidence.

4. The Victims and Witnesses Unit may advise the Prosecutor and the Court on appropriate protective measures, security arrangements, counselling and assistance as referred to in article 43, paragraph 6.

5. Where the disclosure of evidence or information pursuant to this Statute may lead to the grave endangerment of the security of a witness or his or her family, the Prosecutor may, for the purposes of any proceedings conducted prior to the commencement of the trial, withhold such evidence or information and instead submit a summary thereof. Such measures shall be exercised in a manner which is not prejudicial to or inconsistent with the rights of the accused and a fair and impartial trial.

6. A State may make an application for necessary measures to be taken in respect of the protection of its servants or agents and the protection of confidential or sensitive information.

Article 69
Evidence

1. Before testifying, each witness shall, in accordance with the Rules of Procedure and Evidence, give an undertaking as to the truthfulness of the evidence to be given by that witness.

2. The testimony of a witness at trial shall be given in person, except to the extent provided by the measures set forth in article 68 or in the Rules of Procedure and Evidence. The Court may also permit the giving of viva voce (oral) or recorded testimony of a witness by means of video or audio technology, as well as the introduction of documents or written transcripts, subject to this Statute and in accordance with the Rules of Procedure and Evidence. These measures shall not be prejudicial to or inconsistent with the rights of the accused.

3. The parties may submit evidence relevant to the case, in accordance with article 64. The Court shall have the authority to request the submission of all evidence that it considers necessary for the determination of the truth.

4. The Court may rule on the relevance or admissibility of any evidence, taking into account, inter alia, the probative value of the evidence and any prejudice that such evidence may cause to a fair trial or to a fair evaluation of the testimony of a witness, in accordance with the Rules of Procedure and Evidence.

5. The Court shall respect and observe privileges on confidentiality as provided for in the Rules of Procedure and Evidence.

6. The Court shall not require proof of facts of common knowledge but may take judicial notice of them.

7. Evidence obtained by means of a violation of this Statute or internationally recognized human rights shall not be admissible if:

(a) The violation casts substantial doubt on the reliability of the evidence; or

(b) The admission of the evidence would be antithetical to and would seriously damage the integrity of the proceedings.

8. When deciding on the relevance or admissibility of evidence collected by a State, the Court shall not rule on the application of the State's national law.

Article 70
Offences against the administration of justice

1. The Court shall have jurisdiction over the following offences against its administration of justice when committed intentionally:

(a) Giving false testimony when under an obligation pursuant to article 69, paragraph 1, to tell the truth;

(b) Presenting evidence that the party knows is false or forged;

(c) Corruptly influencing a witness, obstructing or interfering with the attendance or testimony of a witness, retaliating against a witness for giving testimony or destroying, tampering with or interfering with the collection of evidence;

(d) Impeding, intimidating or corruptly influencing an official of the Court for the purpose of forcing or persuading the official not to perform, or to perform improperly, his or her duties;

(e) Retaliating against an official of the Court on account of duties performed by that or another official;

(f) Soliciting or accepting a bribe as an official of the Court in connection with his or her official duties.

2. The principles and procedures governing the Court's exercise of jurisdiction over offences under this article shall be those provided for in the Rules of Procedure and Evidence. The conditions for providing international cooperation to the Court with respect to its proceedings under this article shall be governed by the domestic laws of the requested State.

3. In the event of conviction, the Court may impose a term of imprisonment not exceeding five years, or a fine in accordance with the Rules of Procedure and Evidence, or both.

4. (a) Each State Party shall extend its criminal laws penalizing offences against the integrity of its own investigative or judicial process to offences against the administration of justice referred to in this article, committed on its territory, or by one of its nationals;

(b) Upon request by the Court, whenever it deems it proper, the State Party shall submit the case to its competent authorities for the purpose of prosecution. Those authorities shall treat such cases with diligence and devote sufficient resources to enable them to be conducted effectively.

Article 71
Sanctions for misconduct before the Court

1. The Court may sanction persons present before it who commit misconduct, including disruption of its proceedings or deliberate refusal to comply with its directions, by administrative measures other than imprisonment, such as temporary or permanent removal from the courtroom, a fine or other similar measures provided for in the Rules of Procedure and Evidence.

2. The procedures governing the imposition of the measures set forth in paragraph 1 shall be those provided for in the Rules of Procedure and Evidence.

Article 72
Protection of national security information

1. This article applies in any case where the disclosure of the information or documents of a State would, in the opinion of that State, prejudice its national security interests. Such cases include those falling within the scope of article 56, paragraphs

2 and 3, article 61, paragraph 3, article 64, paragraph 3, article 67, paragraph 2, article 68, paragraph 6, article 87, paragraph 6 and article 93, as well as cases arising at any other stage of the proceedings where such disclosure may be at issue.

2. This article shall also apply when a person who has been requested to give information or evidence has refused to do so or has referred the matter to the State on the ground that disclosure would prejudice the national security interests of a State and the State concerned confirms that it is of the opinion that disclosure would prejudice its national security interests.

3. Nothing in this article shall prejudice the requirements of confidentiality applicable under article 54, paragraph 3 (e) and (f), or the application of article 73.

4. If a State learns that information or documents of the State are being, or are likely to be, disclosed at any stage of the proceedings, and it is of the opinion that disclosure would prejudice its national security interests, that State shall have the right to intervene in order to obtain resolution of the issue in accordance with this article.

5. If, in the opinion of a State, disclosure of information would prejudice its national security interests, all reasonable steps will be taken by the State, acting in conjunction with the Prosecutor, the defence or the Pre-Trial Chamber or Trial Chamber, as the case may be, to seek to resolve the matter by cooperative means. Such steps may include:

(a) Modification or clarification of the request;

(b) A determination by the Court regarding the relevance of the information or evidence sought, or a determination as to whether the evidence, though relevant, could be or has been obtained from a source other than the requested State;

(c) Obtaining the information or evidence from a different source or in a different form; or

(d) Agreement on conditions under which the assistance could be provided including, among other things, providing summaries or redactions, limitations on disclosure, use of in camera or ex parte proceedings, or other protective measures permissible under the Statute and the Rules of Procedure and Evidence.

6. Once all reasonable steps have been taken to resolve the matter through cooperative means, and if the State considers that there are no means or conditions under which the information or documents could be provided or disclosed without prejudice to its national security interests, it shall so notify the Prosecutor or the Court of the specific reasons for its decision, unless a specific description of the reasons would itself necessarily result in such prejudice to the State's national security interests.

7. Thereafter, if the Court determines that the evidence is relevant and necessary for the establishment of the guilt or innocence of the accused, the Court may undertake the following actions:

(a) Where disclosure of the information or document is sought pursuant to a request for cooperation under Part 9 or the circumstances described in paragraph 2, and the State has invoked the ground for refusal referred to in article 93, paragraph 4:

(i) The Court may, before making any conclusion referred to in subparagraph 7 (a) (ii), request further consultations for the purpose of considering the State's representations, which may include, as appropriate, hearings in camera and ex parte;

(ii) If the Court concludes that, by invoking the ground for refusal under article 93, paragraph 4, in the circumstances of the case, the requested State is not acting in accordance with its obligations under this Statute, the Court may refer the matter in accordance with article 87, paragraph 7, specifying the reasons for its conclusion; and

(iii) The Court may make such inference in the trial of the accused as to the existence or non-existence of a fact, as may be appropriate in the circumstances; or

(b)In all other circumstances:

(i) Order disclosure; or

(ii) To the extent it does not order disclosure, make such inference in the trial of the accused as to the existence or non-existence of a fact, as may be appropriate in the circumstances.

Article 73
Third-party information or documents

If a State Party is requested by the Court to provide a document or information in its custody, possession or control, which was disclosed to it in confidence by a State, intergovernmental organization or international organization, it shall seek the consent of the originator to disclose that document or information. If the originator is a State Party, it shall either consent to disclosure of the information or document or undertake to resolve the issue of disclosure with the Court, subject to the provisions of article 72. If the originator is not a State Party and refuses to consent to disclosure, the requested State shall inform the Court that it is unable to provide the document or information because of a pre-existing obligation of confidentiality to the originator.

Article 74
Requirements for the decision

1. All the judges of the Trial Chamber shall be present at each stage of the trial and throughout their deliberations. The Presidency may, on a case-by-case basis, designate, as available, one or more alternate judges to be present at each stage of the

trial and to replace a member of the Trial Chamber if that member is unable to continue attending.

2. The Trial Chamber's decision shall be based on its evaluation of the evidence and the entire proceedings. The decision shall not exceed the facts and circumstances described in the charges and any amendments to the charges. The Court may base its decision only on evidence submitted and discussed before it at the trial.

3. The judges shall attempt to achieve unanimity in their decision, failing which the decision shall be taken by a majority of the judges.

4. The deliberations of the Trial Chamber shall remain secret.

5. The decision shall be in writing and shall contain a full and reasoned statement of the Trial Chamber's findings on the evidence and conclusions. The Trial Chamber shall issue one decision. When there is no unanimity, the Trial Chamber's decision shall contain the views of the majority and the minority. The decision or a summary thereof shall be delivered in open court.

Article 75
Reparations to victims

1. The Court shall establish principles relating to reparations to, or in respect of, victims, including restitution, compensation and rehabilitation. On this basis, in its decision the Court

may, either upon request or on its own motion in exceptional circumstances, determine the scope and extent of any damage, loss and injury to, or in respect of, victims and will state the principles on which it is acting.

2. The Court may make an order directly against a convicted person specifying appropriate reparations to, or in respect of, victims, including restitution, compensation and rehabilitation.

Where appropriate, the Court may order that the award for reparations be made through the Trust Fund provided for in article 79.

3. Before making an order under this article, the Court may invite and shall take account of representations from or on behalf of the convicted person, victims, other interested persons or interested States.

4. In exercising its power under this article, the Court may, after a person is convicted of a crime within the jurisdiction of the Court, determine whether, in order to give effect to an order which it may make under this article, it is necessary to seek measures under article 93, paragraph 1.

5. A State Party shall give effect to a decision under this article as if the provisions of article 109 were applicable to this article.

6. Nothing in this article shall be interpreted as prejudicing the rights of victims under national or international law.

Article 76
Sentencing

1. In the event of a conviction, the Trial Chamber shall consider the appropriate sentence to be imposed and shall take into account the evidence presented and submissions made during the trial that are relevant to the sentence.

2. Except where article 65 applies and before the completion of the trial, the Trial Chamber may on its own motion and shall, at the request of the Prosecutor or the accused, hold a further hearing to hear any additional evidence or submissions relevant to the sentence, in accordance with the Rules of Procedure and Evidence.

3. Where paragraph 2 applies, any representations under article 75 shall be heard during the further hearing referred to in paragraph 2 and, if necessary, during any additional hearing.

4. The sentence shall be pronounced in public and, wherever possible, in the presence of the accused.

PART 7. PENALTIES

Article 77
Applicable penalties

1. Subject to article 110, the Court may impose one of the

following penalties on a person convicted of a crime referred to in article 5 of this Statute:

(a) Imprisonment for a specified number of years, which may not exceed a maximum of 30 years; or

(b) A term of life imprisonment when justified by the extreme gravity of the crime and the individual circumstances of the convicted person.

2. In addition to imprisonment, the Court may order:

(a) A fine under the criteria provided for in the Rules of Procedure and Evidence;

(b) A forfeiture of proceeds, property and assets derived directly or indirectly from that crime, without prejudice to the rights of bona fide third parties.

Article 78
Determination of the sentence

1. In determining the sentence, the Court shall, in accordance with the Rules of Procedure and Evidence, take into account such factors as the gravity of the crime and the individual circumstances of the convicted person.

2. In imposing a sentence of imprisonment, the Court shall deduct the time, if any, previously spent in detention in

accordance with an order of the Court. The Court may deduct any time otherwise spent in detention in connection with conduct underlying the crime.

3. When a person has been convicted of more than one crime, the Court shall pronounce a sentence for each crime and a joint sentence specifying the total period of imprisonment. This period shall be no less than the highest individual sentence pronounced and shall not exceed 30 years imprisonment or a sentence of life imprisonment in conformity with article 77, paragraph 1 (b).

Article 79
Trust Fund

1. A Trust Fund shall be established by decision of the Assembly of States Parties for the benefit of victims of crimes within the jurisdiction of the Court, and of the families of such victims.

2. The Court may order money and other property collected through fines or forfeiture to be transferred, by order of the Court, to the Trust Fund.

3. The Trust Fund shall be managed according to criteria to be determined by the Assembly of States Parties.

Article 80
Non-prejudice to national application of penalties and national laws

Nothing in this Part affects the application by States of penalties prescribed by their national law, nor the law of States which do not provide for penalties prescribed in this Part.

PART 8. APPEAL AND REVISION

Article 81
Appeal against decision of acquittal or conviction or against sentence

1. A decision under article 74 may be appealed in accordance with the Rules of Procedure and Evidence as follows:

(a) The Prosecutor may make an appeal on any of the following grounds:

(i) Procedural error,
(ii) Error of fact, or
(iii) Error of law;

(b) The convicted person, or the Prosecutor on that person's behalf, may make an appeal on any of the following grounds:

(i) Procedural error,

(ii) Error of fact,

(iii) Error of law, or

(iv) Any other ground that affects the fairness or reliability of the proceedings or decision.

2. (a) A sentence may be appealed, in accordance with the Rules of Procedure and Evidence, by the Prosecutor or the convicted person on the ground of disproportion between the crime and the sentence;

(b) If on an appeal against sentence the Court considers that there are grounds on which the conviction might be set aside, wholly or in part, it may invite the Prosecutor and the convicted person to submit grounds under article 81, paragraph 1 (a) or (b), and may render a decision on conviction in accordance with article 83;

(c)The same procedure applies when the Court, on an appeal against conviction only, considers that there are grounds to reduce the sentence under paragraph 2 (a).

3. (a) Unless the Trial Chamber orders otherwise, a convicted person shall remain in custody pending an appeal;

(b) When a convicted person's time in custody exceeds the sentence of imprisonment imposed, that person shall be released, except that if the Prosecutor is also appealing, the release may be subject to the conditions under subparagraph (c) below;

(c) In case of an acquittal, the accused shall be released immediately, subject to the following:

(i) Under exceptional circumstances, and having regard, inter alia, to the concrete risk of flight, the seriousness of the offence charged and the probability of success on appeal, the Trial Chamber, at the request of the Prosecutor, may maintain the detention of the person pending appeal;

(ii) A decision by the Trial Chamber under subparagraph (c) (i) may be appealed in accordance with the Rules of Procedure and Evidence.

4. Subject to the provisions of paragraph 3 (a) and (b), execution of the decision or sentence shall be suspended during the period allowed for appeal and for the duration of the appeal proceedings.

Article 82
Appeal against other decisions

1. Either party may appeal any of the following decisions in accordance with the Rules of Procedure and Evidence:

(a) A decision with respect to jurisdiction or admissibility;

(b) A decision granting or denying release of the person being investigated or prosecuted;

(c) A decision of the Pre-Trial Chamber to act on its own initiative under article 56, paragraph 3;

(d) A decision that involves an issue that would significantly affect the fair and expeditious conduct of the proceedings or the outcome of the trial, and for which, in the opinion of the Pre-Trial or Trial Chamber, an immediate resolution by the Appeals Chamber may materially advance the proceedings.

2. A decision of the Pre-Trial Chamber under article 57, paragraph 3 (d), may be appealed against by the State concerned or by the Prosecutor, with the leave of the Pre-Trial Chamber. The appeal shall be heard on an expedited basis.

3. An appeal shall not of itself have suspensive effect unless the Appeals Chamber so orders, upon request, in accordance with the Rules of Procedure and Evidence.

4. A legal representative of the victims, the convicted person or a bona fide owner of property adversely affected by an order under article 75 may appeal against the order for reparations, as provided in the Rules of Procedure and Evidence.

Article 83
Proceedings on appeal

1. For the purposes of proceedings under article 81 and this

article, the Appeals Chamber shall have all the powers of the Trial Chamber.

2. If the Appeals Chamber finds that the proceedings appealed from were unfair in a way that affected the reliability of the decision or sentence, or that the decision or sentence appealed from was materially affected by error of fact or law or procedural error, it may:

(a) Reverse or amend the decision or sentence; or

(b) Order a new trial before a different Trial Chamber.

For these purposes, the Appeals Chamber may remand a factual issue to the original Trial Chamber for it to determine the issue and to report back accordingly, or may itself call evidence to determine the issue. When the decision or sentence has been appealed only by the person convicted, or the Prosecutor on that person's behalf, it cannot be amended to his or her detriment.

3. If in an appeal against sentence the Appeals Chamber finds that the sentence is disproportionate to the crime, it may vary the sentence in accordance with Part 7.

4. The judgement of the Appeals Chamber shall be taken by a majority of the judges and shall be delivered in open court. The judgement shall state the reasons on which it is based. When there is no unanimity, the judgement of the Appeals Chamber shall contain the views of the majority and the minority, but a judge may deliver a separate or dissenting opinion on a

question of law.

5. The Appeals Chamber may deliver its judgement in the absence of the person acquitted or convicted.

Article 84
Revision of conviction or sentence

1. The convicted person or, after death, spouses, children, parents or one person alive at the time of the accused's death who has been given express written instructions from the accused to bring such a claim, or the Prosecutor on the person's behalf, may apply to the Appeals Chamber to revise the final judgement of conviction or sentence on the grounds that:

(a) New evidence has been discovered that:

(i) Was not available at the time of trial, and such unavailability was not wholly or partially attributable to the party making application; and

(ii) Is sufficiently important that had it been proved at trial it would have been likely to have resulted in a different verdict;

(b) It has been newly discovered that decisive evidence, taken into account at trial and upon which the conviction depends, was false, forged or falsified;

(c) One or more of the judges who participated in conviction or confirmation of the charges has committed, in that case, an act of serious misconduct or serious breach of duty of sufficient gravity to justify the removal of that judge or those judges from office under article 46.

2. The Appeals Chamber shall reject the application if it considers it to be unfounded. If it determines that the application is meritorious, it may, as appropriate:

(a) Reconvene the original Trial Chamber;
(b) Constitute a new Trial Chamber; or
(c) Retain jurisdiction over the matter,

with a view to, after hearing the parties in the manner set forth in the Rules of Procedure and Evidence, arriving at a determination on whether the judgement should be revised.

Article 85
Compensation to an arrested or convicted person

1. Anyone who has been the victim of unlawful arrest or detention shall have an enforceable right to compensation.

2. When a person has by a final decision been convicted of a criminal offence, and when subsequently his or her conviction has been reversed on the ground that a new or newly discovered fact shows conclusively that there has been a miscarriage of justice, the person who has suffered punishment as a result of

such conviction shall be compensated according to law, unless it is proved that the non-disclosure of the unknown fact in time is wholly or partly attributable to him or her.

3. In exceptional circumstances, where the Court finds conclusive facts showing that there has been a grave and manifest miscarriage of justice, it may in its discretion award compensation, according to the criteria provided in the Rules of Procedure and Evidence, to a person who has been released from detention following a final decision of acquittal or a termination of the proceedings for that reason.

PART 9. INTERNATIONAL COOPERATION AND JUDICIAL ASSISTANCE

Article 86
General obligation to cooperate

States Parties shall, in accordance with the provisions of this Statute, cooperate fully with the Court in its investigation and prosecution of crimes within the jurisdiction of the Court.

Article 87
Requests for cooperation: general provisions

1. (a) The Court shall have the authority to make requests to States Parties for cooperation. The requests shall be transmitted through the diplomatic channel or any other appropriate channel as may be designated by each State Party upon ratification, acceptance, approval or accession.

Subsequent changes to the designation shall be made by each State Party in accordance with the Rules of Procedure and Evidence.

(b) When appropriate, without prejudice to the provisions of subparagraph (a), requests may also be transmitted through the International Criminal Police Organization or any appropriate regional organization.

2. Requests for cooperation and any documents supporting the request shall either be in or be accompanied by a translation into an official language of the requested State or one of the working languages of the Court, in accordance with the choice made by that State upon ratification, acceptance, approval or accession.

Subsequent changes to this choice shall be made in accordance with the Rules of Procedure and Evidence.

3. The requested State shall keep confidential a request for cooperation and any documents supporting the request, except to the extent that the disclosure is necessary for execution of the request.

4. In relation to any request for assistance presented under

this Part, the Court may take such measures, including measures related to the protection of information, as may be necessary to ensure the safety or physical or psychological well-being of any victims, potential witnesses and their families. The Court may request that any information that is made available under this Part shall be provided and handled in a manner that protects the safety and physical or psychological well-being of any victims, potential witnesses and their families.

5. (a) The Court may invite any State not party to this Statute to provide assistance under this Part on the basis of an ad hoc arrangement, an agreement with such State or any other appropriate basis.

(b) Where a State not party to this Statute, which has entered into an ad hoc arrangement or an agreement with the Court, fails to cooperate with requests pursuant to any such arrangement or agreement, the Court may so inform the Assembly of States Parties or, where the Security Council referred the matter to the Court, the Security Council.

6. The Court may ask any intergovernmental organization to provide information or documents. The Court may also ask for other forms of cooperation and assistance which may be agreed upon with such an organization and which are in accordance with its competence or mandate.

7. Where a State Party fails to comply with a request to cooperate by the Court contrary to the provisions of this

Statute, thereby preventing the Court from exercising its functions and powers under this Statute, the Court may make a finding to that effect and refer the matter to the Assembly of States Parties or, where the Security Council referred the matter to the Court, to the Security Council.

Article 88
Availability of procedures under national law

States Parties shall ensure that there are procedures available under their national law for all of the forms of cooperation which are specified under this Part.

Article 89
Surrender of persons to the Court

1. The Court may transmit a request for the arrest and surrender of a person, together with the material supporting the request outlined in article 91, to any State on the territory of which that person may be found and shall request the cooperation of that State in the arrest and surrender of such a person. States Parties shall, in accordance with the provisions of this Part and the procedure under their national law, comply with requests for arrest and surrender.

2. Where the person sought for surrender brings a challenge

before a national court on the basis of the principle of ne bis in idem as provided in article 20, the requested State shall immediately consult with the Court to determine if there has been a relevant ruling on admissibility. If the case is admissible, the requested State shall proceed with the execution of the request. If an admissibility ruling is pending, the requested State may postpone the execution of the request for surrender of the person until the Court makes a determination on admissibility.

3. (a) A State Party shall authorize, in accordance with its national procedural law, transportation through its territory of a person being surrendered to the Court by another State, except where transit through that State would impede or delay the surrender.

(b) A request by the Court for transit shall be transmitted in accordance with article 87. The request for transit shall contain:

(i) A description of the person being transported;

(ii) A brief statement of the facts of the case and their legal characterization; and

(iii) The warrant for arrest and surrender;

(c) A person being transported shall be detained in custody during the period of transit;

(d) No authorization is required if the person is transported by air and no landing is scheduled on the territory of the transit State;

(e) If an unscheduled landing occurs on the territory of the transit State, that State may require a request for transit from the Court as provided for in subparagraph (b). The transit State shall detain the person being transported until the request for transit is received and the transit is effected, provided that detention for purposes of this subparagraph may not be extended beyond 96 hours from the unscheduled landing unless the request is received within that time.

4. If the person sought is being proceeded against or is serving a sentence in the requested State for a crime different from that for which surrender to the Court is sought, the requested State, after making its decision to grant the request, shall consult with the Court.

Article 90
Competing requests

1. A State Party which receives a request from the Court for the surrender of a person under article 89 shall, if it also receives a request from any other State for the extradition of the same person for the same conduct which forms the basis of the crime for which the Court seeks the person's surrender, notify the Court and the requesting State of that fact.

2. Where the requesting State is a State Party, the requested

State shall give priority to the request from the Court if:

(a) The Court has, pursuant to article 18 or 19, made a determination that the case in respect of which surrender is sought is admissible and that determination takes into account the investigation or prosecution conducted by the requesting State in respect of its request for extradition; or

(b) The Court makes the determination described in subparagraph (a) pursuant to the requested State's notification under paragraph 1.

3. Where a determination under paragraph 2 (a) has not been made, the requested State may, at its discretion, pending the determination of the Court under paragraph 2 (b), proceed to deal with the request for extradition from the requesting State but shall not extradite the person until the Court has determined that the case is inadmissible. The Court's determination shall be made on an expedited basis.

4. If the requesting State is a State not Party to this Statute the requested State, if it is not under an international obligation to extradite the person to the requesting State, shall give priority to the request for surrender from the Court, if the Court has determined that the case is admissible.

5. Where a case under paragraph 4 has not been determined to be admissible by the Court, the requested State may, at its discretion, proceed to deal with the request for extradition from the requesting State.

6. In cases where paragraph 4 applies except that the requested State is under an existing international obligation to extradite the person to the requesting State not Party to this Statute, the requested State shall determine whether to surrender the person to the Court or extradite the person to the requesting State. In making its decision, the requested State shall consider all the relevant factors, including but not limited to:

(a) The respective dates of the requests;

(b) The interests of the requesting State including, where relevant, whether the crime was committed in its territory and the nationality of the victims and of the person sought; and

(c) The possibility of subsequent surrender between the Court and the requesting State.

7. Where a State Party which receives a request from the Court for the surrender of a person also receives a request from any State for the extradition of the same person for conduct other than that which constitutes the crime for which the Court seeks the person's surrender:

(a) The requested State shall, if it is not under an existing international obligation to extradite the person to the requesting State, give priority to the request from the Court;

(b) The requested State shall, if it is under an existing international obligation to extradite the person to the requesting State, determine whether to surrender the person to the Court or to extradite the person to the requesting State. In making its decision, the requested State shall consider all the relevant factors, including but not limited to those set out in paragraph 6, but shall give special consideration to the relative nature and gravity of the conduct in question.

8. Where pursuant to a notification under this article, the Court has determined a case to be inadmissible, and subsequently extradition to the requesting State is refused, the requested State shall notify the Court of this decision.

Article 91
Contents of request for arrest and surrender

1. A request for arrest and surrender shall be made in writing. In urgent cases, a request may be made by any medium capable of delivering a written record, provided that the request shall be confirmed through the channel provided for in article 87, paragraph 1 (a).

2. In the case of a request for the arrest and surrender of a person for whom a warrant of arrest has been issued by the Pre-Trial Chamber under article 58, the request shall contain or be supported by:

(a) Information describing the person sought, sufficient to identify the person, and information as to that person's probable location;

(b) A copy of the warrant of arrest; and

(c) Such documents, statements or information as may be necessary to meet the requirements for the surrender process in the requested State, except that those requirements should not be more burdensome than those applicable to requests for extradition pursuant to treaties or arrangements between the requested State and other States and should, if possible, be less burdensome, taking into account the distinct nature of the Court.

3. In the case of a request for the arrest and surrender of a person already convicted, the request shall contain or be supported by:

(a) A copy of any warrant of arrest for that person;

(b) A copy of the judgement of conviction;

(c) Information to demonstrate that the person sought is the one referred to in the judgement of conviction; and

(d) If the person sought has been sentenced, a copy of the sentence imposed and, in the case of a sentence for imprisonment, a statement of any time already served and the time remaining to be served.

4. Upon the request of the Court, a State Party shall consult with the Court, either generally or with respect to a specific matter, regarding any requirements under its national law that may apply under paragraph 2 (c). During the consultations, the

State Party shall advise the Court of the specific requirements of its national law.

Article 92
Provisional arrest

1. In urgent cases, the Court may request the provisional arrest of the person sought, pending presentation of the request for surrender and the documents supporting the request as specified in article 91.

2. The request for provisional arrest shall be made by any medium capable of delivering a written record and shall contain:

(a) Information describing the person sought, sufficient to identify the person, and information as to that person's probable location;

(b) A concise statement of the crimes for which the person's arrest is sought and of the facts which are alleged to constitute those crimes, including, where possible, the date and location of the crime;

(c) A statement of the existence of a warrant of arrest or a judgement of conviction against the person sought; and

(d) A statement that a request for surrender of the person sought will follow.

3. A person who is provisionally arrested may be released

from custody if the requested State has not received the request for surrender and the documents supporting the request as specified in article 91 within the time limits specified in the Rules of Procedure and Evidence. However, the person may consent to surrender before the expiration of this period if permitted by the law of the requested State. In such a case, the requested State shall proceed to surrender the person to the Court as soon as possible.

4. The fact that the person sought has been released from custody pursuant to paragraph 3 shall not prejudice the subsequent arrest and surrender of that person if the request for surrender and the documents supporting the request are delivered at a later date.

Article 93
Other forms of cooperation

1. States Parties shall, in accordance with the provisions of this Part and under procedures of national law, comply with requests by the Court to provide the following assistance in relation to investigations or prosecutions:

(a) The identification and whereabouts of persons or the location of items;

(b) The taking of evidence, including testimony under oath, and the production of evidence, including expert opinions and reports necessary to the Court;

(c) The questioning of any person being investigated or prosecuted;

(d) The service of documents, including judicial documents;

(e) Facilitating the voluntary appearance of persons as witnesses or experts before the Court;

(f) The temporary transfer of persons as provided in paragraph 7;

(g) The examination of places or sites, including the exhumation and examination of grave sites;

(h) The execution of searches and seizures;

(i) The provision of records and documents, including official records and documents;

(j) The protection of victims and witnesses and the preservation of evidence;

(k) The identification, tracing and freezing or seizure of proceeds, property and assets and instrumentalities of crimes for the purpose of eventual forfeiture, without prejudice to the rights of bona fide third parties; and

(l) Any other type of assistance which is not prohibited by the law of the requested State, with a view to facilitating the investigation and prosecution of crimes within the jurisdiction of the Court.

2. The Court shall have the authority to provide an assurance to a witness or an expert appearing before the Court that he or she will not be prosecuted, detained or subjected to any restriction of personal freedom by the Court in respect of any

act or omission that preceded the departure of that person from the requested State.

3. Where execution of a particular measure of assistance detailed in a request presented under paragraph 1, is prohibited in the requested State on the basis of an existing fundamental legal principle of general application, the requested State shall promptly consult with the Court to try to resolve the matter. In the consultations, consideration should be given to whether the assistance can be rendered in another manner or subject to conditions. If after consultations the matter cannot be resolved, the Court shall modify the request as necessary.

4. In accordance with article 72, a State Party may deny a request for assistance, in whole or in part, only if the request concerns the production of any documents or disclosure of evidence which relates to its national security.

5. Before denying a request for assistance under paragraph 1 (l), the requested State shall consider whether the assistance can be provided subject to specified conditions, or whether the assistance can be provided at a later date or in an alternative manner, provided that if the Court or the Prosecutor accepts the assistance subject to conditions, the Court or the Prosecutor shall abide by them.

6. If a request for assistance is denied, the requested State Party shall promptly inform the Court or the Prosecutor of the reasons for such denial.

7. (a) The Court may request the temporary transfer of a person in custody for purposes of identification or for obtaining

testimony or other assistance. The person may be transferred if the following conditions are fulfilled:

(i) The person freely gives his or her informed consent to the transfer; and

(ii) The requested State agrees to the transfer, subject to such conditions as that State and the Court may agree.

(b) The person being transferred shall remain in custody. When the purposes of the transfer have been fulfilled, the Court shall return the person without delay to the requested State.

8. (a) The Court shall ensure the confidentiality of documents and information, except as required for the investigation and proceedings described in the request.

(b) The requested State may, when necessary, transmit documents or information to the Prosecutor on a confidential basis. The Prosecutor may then use them solely for the purpose of generating new evidence.

(c) The requested State may, on its own motion or at the request of the Prosecutor, subsequently consent to the disclosure of such documents or information. They may then be used as evidence pursuant to the provisions of Parts 5 and 6 and in accordance with the Rules of Procedure and Evidence.

9. (a) (i) In the event that a State Party receives competing requests, other than for surrender or extradition, from the Court and from another State pursuant to an international obligation, the State Party shall endeavour, in consultation with the Court and the other State, to meet both requests, if necessary by postponing or attaching conditions to one or the other request.

(ii) Failing that, competing requests shall be resolved in accordance with the principles established in article 90.

(b) Where, however, the request from the Court concerns information, property or persons which are subject to the control of a third State or an international organization by virtue of an international agreement, the requested States shall so inform the Court and the Court shall direct its request to the third State or international organization.

10. (a) The Court may, upon request, cooperate with and provide assistance to a State Party conducting an investigation into or trial in respect of conduct which constitutes a crime within the jurisdiction of the Court or which constitutes a serious crime under the national law of the requesting State.

(b) (i) The assistance provided under subparagraph (a) shall include, inter alia:

a. The transmission of statements, documents or other

types of evidence obtained in the course of an investigation or a trial conducted by the Court; and

b. The questioning of any person detained by order of the Court;

(ii) In the case of assistance under subparagraph (b) (i) a:

a. If the documents or other types of evidence have been obtained with the assistance of a State, such transmission shall require the consent of that State;

b. If the statements, documents or other types of evidence have been provided by a witness or expert, such transmission shall be subject to the provisions of article 68.

(c) The Court may, under the conditions set out in this paragraph, grant a request for assistance under this paragraph from a State which is not a Party to this Statute.

Article 94
Postponement of execution of a request in respect of ongoing investigation or prosecution

1. If the immediate execution of a request would interfere with an ongoing investigation or prosecution of a case different from that to which the request relates, the requested State may

postpone the execution of the request for a period of time agreed upon with the Court. However, the postponement shall be no longer than is necessary to complete the relevant investigation or prosecution in the requested State. Before making a decision to postpone, the requested State should consider whether the assistance may be immediately provided subject to certain conditions.

2. If a decision to postpone is taken pursuant to paragraph 1, the Prosecutor may, however, seek measures to preserve evidence, pursuant to article 93, paragraph 1 (j).

Article 95
Postponement of execution of a request in respect of an admissibility challenge

Where there is an admissibility challenge under consideration by the Court pursuant to article 18 or 19, the requested State may postpone the execution of a request under this Part pending a determination by the Court, unless the Court has specifically ordered that the Prosecutor may pursue the collection of such evidence pursuant to article 18 or 19.

Article 96
Contents of request for other forms of assistance under article 93

1. A request for other forms of assistance referred to in article 93 shall be made in writing. In urgent cases, a request may be

made by any medium capable of delivering a written record, provided that the request shall be confirmed through the channel provided for in article 87, paragraph 1 (a).

2. The request shall, as applicable, contain or be supported by the following:

(a) A concise statement of the purpose of the request and the assistance sought, including the legal basis and the grounds for the request;

(b) As much detailed information as possible about the location or identification of any person or place that must be found or identified in order for the assistance sought to be provided;

(c) A concise statement of the essential facts underlying the request;

(d) The reasons for and details of any procedure or requirement to be followed;

(e) Such information as may be required under the law of the requested State in order to execute the request; and

(f)Any other information relevant in order for the assistance sought to be provided.

3. Upon the request of the Court, a State Party shall consult with the Court, either generally or with respect to a specific matter, regarding any requirements under its national law that may apply under paragraph 2 (e). During the consultations, the State Party shall advise the Court of the specific requirements

of its national law.

4. The provisions of this article shall, where applicable, also apply in respect of a request for assistance made to the Court.

Article 97
Consultations

Where a State Party receives a request under this Part in relation to which it identifies problems which may impede or prevent the execution of the request, that State shall consult with the Court without delay in order to resolve the matter. Such problems may include, inter alia:

(a) Insufficient information to execute the request;

(b) In the case of a request for surrender, the fact that despite best efforts, the person sought cannot be located or that the investigation conducted has determined that the person in the requested State is clearly not the person named in the warrant; or

(c) The fact that execution of the request in its current form would require the requested State to breach a pre-existing treaty obligation undertaken with respect to another State.

Article 98
Cooperation with respect to waiver of immunity
and consent to surrender

1. The Court may not proceed with a request for surrender

or assistance which would require the requested State to act inconsistently with its obligations under international law with respect to the State or diplomatic immunity of a person or property of a third State, unless the Court can first obtain the cooperation of that third State for the waiver of the immunity.

2. The Court may not proceed with a request for surrender which would require the requested State to act inconsistently with its obligations under international agreements pursuant to which the consent of a sending State is required to surrender a person of that State to the Court, unless the Court can first obtain the cooperation of the sending State for the giving of consent for the surrender.

Article 99
Execution of requests under articles 93 and 96

1. Requests for assistance shall be executed in accordance with the relevant procedure under the law of the requested State and, unless prohibited by such law, in the manner specified in the request, including following any procedure outlined therein or permitting persons specified in the request to be present at and assist in the execution process.

2. In the case of an urgent request, the documents or evidence produced in response shall, at the request of the Court, be sent urgently.

3. Replies from the requested State shall be transmitted in their original language and form.

4. Without prejudice to other articles in this Part, where it is necessary for the successful execution of a request which can be executed without any compulsory measures, including specifically the interview of or taking evidence from a person on a voluntary basis, including doing so without the presence of the authorities of the requested State Party if it is essential for the request to be executed, and the examination without modification of a public site or other public place, the Prosecutor may execute such request directly on the territory of a State as follows:

(a) When the State Party requested is a State on the territory of which the crime is alleged to have been committed, and there has been a determination of admissibility pursuant to article 18 or 19, the Prosecutor may directly execute such request following all possible consultations with the requested State Party;

(b) In other cases, the Prosecutor may execute such request following consultations with the requested State Party and subject to any reasonable conditions or concerns raised by that State Party. Where the requested State Party identifies problems with the execution of a request pursuant to this subparagraph it shall, without delay, consult with the Court to resolve the matter.

5. Provisions allowing a person heard or examined by the Court under article 72 to invoke restrictions designed to

prevent disclosure of confidential information connected with national security shall also apply to the execution of requests for assistance under this article.

Article 100
Costs

1. The ordinary costs for execution of requests in the territory of the requested State shall be borne by that State, except for the following, which shall be borne by the Court:

(a) Costs associated with the travel and security of witnesses and experts or the transfer under article 93 of persons in custody;

(b) Costs of translation, interpretation and transcription;

(c) Travel and subsistence costs of the judges, the Prosecutor, the Deputy Prosecutors, the Registrar, the Deputy Registrar and staff of any organ of the Court;

(d) Costs of any expert opinion or report requested by the Court;

(e) Costs associated with the transport of a person being surrendered to the Court by a custodial State; and

(f) Following consultations, any extraordinary costs that may result from the execution of a request.

2. The provisions of paragraph 1 shall, as appropriate, apply to requests from States Parties to the Court. In that case, the

Court shall bear the ordinary costs of execution.

Article 101
Rule of speciality

1. A person surrendered to the Court under this Statute shall not be proceeded against, punished or detained for any conduct committed prior to surrender, other than the conduct or course of conduct which forms the basis of the crimes for which that person has been surrendered.

2. The Court may request a waiver of the requirements of paragraph 1 from the State which surrendered the person to the Court and, if necessary, the Court shall provide additional information in accordance with article 91. States Parties shall have the authority to provide a waiver to the Court and should endeavour to do so.

Article 102
Use of terms

For the purposes of this Statute:

(a) "surrender" means the delivering up of a person by a State to the Court, pursuant to this Statute.

(b) "extradition" means the delivering up of a person by one State to another as provided by treaty, convention or national legislation.

PART 10. ENFORCEMENT

Article 103
Role of States in enforcement of sentences of imprisonment

1. (a) A sentence of imprisonment shall be served in a State designated by the Court from a list of States which have indicated to the Court their willingness to accept sentenced persons.

(b) At the time of declaring its willingness to accept sentenced persons, a State may attach conditions to its acceptance as agreed by the Court and in accordance with this Part.

(c) A State designated in a particular case shall promptly inform the Court whether it accepts the Court's designation.

2. (a) The State of enforcement shall notify the Court of any circumstances, including the exercise of any conditions agreed under paragraph 1, which could materially affect the terms or extent of the imprisonment. The Court shall be given at least 45 days' notice of any such known or foreseeable circumstances. During this period, the State of enforcement shall take no action that might prejudice its obligations under article 110.

(b) Where the Court cannot agree to the circumstances referred to in subparagraph (a), it shall notify the State of enforcement and proceed in accordance with article 104, paragraph 1.

3. In exercising its discretion to make a designation under paragraph 1, the Court shall take into account the following:

(a) The principle that States Parties should share the responsibility for enforcing sentences of imprisonment, in accordance with principles of equitable distribution, as provided in the Rules of Procedure and Evidence;

(b) The application of widely accepted international treaty standards governing the treatment of prisoners;

(c) The views of the sentenced person;

(d) The nationality of the sentenced person;

(e) Such other factors regarding the circumstances of the crime or the person sentenced, or the effective enforcement of the sentence, as may be appropriate in designating the State of enforcement.

4. If no State is designated under paragraph 1, the sentence of imprisonment shall be served in a prison facility made available by the host State, in accordance with the conditions set out in the headquarters agreement referred to in article 3, paragraph 2. In such a case, the costs arising out of the enforcement of a sentence of imprisonment shall be borne by the Court.

Article 104
Change in designation of State of enforcement

1. The Court may, at any time, decide to transfer a sentenced person to a prison of another State.

2. A sentenced person may, at any time, apply to the Court to be transferred from the State of enforcement.

Article 105
Enforcement of the sentence

1. Subject to conditions which a State may have specified in accordance with article 103, paragraph 1 (b), the sentence of imprisonment shall be binding on the States Parties, which shall in no case modify it.

2. The Court alone shall have the right to decide any application for appeal and revision. The State of enforcement shall not impede the making of any such application by a sentenced person.

Article 106
Supervision of enforcement of sentences and conditions of imprisonment

1. The enforcement of a sentence of imprisonment shall be subject to the supervision of the Court and shall be consistent with widely accepted international treaty standards governing treatment of prisoners.

2. The conditions of imprisonment shall be governed by the law of the State of enforcement and shall be consistent with widely accepted international treaty standards governing treatment of prisoners; in no case shall such conditions be more or less favourable than those available to prisoners convicted of similar offences in the State of enforcement.

3. Communications between a sentenced person and the Court shall be unimpeded and confidential.

Article 107
Transfer of the person upon completion of sentence

1. Following completion of the sentence, a person who is not a national of the State of enforcement may, in accordance with the law of the State of enforcement, be transferred to a State which is obliged to receive him or her, or to another State which agrees to receive him or her, taking into account any wishes of the person to be transferred to that State, unless the State of enforcement authorizes the person to remain in its territory.

2. If no State bears the costs arising out of transferring the person to another State pursuant to paragraph 1, such costs shall be borne by the Court.

3. Subject to the provisions of article 108, the State of enforcement may also, in accordance with its national law, extradite or otherwise surrender the person to a State which has requested the extradition or surrender of the person for

purposes of trial or enforcement of a sentence.

Article 108
Limitation on the prosecution or punishment of other offences

1. A sentenced person in the custody of the State of enforcement shall not be subject to prosecution or punishment or to extradition to a third State for any conduct engaged in prior to that person's delivery to the State of enforcement, unless such prosecution, punishment or extradition has been approved by the Court at the request of the State of enforcement.

2. The Court shall decide the matter after having heard the views of the sentenced person.

3. Paragraph 1 shall cease to apply if the sentenced person remains voluntarily for more than 30 days in the territory of the State of enforcement after having served the full sentence imposed by the Court, or returns to the territory of that State after having left it.

Article 109
Enforcement of fines and forfeiture measures

1. States Parties shall give effect to fines or forfeitures ordered by the Court under Part 7, without prejudice to the rights of bona fide third parties, and in accordance with the procedure of their national law.

2. If a State Party is unable to give effect to an order for forfeiture, it shall take measures to recover the value of the proceeds, property or assets ordered by the Court to be forfeited, without prejudice to the rights of bona fide third parties.

3. Property, or the proceeds of the sale of real property or, where appropriate, the sale of other property, which is obtained by a State Party as a result of its enforcement of a judgement of the Court shall be transferred to the Court.

Article 110
Review by the Court concerning reduction of sentence

1. The State of enforcement shall not release the person before expiry of the sentence pronounced by the Court.

2. The Court alone shall have the right to decide any reduction of sentence, and shall rule on the matter after having heard the person.

3. When the person has served two thirds of the sentence, or 25 years in the case of life imprisonment, the Court shall review the sentence to determine whether it should be reduced. Such a review shall not be conducted before that time.

4. In its review under paragraph 3, the Court may reduce the sentence if it finds that one or more of the following factors are present:

(a) The early and continuing willingness of the person to cooperate with the Court in its investigations and prosecutions;

(b) The voluntary assistance of the person in enabling the enforcement of the judgements and orders of the Court in other cases, and in particular providing assistance in locating assets subject to orders of fine, forfeiture or reparation which may be used for the benefit of victims; or

(c) Other factors establishing a clear and significant change of circumstances sufficient to justify the reduction of sentence, as provided in the Rules of Procedure and Evidence.

5. If the Court determines in its initial review under paragraph 3 that it is not appropriate to reduce the sentence, it shall thereafter review the question of reduction of sentence at such intervals and applying such criteria as provided for in the Rules of Procedure and Evidence.

Article 111
Escape

If a convicted person escapes from custody and flees the State of enforcement, that State may, after consultation with the Court, request the person's surrender from the State in which the person is located pursuant to existing bilateral or multilateral arrangements, or may request that the Court seek the person's surrender, in accordance with Part 9. It may direct that the person be delivered to the State in which he or she was serving the sentence or to another State designated by the

Court.

PART 11. ASSEMBLY OF STATES PARTIES

Article 112
Assembly of States Parties

1. An Assembly of States Parties to this Statute is hereby established. Each State Party shall have one representative in the Assembly who may be accompanied by alternates and advisers. Other States which have signed this Statute or the Final Act may be observers in the Assembly.

2. The Assembly shall:

(a) Consider and adopt, as appropriate, recommendations of the Preparatory Commission;

(b) Provide management oversight to the Presidency, the Prosecutor and the Registrar regarding the administration of the Court;

(c) Consider the reports and activities of the Bureau established under paragraph 3 and take appropriate action in regard thereto;

(d) Consider and decide the budget for the Court;

(e) Decide whether to alter, in accordance with article 36, the number of judges;

(f) Consider pursuant to article 87, paragraphs 5 and 7, any question relating to non-cooperation;

(g) Perform any other function consistent with this Statute or the Rules of Procedure and Evidence.

3. (a) The Assembly shall have a Bureau consisting of a President, two Vice-Presidents and 18 members elected by the Assembly for three-year terms.

(b) The Bureau shall have a representative character, taking into account, in particular, equitable geographical distribution and the adequate representation of the principal legal systems of the world.

(c) The Bureau shall meet as often as necessary, but at least once a year. It shall assist the Assembly in the discharge of its responsibilities.

4. The Assembly may establish such subsidiary bodies as may be necessary, including an independent oversight mechanism for inspection, evaluation and investigation of the Court, in order to enhance its efficiency and economy.

5. The President of the Court, the Prosecutor and the Registrar or their representatives may participate, as appropriate, in meetings of the Assembly and of the Bureau.

6. The Assembly shall meet at the seat of the Court or at the Headquarters of the United Nations once a year and, when circumstances so require, hold special sessions. Except as otherwise specified in this Statute, special sessions shall be convened by the Bureau on its own initiative or at the request of one third of the States Parties.

7. Each State Party shall have one vote. Every effort shall be made to reach decisions by consensus in the Assembly and in the Bureau. If consensus cannot be reached, except as otherwise provided in the Statute:

(a) Decisions on matters of substance must be approved by a two-thirds majority of those present and voting provided that an absolute majority of States Parties constitutes the quorum for voting;

(b) Decisions on matters of procedure shall be taken by a simple majority of States Parties present and voting.

8. A State Party which is in arrears in the payment of its financial contributions towards the costs of the Court shall have no vote in the Assembly and in the Bureau if the amount of its arrears equals or exceeds the amount of the contributions due from it for the preceding two full years. The Assembly may, nevertheless, permit such a State Party to vote in the Assembly and in the Bureau if it is satisfied that the failure to pay is due to conditions beyond the control of the State Party.

9. The Assembly shall adopt its own rules of procedure.

10. The official and working languages of the Assembly shall be those of the General Assembly of the United Nations.

PART 12. FINANCING

Article 113
Financial Regulations

Except as otherwise specifically provided, all financial matters related to the Court and the meetings of the Assembly of States Parties, including its Bureau and subsidiary bodies, shall be governed by this Statute and the Financial Regulations and Rules adopted by the Assembly of States Parties.

Article 114
Payment of expenses

Expenses of the Court and the Assembly of States Parties, including its Bureau and subsidiary bodies, shall be paid from the funds of the Court.

Article 115
Funds of the Court and of the Assembly of States Parties

The expenses of the Court and the Assembly of States Parties, including its Bureau and subsidiary bodies, as provided for in the budget decided by the Assembly of States Parties, shall be provided by the following sources:

(a) Assessed contributions made by States Parties;
(b) Funds provided by the United Nations, subject to the

approval of the General Assembly, in particular in relation to the expenses incurred due to referrals by the Security Council.

Article 116
Voluntary contributions

Without prejudice to article 115, the Court may receive and utilize, as additional funds, voluntary contributions from Governments, international organizations, individuals, corporations and other entities, in accordance with relevant criteria adopted by the Assembly of States Parties.

Article 117
Assessment of contributions

The contributions of States Parties shall be assessed in accordance with an agreed scale of assessment, based on the scale adopted by the United Nations for its regular budget and adjusted in accordance with the principles on which that scale is based.

Article 118
Annual audit

The records, books and accounts of the Court, including its annual financial statements, shall be audited annually by an independent auditor.

PART 13. FINAL CLAUSES

Article 119
Settlement of disputes

1. Any dispute concerning the judicial functions of the Court shall be settled by the decision of the Court.

2. Any other dispute between two or more States Parties relating to the interpretation or application of this Statute which is not settled through negotiations within three months of their commencement shall be referred to the Assembly of States Parties. The Assembly may itself seek to settle the dispute or may make recommendations on further means of settlement of the dispute, including referral to the International Court of Justice in conformity with the Statute of that Court.

Article 120
Reservations

No reservations may be made to this Statute.

Article 121
Amendments

1. After the expiry of seven years from the entry into force of this Statute, any State Party may propose amendments thereto. The text of any proposed amendment shall be submitted to the Secretary-General of the United Nations, who shall promptly circulate it to all States Parties.

2. No sooner than three months from the date of notification, the Assembly of States Parties, at its next meeting, shall, by a majority of those present and voting, decide whether to take up the proposal. The Assembly may deal with the proposal directly or convene a Review Conference if the issue involved so warrants.

3. The adoption of an amendment at a meeting of the Assembly of States Parties or at a Review Conference on which consensus cannot be reached shall require a two-thirds majority of States Parties.

4. Except as provided in paragraph 5, an amendment shall enter into force for all States Parties one year after instruments of ratification or acceptance have been deposited with the Secretary-General of the United Nations by seven-eighths of them.

5. Any amendment to articles 5, 6, 7 and 8 of this Statute shall enter into force for those States Parties which have accepted the amendment one year after the deposit of their instruments of ratification or acceptance. In respect of a State Party which has not accepted the amendment, the Court shall not exercise its jurisdiction regarding a crime covered by the amendment when committed by that State Party's nationals or on its territory.

6. If an amendment has been accepted by seven-eighths of States Parties in accordance with paragraph 4, any State Party which has not accepted the amendment may withdraw from this Statute with immediate effect, notwithstanding article 127, paragraph 1, but subject to article 127, paragraph 2, by giving

notice no later than one year after the entry into force of such amendment.

7. The Secretary-General of the United Nations shall circulate to all States Parties any amendment adopted at a meeting of the Assembly of States Parties or at a Review Conference.

Article 122
Amendments to provisions of an institutional nature

1. Amendments to provisions of this Statute which are of an exclusively institutional nature, namely, article 35, article 36, paragraphs 8 and 9, article 37, article 38, article 39, paragraphs 1 (first two sentences), 2 and 4, article 42, paragraphs 4 to 9, article 43, paragraphs 2 and 3, and articles 44, 46, 47 and 49, may be proposed at any time, notwithstanding article 121, paragraph 1, by any State Party. The text of any proposed amendment shall be submitted to the Secretary-General of the United Nations or such other person designated by the Assembly of States Parties who shall promptly circulate it to all States Parties and to others participating in the Assembly.

2. Amendments under this article on which consensus cannot be reached shall be adopted by the Assembly of States Parties or by a Review Conference, by a two-thirds majority of States Parties. Such amendments shall enter into force for all States Parties six months after their adoption by the Assembly or, as the case may be, by the Conference.

Article 123
Review of the Statute

1. Seven years after the entry into force of this Statute the Secretary-General of the United Nations shall convene a Review Conference to consider any amendments to this Statute. Such review may include, but is not limited to, the list of crimes contained in article 5. The Conference shall be open to those participating in the Assembly of States Parties and on the same conditions.

2. At any time thereafter, at the request of a State Party and for the purposes set out in paragraph 1, the Secretary-General of the United Nations shall, upon approval by a majority of States Parties, convene a Review Conference.

3. The provisions of article 121, paragraphs 3 to 7, shall apply to the adoption and entry into force of any amendment to the Statute considered at a Review Conference.

Article 124
Transitional Provision

Notwithstanding article 12, paragraphs 1 and 2, a State, on becoming a party to this Statute, may declare that, for a period of seven years after the entry into force of this Statute for the State concerned, it does not accept the jurisdiction of the Court with respect to the category of crimes referred to in article 8 when a crime is alleged to have been committed by its nationals or on its territory. A declaration under this article may be withdrawn at any time. The provisions of this article shall be reviewed at the Review Conference convened in accordance with article 123, paragraph 1.

Article 125
Signature, ratification, acceptance, approval or accession

1. This Statute shall be open for signature by all States in Rome, at the headquarters of the Food and Agriculture Organization of the United Nations, on 17 July 1998. Thereafter, it shall remain open for signature in Rome at the Ministry of Foreign Affairs of Italy until 17 October 1998. After that date, the Statute shall remain open for signature in New York, at United Nations Headquarters, until 31 December 2000.

2. This Statute is subject to ratification, acceptance or approval by signatory States. Instruments of ratification, acceretary-General of the United Nations.

Article 126
Entry into force

1. This Statute shall enter into force on the first day of the month after the 60th day following the date of the deposit of the 60th instrument of ratification, acceptance, approval or accession with the Secretary-Genera of the United Nations.

2. For each State ratifying, accepting, approving or acceding

to this Statute after the deposit of the 60th instrument of ratification, acceptance, approval or accession, the Statute shall enter into force on the first day of the month after the 60th day following the deposit by such State of its instrument of ratification, acceptance, approval or accession.

Article 127
Withdrawal

1. A State Party may, by written notification addressed to the Secretary-General of the United Nations, withdraw from this Statute. The withdrawal shall take effect one year after the date of receipt of the notification, unless the notification specifies a later date.

2. A State shall not be discharged, by reason of its withdrawal, from the obligations arising from this Statute while it was a Party to the Statute, including any financial obligations which may have accrued. Its withdrawal shall not affect any cooperation with the Court in connection with criminal investigations and proceedings in relation to which the withdrawing State had a duty to cooperate and which were commenced prior to the date on which the withdrawal became effective, nor shall it prejudice in any way the continued consideration of any matter which was already under consideration by the Court prior to the date on which the withdrawal became effective.

Article 128
Authentic texts

The original of this Statute, of which the Arabic, Chinese, English, French, Russian and Spanish texts are equally authentic, shall be deposited with the Secretary-General of the United Nations, who shall send certified copies thereof to all States.

IN WITNESS WHEREOF, the undersigned, being duly authorized thereto by their respective Governments, have signed this Statute.

DONE at Rome, this 17th day of July 1998.

TABLE OF CONTENTS

---

* Translation by Jessica MIller (Michigan, USA), revised by the author.

LibrosEnRed Publishing House

LibrosEnRed is the most complete digital publishing house in the Spanish language. Since June 2000 we have published and sold digital and printed-on-demand books.

Our mission is to help all authors publish their work and offer the readers fast and economic access to all types of books.

We publish novels, stories, poems, research theses, manuals, and monographs. We cover a wide range of contents. We offer the possibility to commercialize and promote new titles through the Internet to millions of potential readers.

Our royalties system allows authors to receive a profit 300% to 400% greater than they would obtain in the traditional circuit.

Enter www.librosenred.com to see our catalog, comprising of hundreds of classic titles and contemporary authors.

www.ingramcontent.com/pod-product-compliance
Lightning Source LLC
LaVergne TN
LVHW090255210926
848480LV00001B/30
* 9 7 8 9 8 7 5 6 1 0 7 1 2 *